THOSE UNITED STATES

International Perspectives on American History

VOLUME I

THOSE UNITED STATES

International Perspectives on American History

VOLUME I

GERALD MICHAEL GREENFIELD
University of Wisconsin
Parkside

JOHN D. BUENKER
University of Wisconsin
Parkside

HARCOURT BRACE COLLEGE PUBLISHERS

Fort Worth   Philadelphia   San Diego   New York   Orlando   Austin   San Antonio
Toronto   Montreal   London   Sydney   Tokyo

Publisher	Earl McPeek
Executive Editor	David Tatom
Market Strategist	Laura M. Brennan
Project Editor	Laura Miley
Art Director	Michelle L. Krabill
Production Manager	Serena Barnett

Cover Credit: *Washington Crossing the Delaware* by Emanuel Gottlieb Leutze, detail. The Metropolitan Museum of Art, gift of John Stewart Kennedy, 1897 (97.34). Photograph (c) 1992 The Metropolitan Museum of Art.

ISBN: 0-15-508258-2
Library of Congress Catalog Card Number: 98-88278

Address for Domestic Orders
Harcourt Brace College Publishers, 6277 Sea Harbor Drive,
Orlando, FL 32887-6777
800-782-4479

Address for International Orders
International Customer Service
Harcourt Brace & Company, 6277 Sea Harbor Drive, Orlando, FL 32887-6777
407-345-3800
(fax) 407-345-4060
(e-mail) hbintl@harcourtbrace.com

Address for Editorial Correspondence
Harcourt Brace College Publishers, 301 Commerce Street, Suite 3700,
Fort Worth, TX 76102

Web Site Address
http://www.hbcollege.com

Printed in the United States of America

9 0 1 2 3 4 5 6 7 8 039 9 8 7 6 5 4 3 2 1

Harcourt Brace College Publishers

PREFACE

The Brazilian educator Paulo Freire once observed: "Any way of seeing is a way of *not seeing*." Americans long have embraced a vision of their country as representing something distinctive in world history: a nation of individual liberty and boundless opportunity; a refuge for the displaced and oppressed from other lands; and a steadfast opponent of dictators and tyrants. This view emphasizes as well the longevity of the nation's constitution, the stability of its political system, the rapidity of its industrial development, the continuing dynamism of its capitalist economy, and its contemporary status as the world's sole remaining superpower.

For many—if not most—contemporary Americans, this good life of freedom, democracy and economic well-being indicates the marked superiority of the United States among the nations of the world, a superiority which proceeds from what historians have termed "American exceptionalism:" the idea that this nation has followed a unique historical path. This sense of exceptionalism has long historical roots, ones which, arguably, date to Europe's first encounter with the Americas. The vast extent and prodigious fertility of the new found land produced a sense of awe among Europeans, and many of the wise and learned speculated as to why, after having hidden it for so many centuries, God now had chosen to "reveal" this "New World."

To many of the religiously-oriented settlers of colonial British America, the answer to that question seemed obvious: the New World represented an opportunity to escape the deformed, corrupt churches of the "Old" World, and, in a new environment, to establish a purified church and commonwealth. The religious vision had a strong secular counterpart among those who defined opportunity in terms of the chance to live as independent farmers who possessed their own land.

When the colonists met in Continental Congress and officially declared their independence from England, they acted in the belief that they were enunciating bold, new principles that marked a clear departure from the political ideas then reigning in Europe. And, later, in formulating the new nation's Constitution, the founders saw themselves as setting forth on untrod ground, establishing the world's first large-scale republic. The early years of the new nation's history lent further support to the exceptionalist interpretation, as Americans congratulated themselves on their privileged position. Free from the corrupting influence of the Old World, they set about to strengthen and extend their democratic experiment, building a new empire of liberty in the vast American continent.

A strong streak of isolationism stood as one concomitant of this exceptionalist attitude. George Washington's Farewell Address warned of the dangers of "permanent, entangling alliances." President James Monroe, in issuing what subsequently would become known as the Monroe Doctrine, specifically cautioned Europe against attempts to "interfere" in the affairs of the Americas, suggesting as well that the United States itself had no desire to intervene in the affairs of Europe. Although the United States ultimately became a major international actor, isolationist sentiments always have remained strong, and given way only when Americans became convinced that international action of some sort was necessary to protect their unique way of life. Further, in the aftermath of those interventions, Americans frequently experienced a sense of betrayal. That the canny, cynical politicians of the Old World always hoodwinked an honest, naive America assumed the status of conventional wisdom, as did the associated concept that while America always won the war, it wound up a loser in the peace settlements.

The strength of exceptionalism and the urge toward isolationism have made it difficult to see American history as enmeshed in the context of larger patterns and processes of world history. And, they also have made it difficult for Americans to see themselves and their history through any perspective other than their own. To be sure, the works of such foreign observers as Alexis de Tocqueville and Michel-Guillaume Jean de Crevecoeur have had great resonance in America, but in many respects that proceeded from the fact that they spoke in terms of American exceptionalism. Crevecoeur, for example, in widely quoted words, directly asked, "Who then is this new man, this American?" In responding to that question, he stressed the unique positive power of the American environment and political system which rewarded and rejuvenated the downtrodden so long as they had a willingness to work and a desire to improve themselves. Americans also found de Tocqueville's words congenial, for he spoke in terms of the great equality that existed in the United States, contrasting it with the still-rigid class systems and hierarchies of Europe. However, those foreign observers who failed to celebrate the nation's unique, positive qualities, and especially those who have taken a negative stance toward American policies or practices, typically have exercised little lasting influence on the nation's self-perception.

As we stand poised on the brink of a new millennium, the new and still rapidly developing information technology has dramatically transformed both the speed and volume of international communication, and we now speak of the worked as a "global village," with a global economy and diverse peoples from many nations all linked through a world-wide web. As isolationism fades into a romantic concept rather than a practical principle of national policy,

America's sense of exceptionalism also demands reexamination. In many nations, vibrant American Studies centers exist, and in the United States, the Organization of American Historians has begun to emphasize the importance of "internationalizing" American history.

Those United States represents one such effort. It provides students with some new ways of viewing the American past by providing international perspectives on various topics or time-periods typically covered in the introductory United States history survey. Chronologically, then, Volume I begins with Europe's first encounter with the Americas and ends with the Civil War. Along the way, it presents discussions focusing on Native Americans, the slave trade, the nature of colonial America, the American Revolution, the growth and development of the new nation, manifest destiny, and slavery and abolition. Volume II takes as its starting point the industrial surge of the Gilded Age. It considers such topics as urbanization and immigration, expansionism, World War I, the 1920s, the Great Depression and the New Deal, the era of World War II, the Cold War, the 1960s counter-culture, and the contemporary post-industrial era.

Within that traditional organizational schema, it presents a decidedly non-traditional approach. Each of the chapters begins with an introductory essay that sketches the broader international dimensions of a particular topic or time period. So, for example, Volume I's discussion of the slave trade focuses on the larger trans-Atlantic system of colonies and commerce and the transnational efforts to abolish that traffic in human beings, while Volume II considers immigration to America as part of a general move from countryside to city that characterized the experience of multiple world nations. These then are followed by excerpts from the works of foreign observers who lived during the relevant time period, as well as from contemporary international scholars. In a few cases, we have included selections written by U.S.-born scholars whose work traces important comparative dimensions.

Some of these external views remark various distinctive features of the United States, but not necessarily ones Americans themselves have seen as especially significant. For example, many foreigners found the federal system of government truly unusual, and were at great pains to explain to their readers that the individual states within America were for almost all purposes as independent as any sovereign nation. In other cases, they directly challenge our conventional understandings. Americans' concerns over the hardships of the Great Depression, for example, seemed rather exaggerated to some Scottish and Latin American observers. They remarked the nation's wealth, and how well the people seemed to live. Some writers laud the United States; others attack it. Taken as a whole, these various external views provides us with a special, indeed precious opportunity—to see ourselves as others have seen us.

TO THE PROFESSOR

Our primary purpose in writing *Those United States* is to add an extra dimension to the survey course in United States history by examining a significant portion of its usual subject matter within an international context. It is intended to be used as a supplementary text to complement, rather than displace, standard U.S. history textbooks. Each volume contains selections taken almost entirely from the writings of foreign observers contemporaneous to the developments under discussion or from modern-day scholars resident in other countries. We chose these selections primarily because they best exemplified the criteria set forth in the Preface, were written in language accessible to college freshmen, and contributed to the presentation of a variety of national perspectives. Although none of the selections necessarily expresses our interpretations of things, we did reject pieces that we regarded as too heavily ideological in nature or at odds with the generally accepted historical record.

We designed the chapters to stand alone; this allows you to assign materials that best complement your own approach to teaching the survey. The introductory essays, entitled "The International Context," are intended to add an international dimension to the subject matter. Although they do include some material found in survey textbooks, the focus is on drawing comparisons and contrasts with the experiences of other nations. The sections headed "International Views" and the head notes for each selection identify the author of the piece, and highlight the themes presented in that chapter's selections. Terms with which students may be unfamiliar are highlighted in the text and defined at the end of each selection. Each chapter concludes with "Thinking Things Through"— a number of pointed questions requiring students to analyze what they have read, compare and contrast two or more selections, or link up the material in the selections with the stated themes.

To the Student

This book takes a different approach to American history. Reading it, you will discover the varying ways in which people from other countries have viewed the United States. You also will become familiar with the ways in which developments in the United States form part of larger international processes which have affected nations throughout the world.

As you read the views of the varied international observers, it is important to keep in mind that they represent opinions, not objective historical fact. Sometimes, observers' opinions conflict with one another; other times, they seem to share a lot in common. Your job as a student is to reflect on these differences and similarities. Do not simply accept them as "true."

You'll also notice some "peculiar" spellings, for example, "colour," instead of "color." These represent the appropriate spellings in British English, which does not always conform to United States forms and usages. You probably will encounter a number of unfamiliar expressions as well. To assist you, we have bolded these, and then provided definitions at the end of each selection.

Collectively, we have been teaching survey courses in United States history for about 60 years. We really think that *Those United States* is the kind of book that today's students need. We hope that it is one you will enjoy.

Gerald Michael Greenfield
John D. Buenker

ABOUT THE EDITORS

Gerald Michael Greenfield is Professor and Chair of the Department of History at the University of Wisconsin–Parkside, where he also directs the Center for Teaching. He holds a master's degree in United States history from Brooklyn College and a Ph.D. from Indiana University, Bloomington, where his doctoral fields included Latin America and Africa. He served as a Fulbright Senior Lecturer at the Federal University of Pernambuco in Recife, Brazil. He regularly teaches introductory courses in United States history and upper-level courses on Latin America and imperialism. He is the editor and author of several books, including a widely used public school text on the Western Hemisphere. His articles have appeared in such journals as *Hispanic American Historical Review, Journal of Urban History,* and *Social Science History.*

John D. Buenker has been Professor of History at the University of Wisconsin–Parkside since 1970. Before that, he taught at Prince Georges Community College and Eastern Illinois University. He received his M. A. and Ph.D. in United States history from Georgetown University. He regularly teaches courses on the history of immigration to the United States and frequently team-teaches courses on the history of American relations with Russia, Japan and China. He is the author, coauthor or editor of eleven books and over 150 articles and book reviews in scholarly journals, and was Contributing Editor for Research and Reference Tools for the *Journal of American History* from 1986 to 1997. During the 1990–91 academic year, he was selected as the Wisconsin Professor of the Year by the Council for the Advancement and Support of Education of the Carnegie Foundation.

TABLE OF CONTENTS

I

EUROPE'S AGE OF DISCOVERY

A. The International Context

The 1992 quincentennial, or five hundreth anniversary, of Christopher Columbus's voyage across the Atlantic aroused a heated debate as to the meaning of that historic event. Columbus had a hand in the beginning of the slave trade and the destruction of the indigenous population of the Americas. Some suggested, therefore, that he began the European "invasion" of America. Others spoke of his voyages in terms of an "encounter," a term that stressed the resulting interchange of animals, plants, diseases, and people between formerly separate parts of the world. As we consider these issues, it becomes important to take a voyage of our own, back in time to a world far different than today's, one in which Europe was a rather backward, insignificant place, and the Old World's great civilizations centered in Asia and the Middle East.

In the thirteenth and fourteenth centuries, China led the world in terms of commerce and manufacturing. It also was a seat of advanced science and learning. China witnessed great prosperity under the Sung dynasty (960–1297). Literature and the arts flourished, as did science. The Chinese knew of the compass by the early twelfth century, and seafaring and commerce held great importance for them by that time. India, another of the great Asian civilizations, also was an important commercial power. Beginning around 300 B.C., Indian merchants had established a strong presence in many parts of Southeast Asia. They dominated seafaring trade in the body of water that came to be known as the Indian Ocean.

By the thirteenth and fourteenth centuries a good deal of China's foreign trade passed through the hands of another great civilization, the Islamic Arab Empire. Islam began in A.D. 622 in the Arabian peninsula with the prophet Muhammad, who preached a strict monotheistic doctrine. A crusading,

1

proselytizing religion, Islam stood at the heart of the rapid Arab expansion throughout the Middle East, North Africa, and, by the early 700s into the Iberian Peninsula. Arab merchants took control of both the Indian Ocean and Mediterranean trade routes.

In 1087, the Italian city-states of Genoa and Pisa asserted their own power in the western Mediterranean. This encouraged further efforts by European Christendom to break the power of Islam. The first of the Crusades, an attempt to retake the Holy Land, began in 1095. Seven others, with varying objectives and successes, occurred over the ensuing years, the last in 1270. Still, as late as the 1400s, the Islamic empire controlled strategically located territory in the region of the Indian Ocean and eastern Mediterranean Sea.

Islamic trade had brought many benefits to a still backward Europe. For example, paper, first manufactured in China, came to the Middle East around the ninth century, and later spread to Europe. Arabs helped disseminate Chinese innovations in navigation and Indian mathematical concepts. They also spread their own distinctive contributions to mathematics and cartography. But above all, through the hands of Muslim traders came luxury goods from the East, including spices, silks, perfumes, and fine high-fired glazed porcelain. This trade helped spark a commercial revival in Europe and encouraged the growth of towns and the spread of banking.

The vital role of the Mediterranean in this trade gave city-states on the Italian peninsula an advantage in exploiting these new opportunities. Their bankers, merchants, and mariners took the lead in mounting trade expeditions. By 1291, Genoa had sent an expedition outside the Mediterranean in search of a sea route to India.

In the 1400s, Portugal, strategically located on the Atlantic Ocean, took the lead in European seafaring expeditions. By the 1420s, Portuguese expeditions had reached the Madeira Islands and the Azores. Though still relatively backward in the 1400s, western Europe stood poised for its rise to world dominance. The Americas played an important role in that process.

When Columbus set forth on his quest to reach the Indies by sailing west across the Atlantic he used maps of the world largely based on ones compiled by the Greek astronomer, Ptolemy (A.D. 85–165). Ptolemy depicted the world as having three parts: Europe, Asia, and Africa. His map of the world showed the Atlantic Ocean stretching un-

interruptedly from Europe to Asia. The authority of the leading scholars of classical Greece and Rome remained almost unquestioned in fifteenth-century Europe. Columbus, therefore, had no reason to suspect that the lands he sailed to were anything other than islands near Asia. Similar assumptions guided the Italian merchant Giovanni Caboto (John Cabot), who, inspired by Columbus, sailed in 1497 from Bristol, England, to the Cape Breton islands and Newfoundland. Convinced that he had reached China, with his son Sebastiano he mounted another voyage the following year in hopes of trading for spices. Subsequent expeditions by Columbus as well as by other mariners, including those of Amerigo Vespucci in the early 1500s, went on the assumption that the lands thus far encountered could only be small islands. They, too, looked for water passages to the supposedly nearby Asian mainland.

By the 1520s, as a result of multiple voyages of exploration, including Magellan's circumnavigation of the globe, it had become clear that Columbus's "Indies" were nowhere near Asia. New maps now indicated a land mass in the Atlantic called America. Even so, "America" referred only to the areas explored by the Spanish and Portuguese. The true extent of the American land mass, especially to the north, remained unknown. The 1524 voyage of Giovanni da Verrazano revealed a long North American coastline all the way to Newfoundland. Still, European expeditions to North America, as in the case of Henry Hudson's 1609 voyage, continued to search for a northwest passage that would lead into the Pacific.

Although the luxury goods of Asia had motivated various voyages to the Americas, the unanticipated New World yielded significant treasure. With Hernán Cortés's overthrow of the Aztec Empire in the central valley of Mexico in 1522, and then Francisco Pizarro's 1533 conquest of the Inca Empire in South America, vast quantities of gold and silver flowed into Spain. The New World also provided fertile ground for cultivating large quantities of sugar, previously a scarce luxury in Europe.

The economic stimulus provided by the Americas greatly accelerated European development and contributed to a demographic explosion in Europe. New World food crops previously unknown in Europe, for example, American corn and the white potato, soon were being used around the world. By around 1600, Chinese farmers cultivated American corn and sweet potatoes. Manioc, a root known in the United States as tapioca, became a major staple food in Africa. At the same time, the Americas became a site for cultivating Asian products brought there by way of Europe, including sugar, coffee, and bananas. The link to Europe also brought new animals to the Americas, among them, cows, horses, and pigs.

The Old and New World had been isolated from one another for over nine thousand years, since the submergence of the Bering Land Bridge linking Alaska and Asia. It was that long period of isolation that accounted for the existence of different animals and plants. Similarly, prior to the coming of Europeans, numerous diseases, including smallpox, measles, typhoid fever, and pneumonia were unknown in the Americas. The Native American peoples living here, therefore, had not developed any resistance to such diseases. This resulted in vast epidemics that killed enormous numbers of people. Low-end estimates for Mexico and the Caribbean suggest a 20 percent decline, while at the upper end, some scholars suggest the disappearance of 90 percent of the pre-Columbian Native American population in that region. With regard to North America, estimates suggest that small pox epidemics in the 1630s and 1640s among the Iroquois and Hurons reduced their populations by some 50 percent. Such catastrophic rates of death devastated and disorganized Amerindian societies, facilitating European conquest and settlement. That population decline also contributed to the rise of the Atlantic slave trade.

B. International Views

The incorporation of the New World into the Old had many significant consequences—ones that affected the entire world. From this perspective, the "discovery" of America is not an event that occurred in 1492, but a process that unfolded over a much longer period of time. Also, the discovery of new lands had enormous intellectual and psychological aspects. At first, the New World's importance rested only on the opportunities it presented for profit. As time went on, however, the nature of the land and peoples of the Americas began to arouse greater interest. Many travelers wrote about the New World, usually trying to make it fit their own preconceived ideas. For many Europeans, then, the New World seemed a savage, inferior place where all things, including religion and morality, degenerated.

Another theme—the New World as a place of hope and redemption—has had far greater longevity. From a religious perspective, the New World was something of a puzzle. Why,

*people wondered, had it lay hidden all this time? And, why
had it been revealed by God at this moment? That there was
an overriding purpose to the New World's discovery seemed
clear. Many Europeans suggested that the New World—free
from the sins of the Old—provided an opportunity to establish better societies. The Puritan sense of mission and the idea
of American exceptionalism clearly reflect that notion.*

*Writing toward the close of the eighteenth century, the
Scottish Enlightenment economist Adam Smith referred to
the discovery of America as one of the greatest events in
world history. Writers since his time have continued to ponder the meaning of America and its importance. The readings
which follow suggest the early sense of wonder aroused by
this previously unknown land, and the ongoing attempts to
understand and discuss its importance. It begins, appropri-
ately, with a letter by Amerigo Vespucci which asserts that
America is not an island, but a new continent. Next, Giovanni da Verrazano reports on his discoveries, and notes the
vast north–south extent of the American land mass. The
works of these two early explorers clearly reflect the thin line
between objective description and outright fantasy which was
typical of accounts written in the early days of exploration
and discovery. Two wide-ranging discussions of the larger
meanings of the discovery conclude this chapter. The Colombian historian, Germán Arciniegas, focuses on the New
World as utopia, a place of hope and renewal. British historian J. H. Elliot discusses the various ways Europeans have
interpreted the nature of America. He also speculates broadly
on how the discovery altered Europe's intellectual horizons.*

AMERIGO VESPUCCI

WE MAY RIGHTLY CALL IT
A NEW WORLD

*Amerigo Vespucci (1454-1512), the Italian mariner whose name became attached to the
lands that Columbus had first "discovered," made several voyages to the New World. In
the letter below, addressed to his patron, **Lorenzo de´ Medici**, he directly asserts that the
lands he has reached are not simply islands, but a previously unknown part of the world.
This letter came to the attention of a German map-maker, Martin Waldseemuller, who
then used the name "America" on his 1507 map illustrating the new lands in the Western Hemisphere. Note especially the almost mythical quality of Vespucci's descriptions,
particularly regarding the people he encountered.*

On a former occasion I wrote to you at some length concerning my return from those new regions which we found and explored with the fleet, at the cost, and by the command, of this Most Serene King of Portugal. And these we may rightly call a new world, because our ancestors had no knowledge of them and it will be a matter wholly new to all those who hear about them. For this transcends the view held by our ancients, in as much as most of them hold that there is no continent to the south beyond the equator, but only the sea which they named the Atlantic; and if some of them did aver that a continent there was, they denied with abundant argument that it was a habitable land. But that this their opinion is false and utterly opposed to the truth, this my last voyage has made manifest—for in those southern parts I have found a continent more densely peopled and abounding in animals than our Europe or Asia or Africa, and in addition, a climate milder and more delightful than in any other region known to us, as you shall learn in the following account. . . .

On the fourteenth of the month of May, one thousand five hundred and one, we set sail from Lisbon under fair sailing conditions . . . for the purpose of seeking new regions toward the south; and for twenty months we continuously pursued this southern course. . . . But what we suffered on that vast expanse of sea, what perils of shipwreck, what discomforts of the body we endured, with what anxiety of mind we toiled, this I leave to the judgment of those who out of rich experience have well learned what it is to seek the uncertain and to attempt discoveries even though ignorant. And that in a word I may briefly narrate all, you must know that of the sixty-seven days of our sailing we had forty-four of constant rain, thunder, and lightning—so dark that never did we see sun by day or fair sky by night. By reason of this, such fear invaded us that we soon abandoned almost all hope of life. But during these tempests of sea and sky, so numerous and so violent, the Most High was pleased to display before us a continent, new lands, and an unknown world. At sight of these things we were filled with as much joy as anyone can imagine usually falls to the lot of those who have gained refuge from varied calamity and hostile fortune. It was on the seventh day of August, one thousand five hundred and one, that we anchored off the shores of those parts, thanking our God with formal ceremonial and with the celebration of a choral mass.

We knew that land to be a continent and not an island both because it stretches forth in the form of a very long and unbending coast, and because it is replete with infinite inhabitants. For in it we found innumerable tribes and peoples and species of all manner of wild beasts which are found in our lands and many others never seen by us concerning which it would take long to tell in detail. . . .

We adopted the plan of following the coast of this continent toward the east and never losing sight of it. We sailed along until at length we reached a bend where the shore made a turn to the south; and from that point where we first touched land to that corner it was about three hundred leagues, in which sailing distance we frequently landed and had friendly relations with those people, as you will hear below. . . . Now where the said corner of land showed us a southern trend of the coast we agreed to sail beyond it and inquire what there might be in those parts. So we sailed along the coast about six hundred leagues, and often landed and mingled and associated with the natives of those regions and by them we were received in brotherly fashion and we would dwell with them too, for fifteen or twenty day continuously, maintaining amicable and hospitable relations. Part of this new continent lies in the torrid zone beyond the equator toward the Antarctic pole, for it begins eight degrees beyond the equator. We sailed along this coast until we passed the tropic of Capricorn and found the Antarctic pole fifty degrees higher than that horizon. We advanced to within seventeen and a half degrees of the Antarctic circle, and what I there have seen and learned concerning the nature of those races, their manners, their tractability, and the fertility of the soil, the salubrity of the climate, the position of the heavenly bodies in the sky, and especially concerning the fixed stars of the eighth sphere, never seen or studied by our ancestors, these things I shall relate in order.

First then as to the people. We found in those parts such a multitude of people as nobody could enumerate (as we read in the Apocalypse), a race I say gentle and amenable. All of both sexes go about naked, covering no part of their bodies; and just as they spring from their mothers' wombs so they go until death. They have indeed large square-built bodies, well formed and proportioned, and in color verging upon reddish. This I think has come to them, because, going about naked, they are colored by the sun. They have, too, hair plentiful and black. In their gait and when playing their games they are agile and dignified. They are comely too, of countenance which they nevertheless themselves destroy; for they bore their cheeks, lips, noses, and ears. Nor think those holes small or that they have one only. For some I have seen having in a single face seven borings any one of which was capable of holding a plum. They stop up these holes of theirs with blue stones, bits of marble, very beautiful crystals of alabaster, very white bones, and other things artificially prepared according to their customs. But if you could see a thing so unwonted and monstrous, that is to say a man having in his cheeks and lips alone seven stones some of which are a span and a half in length, you would not be without wonder. . . . Women do not bore their faces, but their ears only. They have no cloth either of wool, linen, or cotton, since they need it not; neither do they have goods of their own, but all things are held in common. They live together without king, without government, and each is his own master. They marry as many wives as they please; and son cohabits with mother, brother with sister, male cousin with female, and any man with the first woman he meets. They dissolve their marriages as often as they please, and observe no sort of law with respect to them. Beyond the fact that they have no church, no religion, and are not idolaters, what more can I say? . . . They live one hundred and fifty years, and rarely fall ill and if they do fall victims to any disease, they cure themselves with certain roots and herbs. These are the most noteworthy things I know about them.

The climate there was very temperate and good, and as I was able to learn from their accounts, there was never there any pest or epidemic caused by corruption of the air. This I take to be because the south winds are ever blowing there. . . . They are zealous in the art of fishing, and that sea is replete and abounding in every kind of fish. They are not hunters. This I deem to be because there are there many sorts of wild animals, and especially lions and bears and innumerable serpents and other horrid and ugly beasts, and also because forests and trees of huge size there extend far and wide; and they dare not, naked and without covering and arms, expose themselves to such hazards.

The land in those parts is very fertile and pleasing, abounding in numerous hills and mountains, boundless valleys and eighty rivers, watered by refreshing springs and filled with broad, dense, and well nigh impenetrable forests full of every sort of wild animal. Trees grow to immense size without cultivation. Many of these yield fruits delectable to the taste and beneficial to the human body; some indeed do not, and no fruits there are like those of ours. Innumerable species of herbs and roots grow there too, of which they make bread and excellent food. They have, too, many seeds altogether unlike these of ours. They have there no metals of any description except gold, of which those regions have a great plenty, although to be sure we have brought none thence on this our first voyage. This the natives called to our attention, who averred that in the districts remote from the coast there is a great abundance of gold, and by them it is in no respect esteemed or valued. They are rich in pearls as I wrote you before. If I were to seek to recount in detail what things are there and to write concerning the numerous species of animals and the great number of them, it would be a matter all too prolix and vast. And I truly believe that our **Pliny** did not touch upon a thousandth part of the species of parrots and other birds and the animals, too, which exist in those same regions so diverse as to form and color. . . . There all trees are fragrant and they emit each and all gum, oil, or some sort of sap. If the properties of these were known to us, I doubt not but that they would be salutary to the human body. And surely if the terrestrial paradise be in any part of this earth, I esteem that it is not far distant from those parts. Its situation, as I have related, lies toward the south in such a temperate climate that icy winters and fiery summers alike are never there experienced.

The sky and atmosphere are serene during the greater part of the year, and devoid of thick vapors; the rains there fall finely, last three or four hours, and vanish like a mist. The sky is adorned with most beautiful constellations and forms among which I noted about twenty stars as bright as we ever saw Venus or Jupiter. I have considered the movements and orbits of these, I have measured their circumferences and diameters by geometric method, and I ascertained that they are of greater magnitude. I saw in that sky three *Canopi,* two indeed bright, the third dim. The Antarctic pole is not figured with a Great and a Little Bear as this Arctic pole of ours is seen to be, nor is any bright star to be seen near it, and of those which move around it with the shortest circuit there are three which have the form of a . . . triangle. . . .

TERMS AND DEFINITIONS

Canopi: a reference to stars and constellations.

Lorenzo de´ Medici: Known as "the Magnificent," he ruled the important and wealthy Italian city-state of Florence from 1478 to 1492.

Pliny: Gaius Plinius Secundus (A.D. 23–79), also known as Pliny the Elder, was a writer and naturalist.

GIOVANNI DA VERRAZANO'S ACCOUNT OF NORTH AMERICA

By the dawn of the sixteenth century, the existence of lands to the north of those discovered by the Spaniards and Portuguese had been confirmed. However, the extent of those lands remained unknown. In 1524, Giovanni da Verrazano (1485–1528), sponsored by French king Francis I sailed to North America in search of a passage that would lead to the Indies. He never found such a passage, but in the search, he sailed along the coast from North Carolina to New England and up to Newfoundland. The following account comes from his journal of that voyage. It appears in translation in a 1970 book, The Voyages of Giovanni da Verazzano. *Note how positively he describes the lands he encountered and also how he notes contradictions between his discoveries and assumptions made by the ancient Greeks and Romans.*

We set sail with the Dauphine from the deserted rock near the Island of **Madeira**, on the XVII day of January last; we had fifty men, and were provided with food for eight months, with arms and other articles of war, and naval munitions. On the XXIII day of February we went through a storm as violent as ever sailing man encountered. We continued on our westerly course. In another XXV days we sailed more than four hundred leagues, where there appeared a new land which never had been seen before by any man, either ancient or modern.

I will now tell Your Majesty about it, and describe the situation and nature of this land. The seashore is completely covered with fine sand XV feet deep, which rises in the form of small hills about fifty paces wide. After climbing farther, we found other streams and inlets from the sea which come in by several mouths, and follow the ins and outs of the shoreline. Nearby we could see a stretch of country much higher than the sandy shore , with many beautiful fields and plains full of great forests, some sparse and some dense; and the trees have so many colors and are so beautiful and delightful that they defy description. And do not think, Your Majesty, that these forests are like the **Hyrcanian Forest** or the wild wastelands of **Scythia** and the northern countries, full of common trees; they are adorned and clothed with palms, laurel, cypress, and other varieties of tree unknown in our Europe. And these trees emit a sweet fragrance over a large area. We think that they belong to the Orient by virtue of the surroundings, and that they are not without some kind of narcotic or aromatic liquor. There are other riches, like gold, which ground of such color usually denotes. There is an abundance of animals, stags, deer, hares; and also of lakes and pools of running water with various types of bird perfect for all the delights and pleasures of the hunt. The air is salubrious and pure, and free from the extremes of heat and cold; gentle winds blow in these regions, and the prevailing winds in summertime, which was beginning when we were there, are northwest and westerly; the sky is clear and cloudless, with infrequent rain, and if occasionally the south winds bring in clouds and murk-iness, they are dispelled in an instant, and the sky is once more clear and bright; the sea is calm and unruffled, its waves gentle.

We left this place, still following the coast, which veered somewhat to the north, and after fifty leagues we reached another land which seemed much more beautiful and full of great forests. We anchored there, and with XX men we penetrated about two leagues inland, to find that the people had fled in terror into the forests. Searching everywhere, we met with a very old woman and a young girl of XVIII to XX years, who had hidden in the grass in fear. The old woman had two little girls whom she carried on her shoulders, and clinging to her neck a boy—they were all about eight years old. We took the boy from the old woman to carry back to France, and we wanted to take the young woman who was very beautiful and tall, but it was impossible to take her to the sea because of the loud cries she uttered. And as we were a long way from the ship and had to pass through several woods, we decided to leave her behind, and took only the boy.

The land is like the previous one in situation, fertility, and beauty; the woods are sparse; the land is covered with different types of trees, but they are not so fragrant, since there it is more northern and cold. We saw many vines growing wild, which climb up around the trees they would doubtless produce excellent wines if they were properly cultivated, for several times we found the dry fruit sweet and pleasant, not unlike our own. We found wild roses, violets, and lilies, and many kinds of herbs and fragrant flowers differ-ent from ours.

We weighed anchor, and sailed eastward since the land veered in that di-rection, and we covered LXXX leagues, always keeping in sight of land. We discovered a triangular-shaped island, ten leagues from the mainland, similar in size to the island of **Rhodes**; it was full of hills, covered in trees, and highly populated to judge by the fires we saw burning continually along the shore. We reached another land XV leagues from the island, where we found an ex-cellent harbor; before entering it, we saw about XX boats full of people who came around the ship uttering various cries of wonderment.

We . . . went five to six leagues into the interior, and found it as pleasant as I can possibly describe, and suitable for every kind of cultivation—grain, wine, or oil. For there the fields extend for XXV to XXX leagues; they are open and free of any obstacles or trees, and so fertile that any kind of seed would produce excellent crops. Then we entered the forests, which could be penetrated even by a large army; the trees there are oaks, cypresses, and oth-ers unknown in our Europe. We found Lucullian apples [cherries], plums, and filberts, and many kinds of fruit different from ours.

This country is situated on a parallel with Rome at $40\frac{2}{3}$ degrees, but is somewhat colder, by chance and not by nature. I will now describe the position of the aforementioned port. The coast of this land runs from west to east. The harbor mouth faces south, and is half a league wide; from its entrance it extends for XII leagues in a northeasterly direction, and then widens out to form a very large bay of about XX leagues in circumference. In this bay there are five small islands, very fertile and beautiful, full of tall spreading trees, and any large fleet could ride safely among them without fear of tempest or other dangers. Then, going southward to the entrance of the harbor, there are very pleasant hills on either side, with many streams of clear water flowing from the high land into the sea. In the middle of this estuary there is a rock of "*viva pietra*" [a non-porous rock] formed by nature, which is suitable for building any kind of machine or bulwark for the defense of the harbor.

It remains for me to tell Your Majesty of the progress of this voyage as regards Cosmography. [W]e departed [from Europe] from the rocks which lie at the limit of the Occident as the ancients knew it; and in the meridian of the **Fortunate Islands**, at a latitude of 32 degrees north of the Equator in our hemisphere, we sailed westward until we first found land at 1,200 leagues—which is equal to 4,800 miles, counting four miles to a league in accordance with the maritime practice of naval experts. My intention on this voyage was to reach Cathay and the extreme eastern coast of Asia, but I did not expect to find such an obstacle of new land as I have found; and if for some reason I did expect to find it, I estimated there would be some strait to get through to the Eastern Ocean. This was the opinion of all the ancients, who certainly believed that our Western Ocean was joined to the Eastern Ocean of India without any land in between. Nevertheless, land has been found by modern man which was unknown to the ancients, another world with respect to the one they knew, which appears to be larger than our Europe, than Africa, and almost larger than Asia, if we estimate its size correctly. In this way we find that the extension of the land is much greater than the ancients believed, and contrary to the Mathematicians who considered that there was less land than water, we have proven it by experience to be the reverse.

All this land or New World which we have described above is joined together, but is not linked with Asia or Africa (we know this for certain), but could be joined to Europe by Norway or Russia; this would be false according to the ancients. [M]ay God Almighty prosper you in everlasting glory, so that we may see the perfect end to our cosmography, and that the sacred word of the gospel may be fulfilled: "their sound has gone out into every land."

TERMS AND DEFINITIONS

Fortunate Islands: the Canary Islands in the north Atlantic Ocean.
Hyrcanian Forest: Hyrcan was a province of the ancient Persian Empire in the area of the Caspian Sea.
Madeira: islands in the Atlantic Ocean off the west coast of Morocco.

Rhodes: An ancient Greek island and state located in the Aegean Sea, Rhodes is perhaps most remembered as the site of the great bronze statue of Apollo, known as the "Collosus of Rhodes." It was one of the Seven Wonders of the Ancient World.

Scythia: An area along the Black Sea inhabited by a group of people whom the ancient Greeks regarded as wild and uncivilized.

GERMÁN ARCINIEGAS

AMERICA: EUROPE'S UTOPIA

Germán Arciniegas (b.1900), a Colombian historian and diplomat, adopted the approach of writing about America and its meaning for Europeans in a 1986 work he titled, "America in Europe, A History of the New World in Reverse." In the following selection he notes the many mythological visions of the New World. Europeans for some time saw America in terms of legends and fables. Arciniegas especially stresses, however, the importance of America as utopia: Its appeal endures as a place that promises a better life to those who seek its shores.

The Spanish interest is obvious. The stage on which the story is to unfold is entirely theirs. **Diego Velázquez,** governor of Cuba, when he makes his agreements with Hernán Cortés, stipulates: "Because it has been said that there are people whose ears are large and wide, and others who have faces like dogs, look for them and also learn where and in what place are the Amazons of which the Indians tell." Cortés himself, usually so objective in his letters, writes to **Charles V,** telling him how he has been informed by the Indians of an island inhabited entirely by women, not one man among them. He entrusts his relative Francisco Cortés with the mission of exploring the land of the Amazons described in ancient narratives.

Thus the Amazons heralded by Columbus begin to people the heart of South America, filter themselves into the imagination of those who first explore Chile, Paraguay, Peru, New Granada, Venezuela, Guiana. And in North America, just as to the south, the largest river was named the Amazon and the name of California, queen of the Amazons, is given to a peninsula, a sea, a gulf, and two states.

The legends returned to Europe. They were all the rage, and the **books of chivalry** multiplied furiously. In Amsterdam were printed chronicles that confirmed the renaissance in America of every known freak that ever inhabited medieval fiction. A nonfactual geography persisted even after the discoverers should have fully realized that the Indians were fairly ordinary flesh and blood like themselves. But myth was made of stronger stuff than reality. Into this mèlange of Greek, Asian, and European invention, the American ingredients began to filter.

The story of the Amazons was so vivid in Spanish minds that once, in 1533, one of Charles V's agents informed him that the ports of Santander and

Laredo had witnessed the arrival of sixty ships with ten thousand Amazons on board, attracted by the rumor that the men of those regions were known to be "real men." The Amazons had come to reproduce: each one would pay fifteen ducats to any stud who made her pregnant.

At the same time, illustrated geographies began to grow very popular. The first engravings of New World natives were made by Germans. According to the illustrations in Theodore de Bry's *American History* (1590–1634), the fabulous wealth described by **Prester John** is all located in America. Columbus disembarks, and the naked Indians come out to welcome him and render him homage, bringing chests, necklaces, chiseled gold chalices. Gold mines are depicted as marvelous spectacles. Gold dust is scooped up from the hillsides as if it were sand and poured into baskets that the natives place, one by one, at the admiral's feet. In other engravings, the Amazons are the center of attraction, especially so in the cannibal scenes. Curaçao is depicted as the Isle of the Giants. And the first maps are animated by similarly imaginative scenes.

On the one hand were the human monsters and mythological fauna of the New World; or animals no one had ever laid eyes on before, such as iguanas. On the other, the delights: the Fountain of Eternal Youth, the Garden of Eden. The garden, of course, drew everyone. The actual place where Adam and Eve had first dwelt existed; its reality was universally accepted. One only had to establish just which corner of the planet it occupied. So what did Columbus go out to discover at the mouth of the Orinoco? The Garden of Eden! He arrived at the spot, saw its contours [and said]: "Great signs are these of the Earthly Paradise, because the place conforms to the opinions of the saints and wisest of theologians and proves correct those who have said that the world—land and water—is spherical. I found that it was not round in the way they write about it; it is shaped like a pear, as if one had a very round ball and on it were the breast of a woman with the part of the nipple highest and nearest to Heaven."

What follows this encounter with Paradise is more acceptance of all things, possible and impossible. The Europeans perch in their theater stalls to watch as an unparalleled drama unfolds on the American stage. Nine hundred large-format pages did **León Pinelo** write to combat the seventeen most authorized hypotheses that placed Eden in the center of the moon, in the middle regions of the air on top of the highest known mountain peaks in the sky, in Libya, in India, in the Moluccas, in Ceylon. For Pinelo, all this was groundless geography, and he argued: "Where is the richest, most pleasant land, the most delicious and sweetly moderate in climate, if not in the magic bower of Amazonia with its exotic orchids and its butterflies winged with pearly iridescence and emerald?"

As a complement to this preparatory work, Pinelo transferred to America—one by one—the monsters Europe had invented or adopted and, finally, sure that Peru was wealthier by far than India, sure that everything in divine and humanistic letters pointed to the inevitable conclusion that The Earthly Paradise lay somewhere in the vicinity of Iquitos [Peru], he wove with these elements the enchanted tapestry of his books. For those Occidentals who were weary of the hardships of the Old World, marvelous America was to be the Seat of Paradise.

Of all the philosophies of the West, no other possesses the fascinating charm of *Utopia,* the first joyful moment of the sixteenth century. With it the great sleeping expectation is fanned into awareness. The idea of such a place causes man, a captive of injustice for centuries, to become a rebel, to plunge into the most absurd of explorations and adventures. In the end, the idea mobilizes millions of Europeans in search of new worlds, places where they might begin to imagine conditions of well-being nonexistent in their native lands The new movement—a hopeful one—is toward social justice, for centuries suppressed by the monarchy, the aristocracy, the Church, the powerful bourgeoisie.

Humanism brought together a group of select philosophers who tried, throughout Europe, to propagate a new gospel, born out of a radical revision of ideas. **Thomas More** writes *Utopia* at the same time that his friend **Erasmus** writes *The Praise of Folly.* The twin works, conceived in the closest rapport, give us the exact measure of the belligerent idealism of those days. After which a vast literature, ushered in by those two volumes, penetrates the best currents of Western thought through hundreds of prototypes. Still, not one of these authors, not even Erasmus himself, was able to invent such a fortunate word as More did with his *Utopia.*

"Utopia" means a nonexistent place; it is a name conceived in skepticism and reflecting the irony at the heart of every idealist who is afraid that the treacheries of destiny will mock the children of his imagination. His Utopia is the work that sparks the mightiest exodus of all time. Utopians all, Europeans emigrate in a constant and massive flood, now four centuries long, to the continent of their hopes: America.

One of the great strokes of good fortune that favored the discovery of America and its ensuing intellectual activity was the invention of the printing press. So fresh is this invention that in London it was introduced just one year after More's birth; and More's acquaintance with Vespucci's letters brought about his friendship with those who worked in publishing houses. With the rise of Charles V to the Spanish throne Antwerp became Spain's printing press. The first picture of an American potato plant was printed in Antwerp long before anyone could imagine eating, as the Indians did, the tubercles that fattened on its roots.

It is hard to tell fact from fiction in the first accounts of America. While it is difficult to know up to what point More in the creation of his marvelous island, depended on Vespucci's facts, or on his fantasy, something is positive and evident: destiny began to turn his Utopia into a reality. At first, solitary adventurers crossed the Atlantic full of the conviction that they were going to come upon **El Dorados** and other chimeras, striving at the same time to free themselves from an old continent that was too narrow and oppressive for them. They crossed the ocean and put down roots. After this came the multitudes, millions of Europeans embarking for America on the same quests. Whether it was truth that triumphed or fantasy that materialized, finally it makes little difference.

With the passage of time, not only does the idea of Utopia not fade, it affirms itself more and more in millions of Europeans who continue to see in their native countries the same miseries that More exposed, and in America the same hopes. What may have been begun as a quixotic Iberian adventure becomes a universal contagion in the Old World.

TERMS AND DEFINITIONS

books of chivalry: popular stories of the glory days of armored knights and romantic deeds.

El Dorados: literally "the golden or gilded ones." In its broadest sense it refers to the Spanish explorers and adventurers who searched for wealth in the New World.

Erasmus: Desiderius Erasmus (1466–1536), a Dutch religious thinker and humanist.

Thomas More: Sir Thomas More (1478–1535), an English statesman and author. He was beheaded for treason.

Prester John: a legendary Christian king in the Middle Ages said to rule somewhere in the East.

León Pinela: Antonio de León Pinela wrote a two-volume work, *Paradise in the New World*, which was filled with fantastic stories about America, including, for example, that there were Native Americans who had tails.

Diego Velázquez: the Spanish governor who initially authorized Cortés to mount an expedition to the mainland to investigate tales that a wealthy civilization existed there.

J. H. ELLIOT

EUROPE AND AMERICA

As the "discoverers" of America, Europeans also were its interpreters, both to themselves and to much of the rest of the world. They approached the new world through an inherited intellectual and historical tradition, which predisposed them to understand American reality in ways that conformed to their preconceptions. J. H. Elliott (b.1930), a leading scholar of the meaning of the discovery, discusses the intellectual impact of the New World on the Old in a selection from his 1970 book, The Old World and the New 1492-1650.

The reluctance of cosmographers or of social philosophers to incorporate into their work the new information made available to them by the discovery of America provides an example of the problem arising from the revelation of the New World to the Old. Whether it is a question of the geography of America, its flora and fauna, or the nature of its inhabitants, the same kind of pattern seems constantly to recur in the European response. It is as if, at a certain point, the mental shutters come down; as if, with so much to see and absorb and understand, the effort suddenly becomes too much for them, and Europeans retreat to the half-light of their traditional mental world.

If one asks *what* Europeans saw on arriving on the far side of the Atlantic, and *how* they saw it, much will inevitably depend on the kind of Europeans involved. The range of vision is bound to be affected by background, and by professional interests. Soldiers, clerics, merchants, and officials trained in the law—these are the classes of men on whom we are dependent for most of our first-hand observation of the New World and its inhabitants.

The temptation was almost overpoweringly strong to see the newly-discovered lands in terms of the enchanted isles of medieval fantasy. But it was not only the fantastic that tended to obtrude itself between the European and reality. If the unfamiliar were to be approached as anything other than the extraordinary and the monstrous, then the approach must be conducted by reference to the most firmly established elements in Europe's cultural inheritance. Between them, therefore, the Christian and the classical tradition were likely to prove the obvious points of departure for any evaluation of the New World and its inhabitants.

In some respects, both of these traditions could assist Europeans in coming to terms with America. Each provided a possible norm or yardstick, other than those immediately to hand in Renaissance Europe, by which to judge the land and the peoples of the newly-discovered world. Some of the more obvious categories for classifying the inhabitants of the Antilles were clearly inapplicable. These people were not monstrous; and their hairlessness made it difficult to identify them with the wild men of the popular medieval tradition. Nor were they Negroes or Moors, the races best known to medieval Christendom. In these circumstances, it was natural for Europeans to look back into their own traditions, and seek to evaluate the puzzling world of the Indies by reference to the Garden of Eden or the Golden Age of Antiquity.

The humanists, like the friars, projected onto America their disappointed dreams. In the *Decades* of **Peter Martyr**, the first popularizer of America and its myth, the Indies have already undergone their subtle transmutation. Here were a people who lived without weights and measures and 'pestiferous moneye, the seed of innumerable myscheves. So that if we shall not be ashamed to confesse the truthe, they seem to lyve in the goulden worlde of the which owlde wryters speake so much: wherein men lyved simplye and innocentlye without inforcement of lawes, without quarreling Iudges [judges] and libelles, contente onely to satisfie nature,' . . .

It was an idyllic picture, and the **humanists** made the most of it, for it enabled them to express their deep dissatisfaction with European society, and to criticize it by implication. America and Europe became antitheses—the antitheses of innocence and corruption.

But by treating the New World in this way, the humanists were closing the door to understanding an alien civilization. America was not as they imagined it; and even the most enthusiastic of them had to accept from an early stage that the inhabitants of this idyllic world could also be vicious and bellicose, and sometimes ate each other. This of itself was not necessarily sufficient to quench utopianism, for it was always possible to build Utopia on the far side of the Atlantic if it did not already exist. But the dream was a European dream, which had little to do with the American reality. As that reality came to impinge at an increasing number of points, so the dream began to fade.

Sixteenth-century Europeans . . . instinctively accepted the idea of a designed world into which America—however unexpected its first appearance—must somehow be incorporated. Everything that could be known about America must have its place in the universal scheme. Knowledge of the new lands and new peoples could, as [Josè de] Acosta suggested, further the great task of the evangelization of mankind. Knowledge of its infinite diversity, on which **Fernández de Oviedo** and **Las Casas** exclaimed with awe and wonder, could only enhance man's appreciation of the omnipotence of its divine creator. Knowledge of the medicinal and therapeutic properties of its plants and herbs was further testimony to God's care for the well-being of His children. Often, no doubt, the more strictly metaphysical considerations receded far into the background, but there always remained the hard deposit of an engrained conviction that knowledge had a purpose.

It was not until the publication in Spanish in 1590 of Josè de Acosta's great *Natural and Moral History of the Indies,* that the process of integrating the American world into the general framework of European thought was at last triumphantly achieved. In effect he was engaged in the supremely difficult task of displaying to European readers the unique characteristics of America and its inhabitants, while at the same time emphasizing the underlying unity between the Old World and the New. The competing claims of unity and diversity were reconciled in a synthesis which owed much to the Aristotelian cast of Acosta's thought.

But Acosta's synthesis was itself the culmination of a century of intellectual endeavour, in the course of which three different aspects of the American world were being slowly and painfully assimilated into the European consciousness. America, as an entity in space, had demanded incorporation into Europe's mental image of the natural world. American man had to be found his place among the peoples of mankind. And America, as an entity in time, required integration into Europe's conception of the historical process. All this was achieved during the course of the sixteenth century, and it was Acosta's synthesizing genius which brought the great enterprise to completion.

It was not easy to break away from the traditional conception of the *orbis terrarum* . . . with its three landmasses of Europe, Asia, and Africa, any more than it was easy to break away from the idea of an unnavigable and uninhabitable torrid zone in the southern hemisphere. If experience effectively disproved the second of these theses at an early stage, it did not disprove the first of them until the crossing of the Behring Strait in 1728. It was therefore reasonable enough that there should have been continuing uncertainty throughout the sixteenth-century as to whether or not America formed part of Asia.

Certain cosmographical ideas derived from classical antiquity were in fact vindicated by the discoveries. But other ideas—about uninhabitable regions or climatic zones—had to be abandoned or profoundly modified. Nor could classical learning be of any great value in interpreting the phenomena of a part of the world of which it had remained unaware. Here, as Fernández de Oviedo never tired of pointing out, there was no substitute for personal experience. The superiority of direct personal observation over traditional authority was proved time and time again in the new environment of America. And on each fresh occasion, another fragment was chipped away from the massive rock of authority.

But the very fact that the natural phenomena of the New World did not figure in the traditional cosmographies or natural histories, made it all the harder to bring them within the compass of the European consciousness. One device frequently employed was that of analogy or comparison. But the comparative method had its own dangers and disadvantages. When Oviedo and Las Casas compared Hispaniola to those other two famous islands, England and Sicily, in order to prove that it was in no way inferior to them in fertility, the general effect was simply to blur the differences between all three. Acosta, who saw the danger, specifically warned against the assumption that American species differed accidentally, and not in essence, from those of Europe. The differences were sometimes so great, he said, that to reduce them all to European types was like calling an egg a chestnut.

There was evidence enough in the century of European history since the discovery of America to sustain a thesis that the cultivation of the arts was the determinant of progress. And if progress now became a conceivable possibility, this was partly on account of discoveries themselves. The reverence for antiquity, and the belief in the existence of a Golden Age in the distant past, had both been undermined. The very fact of the discovery of America meant that the moderns had achieved something that had not been achieved in antiquity; and it vividly revealed the value of first-hand experience as against inherited tradition.

If the discovery of the New World, therefore, strengthened Christian providentialist interpretation of history as a progressive movement which would culminate in the evangelization of all mankind, it equally strengthened the more purely secular interpretation of history as a progressive movement which would culminate in the civilization of all mankind.

TERMS AND DEFINITIONS

humanists: Renaissance scholars who adopted a secular orientation and stressed the importance of critical thinking.

Fernández de Oviedo: Gonzalo Fernández de Oviedo (1478–1557) traveled extensively in the New World and in 1535 wrote a book, *General and Natural History of the Indies.*

Las Casas: Bartolomé de las Casas (1474–1567), a Spanish priest and ardent defender of the Native American peoples, wrote several books about America, including a *History of the Indies.*

orbis terrarum: the ancient belief that Europe, Africa, and Asia comprised all the major landmasses that the Earth could hold.

Peter Martyr: Martyr (1447–1562), an Italian humanist who had a significant impact on the reformation in England, also collected a number of reports from early explorers.

THINKING THINGS THROUGH

1. Why did the early explorers of the New World believe that it was very close to Asia?

2. What factors persuaded Vespucci and Verrazano that they had found a major land mass?

3. How did biblically-based Christian belief affect European views of the New World?

4. What factors predisposed Europeans to believe fantastic tales regarding the New World?

5. Considering the discovery of the New World as a process, what major changes did it produce?

2

EUROPE AND THE FIRST AMERICANS

A. The International Context

Acting in accord with his belief that he had reached the Indies, Columbus referred to the Taino who inhabited the Bahamas island of San Salvador as "Indians." Although that name stuck, by the 1520s Europeans understood that Columbus's "Indies" really constituted a new and unanticipated portion of the world. At that point, the origins of the New World's peoples became a puzzling and absorbing question. The earliest European commentary about the Native Americans centered on resolving that issue.

Though the Protestant Reformation (which began in 1517) shattered the unity of Western Christendom, the literal truth of Biblical accounts of Genesis and the Flood remained unquestioned by virtually all Christians. Those accounts clearly indicated that all humans shared a common ancestry as descendants of Adam and Eve. Moreover, all living humans had a direct line of descent from the sons of Noah. Contemporary European belief suggested that Noah's Ark had come to land in Armenia. From that point, humans had spread out to populate Africa, Asia, and Europe. But how had they crossed the broad Atlantic Ocean to reach America? And, equally puzzling, how had land animals—including some previously unknown to Europeans—reached the New World?

Some attempts to answer these compelling questions involved unorthodox—indeed heretical—theological possibilities. For example, a French Calvinist, Isaac de la Peyrere, raised the possibility of polygenesis, that is, more than one creation. He suggested that Adam had been the father only of the Hebrews. An earlier genesis had produced other peoples, including the New World's Native Americans and its unusual animals. He also suggested that the Flood had been a more localized phenomenon, one that destroyed only the Hebrews, leaving other peoples unaffected. Keeping more closely within orthodoxy, other thinkers speculated about the possibility that prior to setting down the Ark in Armenia, Noah had touched land at other points, including the New World. Another biblically-based point of origins lay in the possibility that the Native Americans had descended from the Ten Lost Tribes of Israel, a theory first broached by Dutch and French authors in the 1560s, and supported subsequently in the works of several Spanish writers.

In addition to its theological dimensions, the intellectual framework guiding Europeans included knowledge of "the ancients," that is, the classical civilizations of Greece and Rome. This tradition suggested other explanations for the peopling of America, ones which connected it directly with the Old World. Ptolemy (Claudius Ptolemaeus, 127–151), the great Greek astronomer, mathematician, and philosopher, had referred directly to the "lost continent" of Atlantis, a land mass lying in the Atlantic Ocean to the west of Gibraltar. Supposedly, it had sunk beneath the seas as a result of some great cataclysm. Fitting the new discoveries of Columbus into preexisting understandings, some suggested that Atlantis might well have stretched all the way to the West Indies. Hence, it became possible that Noah's descendants had reached Atlantis through Spain and North Africa. The Native Americans, then, represented the remnants of Atlantean civilization, the descendents of those who escaped its sinking by sailing to the American mainland. Another possibility involved a tale of merchants from the ancient North African civilization of Carthage who had traveled through the Mediterranean out into the Atlantic where they encountered a previously unknown land. Since Europeans learned of the tale of the merchants from Carthage in the writings of Aristotle (384–322 B.C.), regarded by Europeans as the foremost authority on the Classical civilizations, and whose system of logic formed the basis for much of Medieval thought, this theory enjoyed a strong aura of credibility.

The subsequent Spanish encounters with the great Native American civilizations of the Aztecs and Incas lent further weight to this argument, for many Europeans found it impossible to believe that these "savage" peoples had achieved so much on their own. Perceived parallels between aspects of the great Native American civilizations and those of the Classical civilizations of the ancient world lent further support to the idea of far-earlier contacts between Old World and New as the point of origin for the peoples of America.

For example, some Spaniards saw reflections of Rome's temple virgins in the Inca women who served the sun. Various of the Inca and Aztec gods in many respects seemed similar to those worshiped by the Greeks and Romans. Certain other Native American religious practices seemed to echo those of Christianity. These included rites reminiscent of baptism and the use of a cross as a sacred symbol. (Subsequent scholarship revealed that the cross, in this case, represented the four cardinal points.) The possibility existed, then, said some Spanish friars and priests, that one of Christ's apostles had visited the Americas. Others saw in these parallels the sinister work of Satan, twisting the sacred into the profane. The origin stories of the Aztecs, which spoke of the role of Quetzalcoatl, who had taught the Aztecs most of their arts, and described him as a light-skinned god who had sailed off to the east seemed to further suggest the likelihood of ancient contacts between Old World and New.

The most significant of the early Spanish writers, José de Acosta, suggested an origin that essentially conforms to present-day understandings. He speculated that the New World at one time must have had some connection to the Old, most probably a land bridge or a narrow strait. Though myth and fable still attached itself to the Americas for some time, ultimately Acosta's speculation, suggested as well in works by English and Dutch writers, gained general acceptance. Writing in 1700, for example, the famous Puritan theologian Cotton Mather subscribed to the probability of that connection, which by that time had been identified as the Strait of Anian, believed to lie between northeast Asia and northwest America.

Definitive confirmation of the existence of this earlier speculation came from a series of voyages of exploration out from Siberia between 1728 and 1741, undertaken by Vitus Bering, a Dane sailing for Russia. Among his discoveries was the strait bearing his name that lies between the easternmost portion of Russia and Alaska. Controversy continued, however, as to the precise identity of the people who had in some distant time used that route to cross over from Asia. Wandering tribes of ancient Hebrews, Scythians, and Tatars all received prominent mention.

Well before any resolution of the issue of Native American origins, Spain had begun what became a major, ongoing effort at conversion, one also engaged in although somewhat later and less extensively by Portugal. Pope Innocent VIII had in 1486 issued a bull declaring the propagation of the faith, including the conversion of infidels or unbelievers, to be the main mission of the Church. This bull, which clearly reflected the crusading zeal of a still medieval church, received further endorsement from his successor, Pope Alexander VI. Spain's just title to its New World empire, said the Pope, rested on its mission of spreading Christianity among the Native Americans. That these peoples could in fact receive and understand the Gospel was confirmed by both Alexander VI and his successor Paul III.

Several Spanish religious orders, including the Augustinians, Franciscans, and Dominicans carried out the dictates of both Pope and Crown, and much of what is known of the nature and customs of the Native American peoples in Spanish territory comes to us filtered through the journals, letters, and histories written by these friars. For example, the Franciscan friar Bernardino de Sahagún, whose sincere desires to spread the faith led him to learn Nahuatl, the Aztec's language, wrote a general history of Mexico (then known as New Spain) which even today remains an important source for students of Aztec culture. Many Spanish friars spoke out against the early practice of enslaving Indians and organized mission settlements to instruct them in Christianity while protecting them from colonists. At the same time, that fierce religious zeal which brought them to the New World caused them to see indigenous beliefs and practices as idolatrous and heretical. They ordered the destruction of numerous temples, religious images, and sacred texts. And, never did they see the Native Americans' rights as including the choice to live as they pleased.

In North America, both the Jesuits and Franciscan Recollets mirrored the behavior of their Spanish counterparts. They traveled through the wilderness in an attempt to turn the Native Americans away from idolatry and bring them to the one true faith. Samuel de Champlain, the founder of Quebec brought Recollets from France to proselytize among the Iroquois, Algonkians, and Hurons. By the 1630s, missions successfully had been established among the settled Native American peoples, and attempts had begun to alter the patterns of more nomadic groups. Missions established by Recollets and Jesuits became the nuclei for many subsequent colonial settlements.

The early outpouring of missionary zeal diminished as colonial settlement increased and disease and dislocation decimated Native American populations throughout the Americas. In Spanish and Portuguese America, settlers valued the indigenous peoples for the wealth they could produce, whether in the form of tribute or labor. Despite a considerable amount of miscegenation, which gave rise to the racially mixed populations that characterize many of the contemporary nations of Latin America, neither Spaniard nor Portuguese doubted for a moment the superiority of their own civilizations. They also generally acted as if it were their right to take the Native Americans' lands and possessions and exploit their labor.

In New France (French Canada), French settlement remained relatively light, and the fur trade soon became the most significant economic activity. French woodsmen valued the Native Americans for their knowledge of the terrain and their skills in hunting and trapping. As such, they tended to cultivate good relations with them and, as in Spanish America, though not to the same degree, a racially mixed population arose. Since export agriculture never gained importance, there was no economic rationale for forcing the Native Americans off their traditional lands. However, the intrusion of the French, as also proved the case with the English, affected prevailing power relations among different Native American groups. The Hurons (more properly, the Wendat or Wyandot), for example, controlled vast trade routes. They prospered as intermediaries in the fur trade, buying furs from more distant Native American peoples and bringing them to the French at the St. Lawrence. This outraged the Iroquois, who played the same role in the trading activity of the Dutch and English. Allied with the English, the Iroquois began attacking Huron trading expeditions and, in a massive action that occurred in 1648 to 1649, they virtually destroyed the Huron nation. In turn, this shifted the activities of priests from proselytizing among the Native Americans to serving the needs of French settlers. As Native American populations declined, Spanish and Portuguese America witnessed a similar pattern, with priests increasingly ministering to the European, mixed-race population.

In British North America, by contrast, missionary activity never had been a priority. On some occasions, instances of friendly relations between colonials and Native Americans did exist. Europeans profited from Native Americans' knowledge regarding the cultivation of such American food crops as maize and squash. However, the insatiable land hunger of colonists relentlessly pressured Native Americans' settlements and lands, producing numerous armed conflicts. Such conflicts along a continuously moving frontier remained an issue throughout American colonial history.

B. International Views

These shifting patterns from earlier European concerns with questions of origins and proselytizing to economic exploitation of the riches of the New World found their counterpoint in European descriptions of the Native American peoples. Early writers expressed considerable admiration for the achievements of the great Native American civilizations of Central and South America. They also suggested the willingness—indeed eagerness—of the Native American peoples to receive the Gospel and learn "civilized" ways of life. As conflict accelerated, the "savagery" of Native American peoples received wider comment, as did their "stubborn" refusal to adopt European modes of existence. Visions of the Native Americans continued to reflect changing European intellectual patterns. By the seventeenth and eighteenth centuries, the Enlightenment had given new importance to rationalism and science. For many Europeans, then, religiously-based discussions of New World Native Americans became less important, and such concepts as progress and civilization—cast entirely in European terms—gained prominence. As a result, Europeans saw Native Americans as either "noble savages," (children of nature who retained much of the innocence of early humanity), or as degenerates who stood in the way of progress. Indeed, by the early 1800s, many educated Europeans saw the Native Americans—along with the indigenous peoples of other non-Western lands— as doomed by the inevitable workings of a natural historical law that dictated the inability of inherently weak, inferior peoples to stand against a superior civilization.

Throughout the centuries of contact, Europeans always portrayed Native Americans in terms that reflected their own understandings of the world, especially with regard to what constituted appropriate or inappropriate behaviors. It is important to bear in mind, then, that the selections in this chapter ought not be seen as "objective" or factual descriptions. Written in the sixteenth century, the initial selection by the Spanish conquistador [conqueror] Hernán Cortés conveys a sense of admiration and wonder for the great size of the Aztec empire and the splendor of its capital city, Tenochtitlán. Writing toward the end of that same century, José de Acosta, speculates on the origins of the people, animals, and plants in the New World. Based on his reading of the Biblical accounts of creation and the Flood, he finds it especially puzzling that various animals found in America existed nowhere else in the world. Gabriel Sagard, who lived for a while among the

Hurons of French Canada in the early seventeenth century, found much to admire in their customs, and saw them as sincere converts to Catholicism. However, he always refers to them as "savages." George Alsop, writing in the mid-1660s portrayed the Susquehannas of Maryland in an entirely negative light, seeing their society and culture as having no redeeming qualities.

HERNÁN CORTÉS

THE GREAT CITY OF TENOCHTITLÁN

Hernán Cortés (1485–1547), who at the age of thirty-four assured himself of lasting fame when he led the overthrow of the Aztec empire, wrote several letters to Spanish king Charles I (also known as Emperor Charles V of the Holy Roman Empire) describing and justifying his actions. Cortés genuinely admired many of the Aztecs' achievements, as is indicated in the selection below from one of his letters which describes their capital city, today the site of Mexico City. Note how he draws several favorable comparisons between Tenochtitlán and cities in Spain. The sense of wonder, so much a part of early European writers, emerges in his descriptions.

The province is roughly circular in shape and entirely surrounded by very lofty and rocky mountains, the level part in the middle being some seventy leagues in circumference and containing two lakes which occupy it almost entirely, for canoes travel over fifty leagues in making a circuit of them. One of the lakes is of fresh water, the other and larger one of salt. A narrow but very lofty range of mountains cuts across the valley and divides the lakes almost completely save for the western end where they are joined by a narrow strait no wider than a sling's throw which runs between the mountains. Commerce is carried on between the two lakes and the cities on their banks by means of canoes, so that land traffic is avoided.

The great city of Tenochtitlán is built in the midst of this salt lake, and it is two leagues from the heart of the city to any point on the mainland. Four causeways lead to it, all made by hand and some twelve feet wide. The city itself is as large as **Seville** or **Cordova**. The principal streets are very broad and straight, the majority of them being of beaten earth but a few and at least half the smaller thoroughfares are waterways along which they pass in their canoes. Moreover, even the principal streets have openings at regular distances so that the water can freely pass from one to another, and these openings which are very broad are spanned by great bridges of huge beams very stoutly put together, so firm indeed that over many of them ten horsemen can ride at once.

The city has many open squares in which markets are continuously held and the general business of buying and selling proceeds. One square in particular is twice as big as that of **Salamanca** and completely surrounded by arcades where there are daily more than sixty thousand folk buying and selling. Every kind of merchandise such as may be met with in every land is for sale there, whether of food and victuals, or ornaments of gold and silver, or lead, brass, copper, tin, precious stones, bones, shells, snails, and feathers; limestone for building is likewise sold there, stone both rough and polished, bricks burnt and unburnt, wood of all kinds and in all stages of preparation. There is a street of game where they sell all manner of birds that are to be found in their country. They also sell rabbits, hares, deer, and small dogs which they breed especially for eating. There is a street of herb-sellers where there are all manner of roots and medicinal plants that are found in the land. There are houses as it were of apothecaries where they sell medicines made from these herbs, both for drinking and for use as ointments and salves. There are barbers' shops where you may have your hair washed and cut. There are other shops where you may obtain food and drink. There are street porters such as we have in Spain to carry packages. There is a great quantity of wood, charcoal, braziers made of clay, and mats of all sorts, some for beds and others more finely woven for seats, still others for furnishing halls and private apartments. All kinds of vegetables may be found there, in particular onions, leeks, garlic, cresses, watercress, borage, sorrel, artichokes, and golden thistles. There are many different sorts of fruits including cherries and plums very similar to those found in Spain. They sell honey obtained from bees, as also the honeycomb and that obtained from maize plants which are as sweet as sugar canes; they also obtain honey from plants which are known both here and in other parts as maguey which is preferable to grape juice; from maguey in addition they make both sugar and a kind of wine, which are sold in their markets. All kinds of cotton thread in various colors may be bought in skeins, very much in the same way as in the great silk exchange of Granada, except that the quantities are far less. They have colors for painting of as good quality as any in Spain, and of as pure shades as may be found anywhere. There are leathers of deer both skinned and in their natural state, and either bleached or dyed in various colors. A great deal of chinaware is sold of very good quality and including earthen jars of all sizes for holding liquids, pitchers, pots, tiles, and an infinite variety of earthenware all made of very special clay and almost all decorated and painted in some way. Maize is sold both as grain and in the form of bread and is vastly superior both in the size of the ear and in taste to that of all the other islands or the mainland. Pastries made from game and fish pies may be seen on sale, and there are large quantities of fresh and salt water fish both in their natural state and cooked ready for eating. Eggs from fowls, geese and all the other birds I have described may be had, and likewise omelettes ready made. There is nothing to be found in all the land which is not sold in these markets, for over and above what I have mentioned there are so many and such various other things that on account of their very number and the fact that I do not know their names, I cannot now detail them. Each kind of merchandise is sold in its own particular street and no other kind may be sold there: this rule is very well enforced.

There are a very large number of mosques or dwelling places for their idols throughout the various districts of this great city, all fine buildings, in the chief of which their priests live continuously, so that in addition to the actual temples containing idols there are sumptuous lodgings. These pagan priests are all dressed in black and go habitually with their hair uncut; they do not even comb it from the day they enter the order to that on which they leave. Chief men's sons, both nobles and distinguished citizens, enter these orders at the age of six or seven and only leave when they are of an age to marry, and this occurs more frequently to the first-born who will inherit their father's estate than to others. Among these temples there is one chief, one in particular whose size and magnificence no human tongue could describe. For it is so big that within the lofty wall which entirely circles it one could set a town of fifteen thousand inhabitants.

Immediately inside this wall and throughout its entire length are some admirable buildings containing large halls and corridors where the priests who live in this temple are housed. There are forty towers at the least, all of stout construction and very lofty, the largest of which has fifty steps leading up to its base; this chief one is indeed higher than the great church of Seville. The workmanship both in wood and stone could not be bettered anywhere, for all the stonework within the actual temples where they keep their idols is cut into ornamental borders of flowers, birds, fishes, and the like, or trellis-work, and the woodwork is likewise all in relief highly decorated with monsters of very various device. The towers all serve as burying places for their nobles, and the little temples which they contain are all dedicated to a different idol to whom they pay their devotions.

There are three large halls in the great mosque where the principal idols are to be found, all of immense size and height and richly decorated with sculptured figures both in wood and stone, and within these halls are other smaller temples branching off from them and entered by doors so small that no daylight ever reaches them.

The images of the idols in which these people believed are many times greater than the body of a large man. They are made from pulp of all the cereals and greenstuffs which they eat, mixed and pounded together. This mass they moisten with blood from the hearts of human beings which they tear from their breasts while still alive, and thus make sufficient quantity of the pulp to mould into their huge statues; and after the idols have been set up still they offer them more living hearts which they sacrifice in like manner and anoint their faces with the blood. Each department of human affairs has its particular idol after the manner of the ancients who thus honored their gods: so that there is one idol from whom they beg success in war, another for crops, and so on for all their needs.

The city contains many large and fine houses, and for this reason. All the nobles of the land owing allegiance to **Muteczuma** have their houses in the city and reside there for a certain portion of the year; and in addition there are a large number of rich citizens who likewise have very fine houses. All possess in addition to large and elegant apartments very delightful flower gardens of every kind, both on the ground level as on the upper stories.

Along one of the causeways connecting this great city with the mainland two pipes are constructed of masonry, each two paces broad and about as high as a man, one of which conveys a stream of water very clear and fresh and about the thickness of a man's body right to the center of the city, which all can use for drinking and other purposes. The other pipe, which is empty, is used when it is desired to clean the former.

At all the entrances to the city and at those parts where canoes are unloaded, which is where the greatest amount of provisions enters the city, certain huts have been built, where there are official guards to exact so much on everything that enters. I know not whether this goes to the lord or to the city itself, and have not yet been able to ascertain, but I think that it is to the ruler, since in the markets of several other towns we have seen such a tax exacted on behalf of the ruler. Every day in all the markets and public places of the city there are a number of workmen and masters of all manner of crafts waiting to be hired by the day. The people of this city are nicer in their dress and manners than those of any other city or province, for since Muteczuma always holds his residence here and his vassals visit the city for lengthy periods, greater culture and politeness of manners in all things has been encouraged.

Finally, to avoid prolixity in telling all the wonders of this city, I will simply say that the manner of living among the people is very similar to that in Spain, and considering that this is a barbarous nation shut off from a knowledge of the true God or communication with enlightened nations, one may well marvel at the orderliness and good government which is everywhere maintained.

The actual service of Muteczuma and those things which call for admiration by their greatness and state would take so long to describe that I assure your Majesty I do not know where to begin with any hope of ending. For as I have already said, what could there be more astonishing than that a barbarous monarch such as he should have reproductions made in gold, silver, precious stones, and feathers of all things to be found in his land, and so perfectly reproduced that there is no goldsmith or silversmith in the world who could better them, nor can one understand what instrument could have been used for fashioning the jewels; as for the featherwork its like is not to be seen in either wax or embroidery, it is so marvelously delicate.

I was unable to find out exactly the extent of Muteczuma's kingdom, for in no part where he sent his messengers (even as much as two hundred leagues in either direction from this city) were his orders disobeyed although it is true there were certain provinces in the middle of this region with whom he was at war. But so far as I could understand his kingdom was almost as large as Spain. Most of the lords of these various provinces resided, as I have said, for the greater part of the year in the capital, and the majority of them had their eldest sons in Muteczuma's service. Another palace of his (not quite so fine as the one we were lodged in) had a magnificent garden with balconies overhanging it, the pillars and flagstones of which were all Jasper beautifully worked. In this palace there was room to lodge two powerful princes with all their retinue. There were also ten pools of water in which were kept every kind of waterfowl known in these parts, fresh water being provided for the river birds, salt for those of the sea, and the water itself being frequently changed to keep it pure; every species of bird moreover, was provided with its own natural food, whether fish, worms, maize, or the smaller cereals. And I can vouch for it to your Majesty that those birds who ate fish alone and nothing else received some two hundred and fifty pounds of it every day which was caught in the salt lake. It was the whole task of three hundred men to look after these birds. Others likewise were employed in ministering to those who were ill. Each pool was overhung by balconies cunningly arranged, from which Muteczuma would delight to watch the birds. In one room of this palace he kept men, women, and children, who had been white since their birth, face body, hair, eyebrows, and eyelashes. He had also another very beautiful house in which there was a large courtyard, paved very prettily with flagstones in the manner of a chessboard. In this palace there were cages some nine feet high and six yards round: each of these was half covered with tiles and the other half by a wooden trellis skillfully made. They contained birds of prey, and there was an example of every one that is known in Spain, from kestrel to eagle, and many others which were new to us. Other large rooms on the ground floor were full of cages containing lions, tigers, wolves, foxes, and wild cats of various kinds; these also were given as many chickens as they wanted. There were likewise another three hundred men to look after these animals and birds. In another palace he had men and women monsters, among them dwarfs, hunchbacks, and others deformed in various ways, each manner of monster being kept in a separate apartment, and likewise with guards charged with looking after them.

TERMS AND DEFINITIONS

Cordova: generally known as Córdoba, a city in southern Spain which served as the capital during the years of Muslim rule. It was known for its architecture and wealth.

Muteczuma: The ruling Aztec emperor when Cortés arrived in Mexico, Muteczuma (whose name today is spelled Moctezuma) ruled a vast area that included a large number of other Native American groups from whom he exacted payments of tribute.

Salamanca: Famed for its great university, this city also boasted a particularly large and impressive central square.

Seville: In Cortés's day, the largest and wealthiest city in the important Spanish kingdom of Castile, it played a key role in the administration of Spain's trade with the New World.

JOSÉ DE ACOSTA

THE ORIGINS OF THE INDIGENOUS INHABITANTS OF THE NEW WORLD

A Jesuit priest, Josè de Acosta (1539 or 1540–1600) traveled to Peru in 1570, where he remained for some fifteen years, and then went on to Mexico. A careful observer, Acosta published his great work, The Natural and Moral History of the Indies, *in 1590; it remains a major source for information about sixteenth-century Spanish America. His observations also led him to speculate about one of the great debates of his day—the origins of the people who lived in the New World prior to its "discovery" by Columbus. His suggestion that some portion of land had once connected the Old World with the New was verified with the eighteenth-century discovery of the Bering Strait.*

The huge greatness of the Ocean did so amaze S[aint] **Augustine** as he could not conceive how mankind could pass to this new-found world. . . . but the scripture teaches us clearly that all men are come from the first man. Without doubt we shall be forced to believe and confess that men have passed here from Europe, Asia, or Africa, yet must we discover by what means they could pass. It is not likely that there was another Noah's Ark by which men might be transported to the Indies, and much less any Angel to carry the first man to this new world.

. . . by what resolution, force, or industry, [could] the Indians pass so large a Sea, and who might be the Inventor of so strange a passage?

There are great signs and arguments . . . to breed a belief that they [the Indians] are descended from the Jews; for commonly you shall see them fearful, submissive, ceremonious, and subtle in lying. And, moreover, they say that their habits are like unto those the Jews used; for they wear a short coat or waistcoat, and a cloak embroidered all about. But all these conjectures are light. For we know well that the Hebrews used letters, whereof there is no show among the Indians; they were great lovers of silver, these make no care of it; the Jews, if they were not circumcised, held not themselves for Jews, and contrariwise the Indians are not at all. What reason of conjecture is there in this, seeing the Jews are so careful to preserve their language and Antiquities, so as in all parts of the world they differ and are known from others, and yet at the Indies alone, they have forgotten their Lineage, their Law, their Ceremonies, their Messiah; and, finally, their whole Judaism.

It is most certain that the first man came to this land of Peru by one of these two means, either by land or by sea. If they came by sea, it was casually, and by chance, or willingly, and of purpose. I understand by chance being cast by force of some storm or tempest. I mean done of purpose, when they prepared fleets to discover new lands. . . . why may we not suppose that the Ancients had the courage and resolution to travel by sea, with the same intent to discover the land opposite to theirs?

But to say the truth, I am of a contrary opinion, neither can I persuade myself that the first Indians came to this new world of purpose, by a determined voyage; neither will I yield, that the Ancients had knowledge in the Art of Navigation whereby men at this day pass the Ocean, from one part to another, where they please. I find not that in ancient books there is any mention made of the use of the Iman or **Lodestone,** nor of the compass to sail by. And if we take away the knowledge of the compass to sail by, we shall easily judge how impossible it was for them to pass the great Ocean. . . . The art to know the stars was invented by the **Phoenicians.** And there is no doubt but whatsoever the Ancients knew of the Art of Navigation was only in regard of the stars and observing the Shores, Capes, and differences of lands.

[Suppose that] it is likely the first that came to the Indies was by shipwreck and tempest of weather, but here upon grows a difficulty which troubles me much. For, suppose we grant that the first men came from far Countries, and that the nations which we now see are issued from them and multiplied, yet can I not conjecture by what means brute beasts, whereof there is great abundance, could come there, not being likely they should have been embarked and carried by sea. . . . the holy scripture says that all beasts and creatures of the earth perished but such as were reserved in the Ark of Noah, for the multiplication and maintenance of their kind; so we must necessarily refer the multiplication of all beasts to those which came out of the Ark of Noah, on the mountains of Ararat, where it stayed. And by this means we must seek out both for men and beasts the way whereby they might pass from the old world to this new. If these beasts then came by Sea, we must believe it was by swimming, which may happen in some Islands not far distant from others, or from the Mainland. But this is to be understood in small Straights and passages, for in our Ocean they would mock at such swimmers, when as birds do fail in their flight, yea, those of the greatest wing, in the passage of so great a Gulf.

All this being true which we have spoken, what way shall we make for beasts and birds to go to the Indies? I conjecture then, . . . that the new world, which we call Indies, is not altogether severed and disjoined from the other world; and to speak my opinion, I have long believed that the one and the other world are joined and continued one with another in some part, or at the least are very near. And yet to this day there is no certain knowledge of the contrary. For towards the Arctic or Northern Pole all the longitude of the earth is not discovered, and many hold that above Florida the Land runs out very large towards the North. . . . Moreover, no man knows how far the land runs . . . in the South sea, but that they affirm it is a great Continent which runs an infinite length; and returning to the Southern Pole, no man knows the lands on the other part of the Straight of Magellan. So as there is no reason or experience that does contradict my conceit and opinion, which is, that the whole earth is united and joined in some part, or at the least the one approaches near unto the other. If this be true, the answer is easy to the doubt we have propounded, how the first Inhabitants could pass to the Indies. For that we must believe they could not so conveniently come here by Sea as traveling by Land. . . .

It were a matter more difficult to show and prove, what beginning many and sundry sorts of beasts had, which are found at the Indies, of whose kinds we have none in this continent. For if the Creator has made them there, we may not then allege nor fly to Noah's Ark; neither was it then necessary to save all sorts of birds and beasts, if others were to be created anew. If we say then that all these kinds of creatures were preserved in the Ark by Noah, it follows that those beasts, of whose kinds we find not any but at the Indies, have passed there from this continent, as we have said of other beasts that are known unto us. This supposed, I demand how it is possible that none of their kinds should remain here?

Truly it is a question that has long held me in suspense. I say for example, if the sheep of Peru, and those which they call **Pacos** and **Huanacus,** are not found in any other regions of the world, how came they there? seeing there is no show nor remainder of them in all this world. That which I speak of these Pacos and Huanacus may be said of a thousand different kinds of birds and beasts of the forest, which have never been known, and whereof there is no mention made, neither among the Latins nor Greeks, nor any other nations of the world. We must then say, that though all beasts came; out of the Ark, yet by a natural instinct and the providence of heaven, diverse kinds dispersed themselves into diverse regions, where they found themselves so well, that they would not part; or if they departed, they did not preserve themselves, but in the process of time, perished wholly. For if we shall look precisely into it, we shall find that it is not proper and peculiar alone to the Indies, but general to many other Nations and Provinces of Asia, Europe, and Africa, where they say there are certain kinds of creatures that are not found in other regions.

It is easier to refute and contradict the false opinions conceived of the origins of the Indians, than to set down a true and certain resolution; for there is no writing among the Indians, nor any certain remembrances of their founders. But in the end I resolve this point, that the true and principal cause to people the Indies, was that the land and limits thereof are joined and continued in some extremities of the world, or at the least were very near. And I believe it is not many thousand years past since men first inhabited this new world and West Indies, and that the first men that entered were rather savage men and hunters, and that they came to this new world, having lost their own land, or being in too great numbers, they were forced of necessities to seek some other habitations; the which having found, they began little and little to plant, having no other law, but some instinct of nature, and some customs remaining of their first Countries. It is no matter of any great importance to know what the Indians themselves report of their beginning, being more like unto dreams, then to true histories.

TERMS AND DEFINITIONS

Huanacus: Both this term and **Paco** refer to the present-day animals known as llamas and alpacas. The Incas used llamas as beasts of burden; the fur of alpacas found use in textiles.

Lodestone: From the word "lode" which then had the meaning of "way," this rock's magnetic properties helped mariners navigate.

Pacos: see **Huanacus.**

Phoenicians: from 1100 to 625 B.C., a powerful people known as explorers, merchants, and colonizers, based in the middle east, in the area around present-day Lebanon and Syria.

Saint Augustine: One of the fathers of the early Christian church, he lived from A.D. 354 to 430. The Spanish religious order of Augustinians saw him as their patron saint.

GABRIEL SAGARD

THE HURONS

In the 1620s, Gabriel Sagard (d. c. 1636), a member of the Recollets, a brotherhood associated with the **Franciscans,** *spent about six months among the Hurons in French Canada. The term* Huron *is of French origin. When French settlers first encountered these Native Americans, they thought the ridged or curled style in which they wore their hair resembled the head of a boar. And to the French, the word* Huron *meant "unkempt knave." Sagard set down his impressions of the Hurons in his 1632 book,* Long Journey to the Country of the Hurons. *As a missionary seeking converts, and working with Native Americans who already have embraced Christianity, Sagard finds many positive qualities in the Hurons. Nonetheless, he writes as "civilized" man, about people whom he regards as "savages."*

As their practices and their mode of living when they take a journey are almost always the same, I shall now briefly describe how they conduct themselves on such occasions. In order to practice patience in good earnest and to endure hardships beyond the limit of human strength it is only necessary to make journeys with the savages, and long ones especially, such as we did; because, besides the danger of death on the way, one must make up one's mind to endure and suffer more than could be imagined, from hunger, from the stench that these dirty disagreeable fellows emit almost constantly in their canoes, which is enough to disgust one utterly with such unpleasant companions, from sleeping always on the bare ground in the open country, from walking with great labor in water and bogs and in some places over rocks, and through dark thick woods, from rain on one's back and all the evils that the season and weather can inflict, and from being bitten by a countless swarm of mosquitoes and midges, together with difficulties of language in explaining clearly and showing them one's needs, and having no Christian beside one for communication and consolation in the midst of one's toil.

Now when they were in the open country and the hour for encamping arrived, they would seek some fitting spot on the bank of a river for a camp, or in another place where dry wood could easily be found to make a fire; then one of them set himself to look for it and collect it, another to put up the lodge and find a stick on which to hang the kettle at the fire, another to look for two flat stones for crushing the Indian corn over a skin spread out on the ground, and afterwards to put it into the kettle and boil it. When it was boiled quite clear it was all served in bowls of birch bark which with this object we carried each one for himself, and also large spoons like small dishes, which are used for eating this broth, *sagamitè* [a kind of soup or stew] in the evening and in the morning, the only times in the day when the kettle is boiled, that is to say after pitching camp in the evening and before starting in the morning. Sometimes also we did without it when we were in a hurry to set out, and sometimes we boiled it before daylight. If two groups used the same lodge each one boiled its own kettle, then all ate together, one kettle after the other, without any discussion or contention and every man had his share of both. As for me I satisfied myself as a rule with the *sagamitè* which pleased me best, although in both there was always dirt and refuse, partly because they used fresh stones every day, and very dirty ones, to crush the corn.

They wear round the neck little collars made of feathers and they have the same ornament in their hair. Their faces are painted in different colors with oil, very prettily; some had one side all green, the other all red, others appeared to have the whole face covered with natural lacework, and others again were quite different. Their custom is to paint and stain themselves, especially when they are approaching or passing through another tribe. This is the reason why they carry their pigments and oil with them on a journey, and also because of feasts, dances, or other assemblies, in order to appear more handsome and attract the attention of onlookers. The next day after we had come upon these savages we stopped for some time at an **Algonquin** village, and hearing a great noise I was curious enough to look through a chink in a lodge to find out what it was about. There within I saw (as I have since seen many times among the Hurons on similar occasions) a number of men divided into two companies sitting on the ground and disposed along the two sides of the lodge; each company had in front of them a long flat piece of wood, three or four inches broad, and every man had a stick in his hand and kept continually striking this flat piece of wood in time to the sound of the tortoise shells and of several songs which they sang at the top of their voices. The Loki or medicine man, who was at the upper end with his large tortoise shell in his hand began and the others followed at the top of their voices; it was like a witches' Sabbath, a regular hubbub and concert of demons. I beg the reader . . . to excuse me if, in order to give a better understanding of the character of our savages, I have been forced to insert here many uncivilized and extravagant details, since one cannot convey complete knowledge of a foreign country or of how it is governed except by showing, along with the good, the evil and the imperfection to be found in it. Otherwise, it would not be necessary for me to describe the manners of savages if there were nothing savage to be seen in them, but . . . polite and refined habits like [those of] nations civilized by religion and piety, or by magistrates and wise men who through their good laws might have given some shapeliness to the uncouth manners of these barbarous nations, for in them one can discern but little of the light of reason and the purity of a purified nature. . . . their language is very poor and defective in words for any things, and particularly so as concerns the mysteries of our holy religion, which we could not explain to them, not even the *Pater noster* except by periphrases; that is to say, for one of our words we had to use several of theirs, for with them there is no knowledge of the meaning of Sanctification, the Kingdom of Heaven, the Most Holy Sacrament, nor of leading into temptation. The words Glory, Trinity, Holy Spirit, Angels, Resurrection, Paradise, Hell, Church, Faith, Hope and Charity, and a multitude of others, are not used by them. So that to make a beginning there is no necessity for very learned men, but there is indeed for persons who fear God and are patient and full of love; and it is in this that one must chiefly excel in order to convert this poor people and draw them out of their sinfulness and blindness.

On this side of their territory our town was the nearest neighbor to the Iroquois, their deadly enemies; for this reason I was often warned to be on my guard for fear of some surprise while I was going to the woods to say my prayers to God or in the fields gathering wild blackberries. But I never encountered any danger or risk (God be thanked); only a Huron once strung his bow against me, thinking me an enemy, but when I spoke he was reassured and saluted me according to the custom of the country. Sometimes also I visited their cemetery . . . and admired the care that these poor people take of the dead bodies of their deceased relatives and friends, and I found that in this respect they surpass the piety of Christians, since they spare nothing for the relief of the souls [of the departed], which they believe to be immortal and in need of help from the living.

These good savages have this praiseworthy custom among them, that when any one of their fellow townsmen has no lodge to live in, all of them with one accord lend a hand and build one for him and do not leave him until the work has been made complete, or at least until he or they for whom it is intended can easily finish it; and to bind everyone to a task so pious and charitable the matter, when it is a question of work, is decided upon always in full council, and then the summons is cried every day throughout the town in order that each man may be on the spot at the appointed hour. This is an excellent institution, and much to be admired among savage people whom we think to be, and who in fact are, less civilized than ourselves. But as regards us, who were strangers to them and newcomers, it was a great thing that they should show themselves so full of human kindness as to put up a building for us with good feeling so general and universal, since as a rule to strangers they give nothing for nothing, except to deserving persons or those who have obliged them greatly, although they themselves always make demands, especially upon the French. They call the French Agnonha in their language, that is, iron people.

Whenever we had to go from one village to another for some necessity or business we used to go freely to their dwellings to lodge and get our food, and they received us in them and treated us very kindly although they were under no obligation to us. For they hold it proper to help wayfarers and to receive among them with politeness anyone who is not an enemy, and much more so those of their own nation. They reciprocate hospitality and give such assistance to one another that the necessities of all are provided for without there being any indigent beggar in their towns and villages; and they considered it a very bad thing when they heard it said that there were in France a great many of these needy beggars, and thought that this was for lack of charity in us, and blamed us for it severely.

The occupations of the savages are fishing, hunting and war; going off to trade, making lodges and canoes, or contriving the proper tools for doing so. The rest of the time they pass in idleness, gambling, sleeping, singing, dancing, smoking, or going to feasts, and they are reluctant to undertake any other work that forms part of the women's duty except under strong necessity.

Gambling is so frequent and customary a practice with them that it takes up much of their time, and sometimes not only the men but the women also stake all they possess, and lose as cheerfully and patiently, when chance does not favor them, as if they had lost nothing. The men are addicted not only to the game of straws, for which three or four hundred little white reeds are cut of equal length, a foot long or thereabouts, but also to many other kinds of play. One is to have a large wooden bowl and put into it five or six fruit-stones or little balls slightly flattened, as big as the tip of your little finger, and painted black on one side and white or yellow on the other; and when they are all squatting on the ground in a circle, their accustomed posture, they take this bowl in turn, according to lot, in both hands, lift it a little from the ground, and at once replace it, giving it rather a sharp knock so that the little balls are made to move and leap up, and then, as in dicing, they see on which side the balls lie, and if it is in their favor. The one who holds the bowl, while he is jolting it and looking at his throw, keeps saying without a pause Tet, tet, tet, tet, thinking that this affects the throw and makes it a favorable one for him. But the special game of the women and girls, in which also men and boys sometimes take part with them, is played with five or six fruit stones like those of our apricots, blackened on one side. They hold them in their hand, as one does dice, then cast them upward a little, and, when they have fallen on a piece of leather or skin stretched on the ground for the purpose, see what the throw gives them; and they keep on at it, trying to win collars, earrings, or other trifles they possess, but never money, for of that they have neither knowledge nor use, but offer and give one thing in exchange for another throughout the whole of the savages' country.

TERMS AND DEFINITIONS

Algonquin: spelled today as Algonquian or Algonkian, most precisely a group of languages spoken by a large number of Native American peoples in eastern North America, including Canada.

Franciscans: St. Francis of Assisi (1182–1226), an Italian friar, founded this religious order, which undertook significant missionary activities in the New World.

GEORGE ALSOP

THE MIGHTY SUSQUEHANNA

George Alsop (b. 1638) traveled from England to Maryland in 1658 where he spent four years as an indentured servant. Later, having returned to England, he wrote a description of that colony, A Character of the Province of Maryland, *published in 1662, in which he praised its climate and rich natural resources. He also wrote about the Susquehannas, though in far less flattering terms. He seemed especially intent in portraying their barbarism and cruelty, not a surprising choice given the conflict between Native Americans and settlers that had marked the experience of Virginia and Maryland during the first half of the seventeenth century. Many of his descriptions, then, are not factually accurate. However, they do provide a good example of how Native Americans were portrayed to a public in England who had no basis for doubting the accuracies of such accounts, and thrilled to tales of the cruel and savage Indians.*

Those *Indians* that I have convers'd withall here in this Province of *Mary-Land,* and have had any view of either of their Customs, Manners, Religions, and Absurdities, are called by the name of *Susquehanocks,* being a people lookt upon by the Christian Inhabitants, as the most Noble and Heroick Nation of Indians that dwell upon the confines of America; also are so allowed and lookt upon by the rest of the Indians, by a submissive and tributary acknowledgment; being a people cast into the mould of a most large and Warlike deportment, the men being for the most part seven foot high in latitude, and in magnitude and bulk suitable to so high a pitch; their voyce large and hollow, as ascending out of a Cave, their gate and behavior strait, stately, and majestick treading on the Earth with pride, contempt, and disdain.

Their bodies are cloth'd with no other Armour to defend them from the nipping frosts of a be numbing Winter, or the penetrating and scorching influence of the Sun in a hot Summer, then what Nature gave them when they parted with the dark receptacle of their mothers womb. They go Men, Women, and Children, all naked, only where shame leads them by a natural instinct to be reservedly modest, there they become cover'd.

The formality of **Jezabel's** artificial Glory is much courted and followed by these Indians; only in matter of colours (I conceive) they differ. The Indians paint upon their faces one stroke of red, another of green, another of white, and another of black, so that when they have accomplished the Equipage of their Countenance in this trim, they are the only Hieroglyphicks and Representatives of the **Furies.** Their skins are naturally white, but altered from their originals by the several dyings of Roots and Barks, that they prepare and make useful to metamorphize their hydes into a dark Cinnamon brown. The hair of their head is black, long, and harsh, but where Nature hath appointed the situation of it any where else, they divert it from its growth, by pulling it up hair by hair by the root in its primitive appearance. Several of them wear divers impressions on their breasts and armes, as the picture of the Devil, Bears, Tigers, and Panthers, which are imprinted on their several lineaments with much difficulty and pain. And this they count a badge of Heroick Valour, and the only Ornament due to their Heroes.

These *Susquehanock* Indians are for the most part great Warriours, and seldom sleep one Summer in the quiet armes of a peaceable Rest, but keep (by their present Power, as well as by their former Conquests) the several Nations of Indians round about them in a forceable obedience and subjection.

When they determine to go upon some Design that will and doth require a Consideration, some six of them get into a corner, and sit in Juncto [council]; and if thought fit, their business is made popular, and immediately put into action; if not, they make a full stop to it, and are silently reserv'd.

The Warlike Equipage they put themselves in is with their faces, armes, and breasts confusedly painted, their hair greazed with Bears oyl, and stuck thick with Swans Feathers, with a wreath or Diadem of black and white Beads upon their heads, a small Hatchet, instead of a Cymetre, stuck in their girts behind them, and either with Guns, or Bows and Arrows. In this posture and dress they march out from their Fort, or dwelling, to the number of Forty in a Troop, singing (or rather howling out) the Decades or Warlike exploits of their Ancestors, ranging the wide Woods until their fury has met with an Enemy worthy of their Revenge. What Prisoners fall into their hands by the destiny of War, they treat them very civilly while they remain with them abroad, but when they once return homewards, they then begin to dress them in the habit for death, putting on their heads and armes wreaths of Beads, greazing their hair with fat, some going before, and the rest behind, at equal distance from their Prisoners, bellowing in a strange and confused manner, which is a true presage and forerunner of destruction to their then conquered Enemy.

In this manner of march they continue till they have brought them to their Barken City, where they deliver them up to those that in cruelty will execute them, without either the legal Judgement of a Council of War, or the benefit of their clergy at the Common Law. The common and usual deaths they put their Prisoners to is to bind them to stakes, making a fire some distance from them: then one or other of them, whose Genius delights in the art of Paganish dissections, with a sharp knife or flint cuts the Cutis or outermost skin of the brow so deep, until their nails or rather Talons, can fasten themselves firm and secure in, then (with a most rigid jerk) disrobeth the head of skin and hair at one pull, leaving the skull almost as bare as those Monumental Skelitons at

Chyrurgione Hall: But for fear they should get cold by leaving so warm and customary a Cap off, they immediately apply to the skull a Cataplasm of hot Embers to keep their Pericranium warm. While they are thus acting this cruelty on their heads, several others are preparing pieces of Iron, and barrels of old Guns, which they make red hot, to sear each part and lineament of their bodies, which they perform and act in a most cruel and barbarous manner. And while they are thus in the midst of their torments and execrable usage, some tearing their skin and hair of their head off by violence, others bearing their bodice with hot irons, some are cutting their flesh off and eating it before their eyes raw while they are alive, yet all this and much more never makes them lower the Top gallant sail of their Heroick courage, to beg with a submissive Repentance any indulgent favour from their persecuting Enemies but with an undaunted contempt to their cruelty, eye it with so slight and mean a respect, as if it were below them to value what they did, they courageously (while breath doth libertize them) sing the summary of their Warlike Atchievements.

As for their religion, together with their Rites and Ceremonies, they are so absurd and ridiculous, that it is almost a sin to name them. They own no other Deity then the Devil, but with a kind of a wilde imaginary conjecture, they suppose from their groundless conceits that the World had a Maker but where he is that made it, or whether he be living to this day, they know not. The Devil as I said before is all the God they own or worship and that more out of a slavish fear than any real Reverence to his Infernal or Diabolical greatness, he forcing them to their Obedience by his rough and rigid dealing with them, often appearing visibly among them to their terrour. Once in four years, they Sacrifice a Childe to him, in an acknowledgement of their firm obedience to all his Devillish powers, and Hellish commands. These Indians oft times raise great Tempests when they have any weighty matter or design in hand, and by blustering storms inquire of their Infernal God (the Devil) How matters shall go with them either in publick or private.

When any among them depart this life, they give him no other intombment, then to set him upright upon his breech in a hole dug in the Earth some five foot long, and three foot deep, covered over with the Bark of Trees Arch wise, with his face Due West, only leaving a hole half a foot square open. They dress him in the same Equipage and Gallantry that he used to be trim'd in when he was alive, and so bury him (if a Soldier) with his Bows, Arrows, and Target, together with all the rest of his implements and weapons of War, with a Kettle of Broth, and Corn standing before him, lest he should meet with bad quarters in his way. His Kindred and Relations follow him to the Grave, sheath'd in Bear skins for close mourning.

Their houses are low and long, built with the Bark of Trees Archwise standing thick and confusedly together. They are situated a hundred and odd miles distant from the Christian Plantations of Mary-Land at the head of a River that runs into the Bay of Chesapike called by their own name. The

Susquehanock River, where they remain inhabit most part of the Summer time, and seldom remove far from it, unless it be to subdue any Forreign Rebellion.

About November the best Hunters draw off to several remote places of the Woods, where they know the Deer, Bear, and Elke useth; there they build them several Cottages, which they call their Winter quarter, where they remain for the space of three months, until they have killed up a sufficientcy of Provisions to supply their Families with in the Summer.

The Women are the Butchers, Cooks, and Tillers of the ground, the Men think it below the honour of a Masculine, to stoop to any thing but that which their Gun, or Bow and Arrows command. The Men kill the several Beasts which they meet withall in the Woods, and the Women are the Pack horses to fetch it in upon their backs, fleying and dressing the hydes as well as the flesh for prevision to make them fit for Trading, and which are brought down to the *English* at several seasons in the year, to truck and dispose of them for course Blankets, Guns, Powder, and Lead, Beads, small Looking glazers, Knives, and Razors.

TERMS AND DEFINITIONS

furies: in Greek mythology, three gods who punished those who committed evil.

Jezabel: a queen of Israel in the ninth century B.C., portrayed as vain and scheming.

THINKING THINGS THROUGH

1. What accounts for the great concern Europeans had with determining the origins of the people they encountered in the New World?

2. In what ways did religion and religious beliefs influence European perceptions of the Native Americans?

3. Why did Cortés refer to the Aztecs as "barbarous" even though he found so much in Tenochtitlán that compared favorably with things in Spain?

4. What characteristics of the Native Americans received the most positive commentary from European observers?

3

THE SLAVE TRADE

A. The International Context

As of January 1, 1808, the United States ended its participation in the Atlantic slave trade, officially closing its ports to a commerce in human beings that had flowed to its shores since the early days of colonial settlement. By that time more than five hundred thousand Africans had been forcibly brought across the ocean to fulfill the labor needs of colony and nation, especially those related to the large-scale export agriculture of such plantation crops as tobacco, rice, and cotton. According to the 1810 census, African slaves comprised some 16 percent of the nation's population.

Despite the magnitude of such numbers, the American colonies never had been a major destination for the slave trade. That status belonged to Portuguese Brazil and the West Indies sugar islands, where Spain, England, France, and Holland all held colonies. Slave-based labor also produced wealth in many of Spain's mainland colonies. In all, some ten to twelve million Africans were transported to the Americas in the slave trade's 360 years of legal and illegal existence, or about 4.5 times as many Europeans who settled in the Americas during the same period. Large numbers of deaths occurred at various points in the process, especially during the so-called "Middle Passage" across the Atlantic. The figure of ten to twelve million, therefore, vastly undercounts the number of Africans who actually formed part of the trade.

In the contemporary United States the word "slave" inevitably involves images of "black" Africans. Throughout history peoples of varying races and ethnicities have been enslaved and traded as commodities. One of the more profound legacies of the Atlantic slave trade is the degree to which it has obscured slavery's longer history, making it seem the unique condition of one particular people.

The great ancient civilizations of the Middle East, including Egypt, Babylonia, and Assyria, as well as those of China and India all defined the concept of slave as property, subject, among other things, to being bought or sold. For western civilization, the cultural roots of slavery are found in the Hebrew and Christian Bibles, Classical Greece, and the Roman Empire. In Europe, after the fall of the Roman Empire serfdom largely replaced slavery. Still, from the 1200s to the 1400s, merchants, especially those from the Italian city-state of Genoa, carried on an international slave trade in the area of the Black Sea and the Mediterranean.

The shifting of the older Mediterranean slave trade to the Atlantic mirrors a similar shift in the movement of goods, services, and people sparked by the incorporation of the New World into the Old. The origins of this new slave trade, therefore, are linked closely to the European conquest and colonization of the Americas. The earliest European participants in the trade were Portugal and Spain, the first of the colonizers. The subsequent Atlantic slave trade was an international phenomenon closely associated with the major seafaring/colonizing nations of western Europe. Further, it involved the active collaboration of numerous African peoples.

By the 1440s, Portuguese ships had established trade relations with various groups along the African coast, and slaves formed one significant item in that commerce. The Portuguese established their trading stations either on the coast or on off-shore islands, relying on African middlemen to furnish the slaves. That pattern continued throughout the years of the slave trade, not only for the Portuguese, but for all the other European nations. Indeed, despite their long commercial interaction along the West African coast, as late as the 1850s European presence remained confined to small coastal enclaves. Two factors largely account for this pattern. Such tropical diseases as malaria decimated Europeans who ventured into the interior. (Discovered in 1820, Quinine prophylaxis to ward off malaria did not come into wide use until the mid-nineteenth century.) And, African traders amply supplied Europeans with the needed articles of trade.

Did Africans then, as some have suggested, "sell their own kind?" That question testifies to the power of color prejudice. Consider, for example, the idea that Romans, who were "white," enslaved Greeks, who also were "white," and that the "white" nations of Europe warred endlessly among one another, slaughtering and at times enslaving their fellow "whites." When put in this fashion, it becomes clear that among "whites" racial identity held no significance. The same proved true in Africa. African peoples—whether organized in kinship groups, or "tribes," or formalized political groupings, which included city-states, kingdoms, and large empires—saw themselves as distinct one from another.

As in other parts of the world, slavery existed in Africa long before the advent of the Atlantic trade. Slaves typically were persons who had been captured during war. Slavery also was a penalty for crime. Accustomed to holding slaves, African peoples saw nothing remarkable in the fact that Europeans might trade for them. As with Europeans, both reasons of state and individuals' quest for profits motivated Africans to enter that commerce. Gained in return for slaves, guns and horses and enhanced revenues meant increased wealth and power. Many existing African merchants profited from the trade by providing slaves to other African merchants in coastal locations who dealt directly with the overseas trade. New merchant groups linked to the trade arose. As the slave trade accelerated, the growing demand for slaves sparked raids and even wars in West Africa, which in some cases dramatically reshaped existing political relationships. The growing trade also deformed the legal system; slavery became the penalty for an ever-larger number of crimes. Furthermore, overwhelmingly it drained active, healthy males from Africa.

If the African participants in the trade acted to secure profit and power, so too did the Europeans. Slave labor produced the most valuable commercial products of the Americas: sugar, tobacco, and precious metals. Sugar became the most important agricultural commodity in international trade virtually from the time of Columbus. It remained so until the early 1800s. Unknown in Europe until the seventh century, cane sugar was carried back from the Middle East by participants in the Crusades. Increases in overland trade with the Middle East and Asia resulted in a small luxury trade in sugar. On his second voyage to the New World Columbus brought sugar cane to Hispaniola. Later, Hernán Cortés established sugar mills in Mexico, and the Portuguese in 1520 planted sugar cane along the coast of northeastern Brazil.

The West Indies became a battleground for various European powers in part because of the suitability of its islands for sugar production. When various European powers, including Holland, France, and England did manage to establish themselves in that region, they immediately planted sugar. Over time, the resulting large increases in sugar production *transformed it from a luxury commodity available only to the wealthiest classes in Europe into a mass-market consumer product. It combined especially well with tea, coffee, and chocolate, three other tropical products that gained great popularity at that time. That ever rising and seemingly inexhaustible demand made for enormous profits. It also encouraged further planting of cane.*

This sugar boom fueled the Atlantic slave trade. Extensive sugar cane plantations required particularly large amounts of labor, especially at harvest time, for if not cut quickly, the cane's sugar content diminished. Since both Spain and Portugal already had contact with Africa, the trade in slaves appeared an obvious solution to the labor question. As other European nations established claims in the New World, they too participated in the trade.

Since the basic reason for the slave trade was to provide labor, males of working age formed its largest component. The imbalance between the numbers of male and female slaves tended to diminish the natural rate of reproduction. At the same time, high profits accruing to sugar and the relatively low cost of slaves promoted an economic logic of literally working slaves to death. This generated a continuous demand for more slaves. Throughout the Americas, only in the United States did the slave population become self-reproducing. There the government ended participation in the Atlantic trade, while allowing slavery itself to continue.

The slave trade remained highly important to the economies of colonial British North America. Tobacco, its single most profitable export product, and the life-blood of Virginia and Maryland, depended on slave labor. So did the economic viability of the Carolinas. Even colonies that did not make much use of slave labor might profit from the existence of the slave trade. For example, the various "triangular" trades engaged in by the merchants of New England all directly related to the slave trade. Perhaps the most famous of such trades saw rum from New England shipped to Africa, where it was traded for slaves who were brought to the West Indies, exchanged there for molasses (a by-product of sugar refining), which then was used to manufacture rum. The sugar-growing West Indies islands comprised perhaps the single most important market for the produce of the northern colonies. Beyond the specific products themselves, the so-called carrying trade—that is, the profits from charges for carrying goods from one port to another—helped spark the development of New England's ship-building industry, which in turn spurred various allied artisan activities. In sum, the slave trade held economic importance for all of colonial America.

In the process of achieving its independence from England, the American colonies initiated the process of disengagement from the Atlantic slave trade. In April 1776, the Second Continental Congress, at the same time that it opened American ports to trade with all the world save England, also declared an end to the importation of slaves. During the Confederation Period, most of the new states individually foreswore further importing of slaves from abroad. By the time Thomas Jefferson urged the Congress of the United States to formally put an end to the nation's participation in the trade, South Carolina was the only state that had not yet independently outlawed it.

The greatest opposition to and pressure against the Atlantic trade came from England, a nation which had been a major participant in it. By an 1807 act of Parliament any participation by British subjects in the slave trade became illegal. Furthermore, Britain took the lead in urging other nations to follow its example (see Chapter 9). By 1820, the major West Indies colonial powers, England, the Netherlands, France, and Spain all had outlawed the trade. However, they did not at that time make slavery itself illegal.

Later, in 1833, England abolished the institution of slavery throughout its colonial empire, as did France in 1848. Still, Brazil remained a major source of demand for slaves, even though, bowing to heavy pressure from England, it had abolished the trade in 1830. Having grown increasingly impatient with the open flouting of the 1830 abolition, the British Parliament in 1845 passed the Aberdeen Bill, which called for the seizure of Brazilian slave ships. Five years later, Brazil's national legislative assembly definitively renounced the trade.

As long as the institution of slavery remained, so too did demand. As the case of Brazil indicates, legislating the trade's end proved easier than enforcing it. An illegal slave trade continued for a number of years. England, in fact, maintained a squadron off the west coast of Africa as well as in the Caribbean to clamp down on the illegal slave trade. The United States also maintained such a fleet, but its actions proved mostly ineffective. Indeed, American citizens themselves actively participated in the slave trade. In terms of volume, the Atlantic slave trade recorded its highest numbers in the early 1840s.

B. International Views

For almost three hundred years, the trade in slaves across the Atlantic was an accepted, and largely unquestioned fact of life for both the nations of western Europe and the Americas. The growth in power of new democratic liberal principles in the eighteenth-century Atlantic world changed this situation. Most powerfully expressed in the American Declaration of Independence and revolutionary France's Declaration of the Rights of Man, these principles clearly suggested the impropriety of slavery. Perhaps even more powerful in changing attitudes was the rise of several evangelical religions, for example, Methodism, which defined slavery as sin. As a result, both the slave trade and slavery itself came under attack. International commentary began to stress the horrors and evil of the trade.

Although the United States had outlawed the Atlantic trade, in various ways, it remained involved in the ensuing illegal trade in slaves. The American flag provided significant protection on the high seas. Since its founding as a nation, the United States had strongly upheld the concept of neutral rights for its shipping. It resisted both British and French attempts to interfere with its maritime commerce during the Napoleonic wars. When England stopped and boarded American ships at sea, the United States objected that such actions violated America's sovereignty. The War of 1812 had been fueled in part by such resentment.

Though England continued to have a far more powerful navy than the United States, in the wake of the1812 war it was reluctant to stop any American ships. As a result, slavers used the American flag as a cover. In some cases, they actually had legally registered their ships in the United States. Furthermore, since the U. S. South practiced slavery on a large scale, its officials often displayed little interest in actually enforcing laws against the trade. Slavers brought into southern ports, therefore, typically could anticipate a sympathetic hearing in court. This situation animated considerable commentary, especially by British observers, and those directly involved in attempts to suppress the trade.

The selections which follow illuminate various aspects of the debate regarding the Atlantic trade. It begins with arguments in favor of the slave trade, written anonymously in 1763 as commentary on the Treaty of Paris, stressing the economic importance of African slaves to England and the colonies. Next, a sermon by John Wesley, one of the founders of Methodism, denounces the immorality and inhumanity of both the trade and of slavery itself. Venture Smith, an African who himself was enslaved, provides a first-person account detailing his capture in Africa. Selections from two contemporary scholars conclude the readings. An American historian, Robert Conrad, presents a detailed discussion of the role of the United States and some of its citizens in the illegal trade to Brazil. French scholar, Serge Daget, concludes with an overall discussion of the trade, its participants, and the factors accounting for its cessation.

ANONYMOUS

THE SLAVE TRADE AS KEY TO THE BRITISH EMPIRE'S WELL-BEING

The 1763 Treaty of Paris, which concluded the Great War for Empire, saw great territorial gains for the British in North America. However, France retained its possessions in the West Indies. Some critics of the treaty suggested that those sugar-growing islands had far greater value than the lands in North America. The following selection comes from an anonymous pamphlet published in London, and written in 1763, "Considerations on the Present Peace as far as it is relative to the Colonies, and the American Trade." As that title suggests, the pamphlet discusses issues of commerce and the empire, making a strong case for the importance of the African slave trade. Note also the arguments presented to justify the trade in moral terms.

Since the preliminary articles of peace were published, . . . we have heard many persons in coffee-houses and other places, censure and blame our negotiators, for their not having obtained better terms . . . if they would give themselves the least time to reflect seriously, and judge dispassionately, they would find, that by retaining our conquests in North America (which are extended beyond our most sanguine expectations) the greatest benefit and utility must arise to this the mother-country;

Whatever self-interested people may clamour to the contrary, there cannot be a doubt but his majesty and his ministers, in their negociations, have given the most serious attention to the universal good of this country, without confining their views, or partially regarding whether *North America* is more valuable than the *Sugar Islands,* because each merited their notice and care, being both of inestimable value to the mother-country, and reciprocally so to each other; and all three so essentially connected, that whatever happens to the disadvantage of the one, must in proportion affect the other. For the West India islands depend upon *North America,* in a great measure, for provisions, mill, and other timber; as well as for horses, cattle, and many things absolutely necessary for the use of the plantations; which are paid for in *specie, sugar, rum,* melasses [molasses], and other plantation-produce: moreover, the melasses being distilled into rum in *North America,* are of great advantage to the merchants there, in carrying on the African trade directly from thence, which enables them to make returns for those manufactures, &c. They receive from hence with greater facility.

The trade carried on between Great Britain, Ireland, North America, and the West India islands and Africa, is of greater advantage to this country, than all our other trades whatsoever, arising from the exportation of *British* manufactures, *East India* goods, provisions as well as *linens* from *Ireland,* which are paid for with *specie, sugar, tobacco, rice, cotton,* and other plantation-produce; and with the commodities of *Africa,* such as *gold-dust, bees wax, elephants teeth, gum Senegal,* various sorts of *dying woods,* and particularly *Negroes for the plantations;* whence it manifestly appears, upon the African trade, and the invaluable commerce of our colonies, above two-thirds of the British navigation depends;

It is well known to those who are acquainted with the sugar islands, that the profits of the planter depend upon the vent he finds for his rum and melasses; for if sugar only, and no rum and melasses could be produced from the sugar cane, it would hardly pay the expense of culture, and manufacturing into sugar. Therefore, as the consumption of rum and melasses is stopped or increase, the sugar colonies . . . must respectively thrive or decline.

It must be acknowledged by those who have a general knowledge of the trade and commerce of *Great-Britain* and *Ireland,* that the *Negro trade* on the coast of *Africa,* is the chief and fundamental support of the *British colonies,* by supplying them with that race of useful people called Negroes, to be employed in cultivating the lands. But when there is either a deficiency of them, or that they are purchasable but at high prices, then such checks must greatly impoverish our British planters; and in consequence, considerably diminish the wealth, power, trade and navigation of these kingdoms, the increase of which has been, in great measure, owing to the extensive commerce to and from our colonies and plantations: therefore their not being properly supplied with Negroes, must be extremely detrimental to them;

For the lands in Britain must always rise and fall in proportion as our manufactures and navigation prosper or decline, and the national revenue increase or diminish as the trade of our colonies is in a more or less flourishing way. Therefore is it not evident, that there is not a man in this kingdom, who, in proportion to his possession and property in the community, does not partake of the benefits and advantages accruing from the *African, North American,* and *West Indian* trades;

When the enquiry, relative to the *African* trade, was under consideration before the honourable house of commons in the year of 1758, **Mr Pitt** . . . was pleased to declare, that he believed the then method for carrying on the *African* trade wanted alteration and amendment. He also added, that when we should be so happy as to have a peace, he would be at all times ready to examine into it, and give all the assistance in his power to put it upon such a footing, that our plantations might be supplied with the best and most valuable Negroes at reasonable rates. We doubt not but he will make good his promise to lend his able assistance and to recommend it to the administration to begin such an enquiry, and continue it, in order to amend the present, or form such other plan, as will preserve and secure that valuable trade to the *British* subjects, as the only and certain means to encrease the produce of the *British,* and lessen that of the *French colonies.* For, with the islands we already possess, and those which it appears by the preliminaries [of the peace treaty] are to be ours, we shall have a sufficient number to raise sugar, & c. for the consumption of all Europe, if our British planters are properly supplied with the best sort of Negroes for their cultivation.

We cannot help once more observing, it is not having the most sugar islands that will be the greatest benefit and advantage to the mother-country, unless such islands can be supplied with a sufficient number of the best Negroes for their cultivation; therefore as *Great Britain, France, Spain, Holland,* and *Denmark,* have encreased their number, and extended their colonies to such a degree, that Africa cannot sufficiently supply them all with Negroes, including those that the Portuguese want and carry off. On that account, in our humble opinion, the contest ought to be, not who has the most islands, but who can secure the trade to those parts of Africa, where the best and greatest number of those useful people are to be procured, as the only means to promote the interest and prosperity of their colonies. . . .

From what has been before observed, I presume it will be admitted that every equitable method ought be pursued and put in practice by Great Britain, to secure to herself as much as possible the African trade, in order to prevent the French purchasing Negroes. It cannot be too much insisted on that the Negroes are of as much consequence and use for the cultivation of our colonies, as the wool is to our manufactory, for these obvious reasons: that the Negroes are the artificers, manufacturers, and labourers in the colonies; because the whole process, from clearing and preparing the ground to planting the sugar cane, and manufacturing it into sugar and rum, and the putting it on board the ships, is the work of Negroes;

In order to remove the prejudices of many worthy and tender-minded persons against the Negro-trade, which from a delicacy natural to civilized nations, they declare to be quite contrary to all dictates of humanity, and a disgrace to the professors of the Christian religion, we shall lay before them and the public a true state of the case. As there is no occasion to enlarge how essentially and absolutely necessary it is to have Negroes for the cultivation of our colonies, therefore we shall only beg to observe, by the best information that could be obtained, Africa in general is divided into little kingdoms and states which, when at peace, the natives whereof breed slaves for sale, as our farmers do stock on their farms, and sell them as their necessity requires, which was a trade carried on among themselves before Europeans traded thither; and when overstocked, their practice was putting to death (often with great torture) the prisoners taken in war. Those that are bred slaves, are always very desirous to be purchased by white people, as they are infinitely better used than by their black masters, who allow them but a bare subsistence, and treat them with the greatest barbarity; and when used to put several to death through custom, when they buried persons above the common rank;

Those Negroes taken in war, or prisoners for feloniously committing crimes in despite of the laws made by the officers commanding **the European forts** . . . are now sold, but often unwilling to go on board ships; perhaps on account of having lived in a better situation in their own country than those who have been bred up in slavery from their infancy, therefore they often contrive to make their escape, and by speaking the language, persuade others to join and assist them to take the ship from the Europeans, of which we have had too many fatal instances, and is entirely owing to their ignorance in not knowing the place they are destined to; and also that they will be much better treated and looked after in our colonies than they ever were in their country; so that when bought by Europeans, they are in a manner rescued from a state of misery as to treatment; for in the colonies, when they are sick, they have great care taken of them, and physicians to administer proper medicines for their relief; which, on a similar occasion, their black masters would give themselves no care or concern about them.

Besides, many of them are instructed in the principles of religion, and become Christians and men of property, which, from experience, we know to be true, having talked with several who had no desire to see their own country, living much more comfortably in our colonies. And we think it would be politic to send two or three Negroes on board every ship that goes to Africa, that can talk the different languages of the countries the master of such ship intends to trade to, that they might inform their countrymen how they had been treated. Such measures, we are convinced, would prevent the loss of many lives, by the Negroes being satisfied they were going where they would be better treated than in their own country; and, at the same time, to eradicate that opinion many of them have, that they are going to be fed and eaten, which if effected, would be a means to quiet their minds, so as not to attempt rising on board of ships.

TERMS AND DEFINITIONS

the European Forts: European nations involved in the slave trade usually had fortified trading posts or "factories" on islands off the coast of West Africa and, at times, directly on the coast itself.

Mr. Pitt: Whig leader, who became prime minister of England in 1758 and helped organize the successful war effort against France.

JOHN WESLEY

THOUGHTS ON SLAVERY

John Wesley (1703–1791), who along with his brother Charles (1707–1788) spearheaded the evangelical religious reform movement that became known as Methodism, staunchly opposed both slavery and the slave trade. A relentless critic of England's participation in that trade, he became even more vehement in his opposition to slavery after a visit to the West Indies and Georgia. In the following selection, Thoughts Upon Slavery, *written in 1774, Wesley denies the necessity of slavery but, above all, proclaims its inherent contradiction of the fundamental moral tenets of Christianity.*

But after Christianity prevailed, it [slavery] gradually fell into decline in almost all parts of Europe. This great change began in Spain, about the end of the eighth century, and was become general in most other kingdoms of Europe before the middle of the fourteenth. From this time slavery was nearly extinct till the commencement of the sixteenth century, when the discovery of America and of the western and eastern coasts of Africa gave occasion to the revival of it. It took its rise from the Portuguese, who, to supply the Spaniards with men to cultivate their new possessions in America, procured negroes from Africa, whom they sold for slaves to the American Spaniards. This began in the year 1508, when they imported the first negroes into Hispaniola. Afterwards other nations, as they acquired possessions in America, followed the examples of the Spaniards, and slavery now has taken deep root in most of our American colonies.

In what manner are they [the slaves] procured? Part of them by fraud. Captains of ships from time to time have invited negroes to come on board, and then carried them away. But far more have been procured by force. The Christians landing upon their coasts seized as many as they found, men, women, and children, and transported them to America. It was some time before the Europeans found a more compendious way of procuring African slaves, by prevailing upon them to make war upon each other and to sell their prisoners. Till then they seldom had any wars, but were in general quiet and peaceable; but the white men first taught them drunkenness and avarice, and then hired them to sell one another. Nay, by this means even their kings are induced to sell their own subjects.

Thus are they procured; but in what numbers and in what manner are they carried to America? **Mr. Anderson,** in his "History of Trade and Commerce," observes, "England supplies her American colonies with negro slaves amounting in number to about an hundred thousand every year." That is, so many are taken on board our ships, but at least ten thousand of them die on the voyage; about a fourth part more die at the different islands, in what is called the seasoning: so that, at an average, in the passage and seasoning together, thirty thousand die,—that is, properly, are murdered. O earth, O sea, cover not thou their blood!

When they are brought down to the shore in order to be sold, our surgeons thoroughly examine them, and that quite naked, women and men, without any distinction. Those that are approved are set on one side. In the mean time a burning iron, with the arms or name of the company, lies in the fire, with which they are marked on the breast. It is common for several hundred of them to be put on board one vessel, where they are stowed together in as little room as it is possible for them to be crowded.

When the vessels arrive at their destined port, the negroes are again exposed naked to the eyes of all that flock together, and the examination of their purchasers; then they are separated to the plantations of their several masters, to see each other no more. And what can be more wretched than the condition they then enter upon! Banished from their country, from their friends and relations forever, from every comfort of life, they are reduced to a state scarce any way preferable to that of beasts of burden. Did the Creator intend that the noblest creatures in the visible world should live such a life as this?

Such is the manner wherein our African slaves are procured, such the manner wherein they are removed from their native land, and wherein they are treated in our plantations. I would now inquire whether these things can be defended on the principles of even heathen honesty;—whether they can be reconciled (setting the Bible out of the question) with any degree of either justice or mercy.

Where is the justice of inflicting the severest evils on those that have done us no wrong? Of depriving those that never injured us, in word or deed, of every comfort of life? Of tearing them from their native country, and depriving them of liberty itself,—to which an Angolan had the same natural right as an Englishman, and on which he sets as high a value? That slave-holding is utterly inconsistent with mercy is almost too plain to need a proof. Indeed it is said," "That these negroes, being prisoners of war, our captains and factors buy them merely to save them from being put to death. And is this not mercy?" I answer, . . . Was it to save them from death that they knocked out the brains of those they could not bring away? Who occasioned and fomented those wars wherein those poor creatures were taken prisoners? Who excited them, by money, by drink, by every possible means, to fall upon one another? Was it not themselves [the European slavers]?

But if this manner of procuring and treating negroes is not consistent either with mercy or justice, yet there is a plea for it which every man of business will acknowledge to be quite sufficient. "It is necessity." Here also the slave-holder fixes his foot; here he rests the strength of his cause. "If it is not quite right, yet it must be so; there is an absolute necessity for it; it is necessary we should procure slaves, and when we have procured them it is necessary to use them with severity, considering their stupidity, stubbornness, and wickedness."

I answer, You stumble at the threshold. I deny that villainy is ever necessary. But, to be more particular, I ask, first, what is necessary? And, secondly, to what end? It may be answered, "The whole method now used by the original purchasers of negroes is necessary to the furnishing of our colonies with a hundred thousand slaves." I grant this is necessary to that end. But how is that end necessary?

"But, however, you must allow those slaves are necessary for the cultivation of our islands, inasmuch as white men are not able to labor in hot climates." ... the supposition on which you ground your argument is false; for white men, even Englishmen, are well able to labor in hot climates, provided they are temperate in both meat and drink, and that they inure themselves to it by degrees. I speak no more than I know by experience. It appears from my thermometer that the summer heat in Georgia is frequently equal to that in Barbadoes, yea to that under the line [the equator]; and yet I and my family, eight in number, did employ all our spare time there in felling of trees and clearing of ground,—as hard labor as any negro need be employed in. The German family, likewise, forty in number, were employed in all manner of labor; and this was so far from impairing our health, that we all continued perfectly well, while the idle ones all round about us were swept away as with pestilence.

"But the furnishing us with slaves is necessary for the trade, and wealth, and glory of our nation." Here are several mistakes; for, first, wealth is not necessary to the glory of any nation, but wisdom, virtue, justice, mercy, generosity, public spirit, love of our country: these are necessary to the real glory of a nation, but abundance of wealth is not. But, secondly, it is not clear that we should have either less money or trade (only less of that detestable trade of man-stealing) if there were not a negro in all our islands, or in all of English America. However, thirdly, I come back to the same point: better no trade than trade procured by villainy.

And this equally concerns every gentleman that has an estate in our American plantations, yea, all slave-holders of whatever rank and degree, seeing men-buyers are exactly on a level with men-stealers. Indeed, you say, "I pay honestly for my goods, and I am not concerned to know how they are come by." Nay, but you are; you are deeply concerned to know they are honestly come by, otherwise you are partaker with a thief, and are not a jot honester than him. But you know they are not honestly come by; you know they are procured by means nothing near so honest as picking of pockets, housebreaking, or robbery upon the highway. You know they are procured by a deliberate series of more complicated villainy, of fraud, robbery, and murder, than was ever practised by either Mahometans [Muslims] or Pagans. Now, it is your money that pays the merchant, and through him the captain and the African butchers. You are the spring that puts all the rest in motion: they would not stir a step without you; therefore the blood of all these wretches who die before their time, whether in this country or elsewhere, lies upon your head.

Liberty is the right of every human creature as soon as he breathes the vital air; and no human law can deprive him of that right, which he derives from the law of nature. If, therefore, you have any regard to justice (to say nothing of mercy, nor of the revealed law of God,) render unto all their due; give liberty to whom liberty is due, that is to every child of man, to every partaker of human nature.

TERMS AND DEFINITIONS

Mr. Anderson: most likely a
reference to a Scottish author,
Adam Anderson (1692–1765).

VENTURE SMITH

AN AFRICAN'S ACCOUNT
OF THE TRADE

Venture Smith (1729–?) provides a narrative of the first eight years of his life, during which his status changed from that of a rather privileged son of an African prince to a slave in the United States. His account, A Narrative of the Life and Adventures of Venture, A Native of Africa . . . Related by Himself, *first appeared in 1798. It helps remind us that each one of the millions of Africans taken prisoner because of the slave trade were individual human beings, with families, and friends. Their lives were dramatically altered—and often ended—as a result of the demand for slave labor in the Americas. Note, for example, the impact of the trade on Venture and his family.*

I was born at Dukandarra, in **Guinea,** about the year 1729. My father's name was Saungm Furro, Prince of the tribe of Dukandarra. The first thing worthy of notice which I remember, was a contention between my father and mother. . . . In consequence of this rupture, my mother left her husband and country, and traveled away with her three children to the eastward. I was then five years old. We went on our journey until the second day after our departure from Dukandarra, when we came to the entrance of a great desert. After five days' travel we came to the end of this desert, and immediately entered into a beautiful and extensive interval country. Here my mother was pleased to stop and seek a refuge for me. She left me at the house of a very rich farmer. My new guardian, as I shall call the man with whom I was left, put me into the business of tending sheep. . . . During my stay with him I was kindly used, and with as much tenderness, for what I saw, as his only son, although I was an entire stranger to him, remote from friends and relatives.

My father sent a man and horse after me. After settling with my guardian for keeping me, he took me away and went for home. It was then about one year since my mother brought me here. I found that the difference between my parents had been made up previous to their sending for me.

Not more than six weeks had passed after my return, before a message was brought by an inhabitant of the place where I lived the preceding year to my father, that that place had been invaded by a numerous army, from a nation not far distant, furnished with . . . all kinds of arms then in use; that they were instigated by some white nation who equipped and sent them to subdue and possess the country; that his nation had made no preparation for war, having been for a long time in profound peace; that they could not defend themselves against such a formidable train of invaders, and must therefore, necessarily evacuate their lands to the fierce enemy, and fly to the protection of some chief; and that if he would permit them they would come under his rule and protection when they had to retreat from their own possessions.

He had scarcely returned to his nation with the message before the whole of his people were obligated to retreat from their country and come to my father's dominions. But they had not been there longer than four days before news came to them that the invaders had laid waste their country, and were coming speedily to destroy them in my father's territories.

A detachment from the enemy came to my father and informed him that the whole army was encamped not far from his dominions, and would invade the territory and deprive the people of their liberties and rights, if he did not comply with the following terms. These were, to pay them a large sum of money, three hundred fat cattle, and a great number of goats, sheep, asses, etc.

My father told the messenger he would comply. . . . But their pledges of faith and honor proved no better than those of other unprincipled hostile nations, for a few days after, a certain relation of the king came and informed him that the enemy . . . yet meditated an attack upon his subjects by surprise.

The same night which was fixed upon to retreat, my father and his family set off about the break of day. But we presently found that our retreat was not secure. For having struck up a little fire for the purpose of cooking victuals, the enemy, who happened to be encamped a little distance off, had sent out a scouting party who discovered us by the smoke of the fire just as we were extinguishing it and about to eat. They then came to us in the reeds, and the very first salute I had from them was a violent blow on the head with the fore part of a gun, and at the same time a grasp around the neck. I then had a rope put about my neck, as all the women in the thicket with me, and were immediately led to my father, who was likewise pinioned and haltered for leading. The women and myself, being submissive had tolerable treatment from the enemy, while my father was closely interrogated respecting his money, which they knew he must have. I saw him while he was thus tortured to death. The shocking scene is to this day fresh in my memory, and I have often been overcome while thinking on it.

After destroying the old prince, they decamped and immediately marched towards the sea, lying to the west, taking with them myself and the women prisoners. The enemy had remarkable success in destroying the country wherever they went. For as far as they had penetrated they laid the habitations waste and captured the people. The distance that had now brought me was about four hundred miles. All the march I had very hard tasks imposed on me, which I must perform on pain of punishment.

Having come to the next tribe, the enemy laid siege and immediately took men, women, children, flocks, and all their valuable effects. They then went on to the next district, which was contiguous to the sea. . . . The enemies' provisions were then almost spent, as well as their strength. The inhabitants, knowing what conduct they had pursued, and what were their present intentions, improved the favorable opportunity, attacked them, and took enemy, prisoners, flocks and all their effects. I was then taken a second time. All of us were then put into the castle and kept for market. On a certain time, I and other prisoners were put on board a canoe, under our master, and rowed away to a vessel belonging to Rhode Island, commanded by Captain **Collingwood**, and the mate, Thomas Mumford. While we were going to the vessel, our master told us to appear to the best possible advantage for sale. I was bought on board by one Robertson Mumford, a steward of said vessel, for four gallons of rum and a piece of calico, and called VENTURE on account of having purchased me with his own private venture. Thus I came by my new name. All the slaves that were bought for that vessel's cargo were two hundred and sixty.

After all the business was ended on the coast of Africa, the ship sailed from thence to Barbadoes. After an ordinary passage, except great mortality by the small pox, which broke out on board, we arrived at the island of Barbadoes; but when we reached it, there we found, out of the two hundred and sixty that sailed from Africa, not more than two hundred alive. These were all sold, except myself and three more, to the planters there.

The vessel then sailed for Rhode Island, and arrived there after a comfortable passage. Here my master sent me to live with one of his sisters until he could carry me to Fishers' Island, the place of his residence. I had then completed my eighth year.

TERMS AND DEFINITIONS

Guinea: a portion of the West African Coast between 15 degrees north and 15 degrees south latitude. Traders and slavers referred to the more northern portion as Upper Guniea, and subdivided it further into smaller areas known as the slave, gold, ivory, and grain coasts.

Mr. Collingwood: A Rhode Islander, well-known as a slave trading captain, he had a reputation for treating slaves decently.

ROBERT CONRAD

NORTH AMERICANS AND THE ILLEGAL SLAVE TRADE TO LATIN AMERICA

An American-born historian, Robert Conrad (1928–) has written extensively about Brazilian slavery as well as about its participation in the Atlantic slave trade. The following selection comes from his 1986 book, World of Sorrow: The African Slave Trade to Brazil. *Here he provides an extensive description of the participation of United States citizens in the Atlantic trade after it had been outlawed. He also notes policies of the U.S. government that contributed to the ongoing illegal trade.*

Like their British cousins, North Americans remained involved in the international slave trade after it became illegal for both English-speaking nations, openly constructing ships in Atlantic ports for use in the forbidden traffic and transporting tens of thousands of Africans in those ships to New World countries. In fact, violations of American slave-trade laws were so common in the first decades of the nineteenth century that early laws banning the traffic from the United States to foreign countries (1794), forbidding the transportation of slaves by Americans between foreign countries (1800), and outlawing the traffic to the United States (1807) were supplemented in 1820 by statutes that made slave-trading punishable by long prison terms and even death. Severe penalties did not, however, eliminate American cooperation with illegal slave traders. According to a visitor to St. Thomas in the Virgin Islands in 1831, that island was then a supply station for the slave trade to Cuba and Puerto Rico, to which "handcuffs and leg-shackles, negro cloth, and a thousand other cheap manufactured articles" were supplied from England for later shipment to Africa, and "rice, tobacco, flour and other provisions" were supplied from the United States, evidently for feeding slaves and crews on return voyages.

Cuba had long been familiar territory to American slave traders. From 1789, when Spain replaced the *asiento,* or contract system, with free trading in slaves, until 1794, when American involvement in slave trading to foreign countries was outlawed, slave merchants from the United States competed strongly with Spanish, French, and British slave traders in the Cuban market. Thus in 1835, when Britain coerced Spain into a treaty permitting the Royal Navy to seize Spanish ships equipped for the commerce in Africans, there was an easy resurgence of North American involvement in the slave trade to Cuba, which had never totally ceased. Before 1839, in fact, most slaves brought illegally to the Western Hemisphere by United States citizens were landed on that Caribbean island, with relatively few reaching the United States, since the great demand for black workers in the South was met almost entirely by the self-generating slave population itself.

In regard to Brazil, Americans may have participated in the slave trade as early as 1810. . . . It is realistic to assume, however, that the United States had little more than fast sailing ships to offer the Brazilian and Portuguese merchants who then dominated the trade. When, however, Parliament passed the

Palmerston Bill in August, 1839, unilaterally authorizing British warships to seize slave ships registered in Portugal and flying the Portuguese flag, this situation drastically changed. With the Portuguese advantage suddenly eliminated, United States citizens became peculiarly qualified to engage in some phase of the trade to Brazil with a far greater likelihood of success than citizens of other countries. As a result, North American merchants and sailors, already involved in slave trading to Cuba, entered the Brazilian traffic decisively and remained involved until its end.

The main American advantage was simple and important: after 1839 the United States was the only major Western nation that resisted British efforts to legalize the boarding and searching of merchant vessels. As a result, the flag of the United States offered the same theoretical immunity from seizure by British ships that the Portuguese flag had provided before passage of the Palmerston Bill—with the added advantage that Great Britain was far less ready to risk a war with the United States than it had been with Portugal. War with Portugal might have given Britain a welcome opportunity to seize Portuguese colonies, especially those the East India Company coveted in Asia. A military struggle with the United States, on the other hand, offered no such incentive and might have had the further disadvantage of stopping the flow of American cotton to British mills.

The refusal of the United States to permit boarding and searching of its ships was the result of peculiar historical developments, notably the well-known British impressment of passengers and sailors aboard United States ships, which had helped to incite the War of 1812. In November, 1818, John Quincy Adams, then secretary of state, rejected a British draft treaty . . . to allow mutual inspections of ships at sea and to create mixed commission courts. . . . In rebuffing Britain, Adams expressed doubt that the Constitution of the United States authorized his government to establish tribunals composed partly of foreigners who would be beyond American constitutional controls and able to render decisions that could not be appealed. Nor could the government of the United States, he pointed out, guarantee the freedom of Africans liberated by such courts, since the condition of blacks in the Republic was regulated by the laws in each state. More important than constitutional arguments, however, was the public attitude toward the delicate question of the citizen's rights at sea. With recent events obviously in mind, Adams argued that permitting foreign officers to board and search American ships would be "obnoxious to the feelings and recollections" of the American people and Senate, who would oppose such an agreement even in a qualified form and even in time of peace. It was mainly these principles, which the Lincoln administration at last reluctantly abandoned during the Civil War, that gave the flag of the United States an indispensable role in the last dozen years of the Brazilian slave trade, during which perhaps many as five hundred thousand Africans entered Brazil.

The United States government conferred another advantage upon foreign slave traders. An old State Department procedure, initiated in 1792 as a means of stimulating the shipbuilding industry, required consulates abroad to grant ship's papers (sea letters) to any citizen who claimed to be a resident of the United States and the bona fide purchaser of an American ship abroad. Stubbornly maintained in the 1840s, contrary to the advice of United States diplomatic personnel in Brazil, this arrangement enabled owners of slave ships to acquire the protection of the American flag by simply persuading citizens of the United States to make false applications in exchange for substantial compensation. Federal law permitted the granting of registration papers only to ships entirely owned by United States citizens, but . . . facile acts of perjury by North Americans enabled notorious slave merchants to obtain United States papers for ships they themselves owned entirely, along with the coveted immunity the United States flag all but guaranteed.

Once in possession of the coveted documents, slave dealers needed American officers and crews to give their ships an authentic Yankee look. Such persons were not hard to recruit, however, since incentives were high and United States seamen who joined such voyages had little to fear from authorities of any nation. More surprising, however, even United States authorities aroused little fear, since any informed person knew that Congress, the navy, the State Department, and American courts and juries rarely acted vigorously to discourage such involvement.

Contributing to the misuse of the American flag, was the inadequacy of the naval squadron that the United States government kept on the African station from 1839 until 1861. This was the result in part of the deliberate refusal of Congress, led by southern and western legislators, to build a strong navy. The squadron's weakness also resulted, however, from the attitudes of administrations in Washington, who consistently saw safeguarding of United States commerce as the squadron's primary mission. Suppressing the slave trade would have required a powerful fleet capable of ranging over the whole African coast, able to inspect each river and cove, in search of elusive vessels. On the other hand, the task of discouraging British boarding of United States ships required only a token presence near the African continent—a mission more in keeping with the navy's weakness.

Perhaps because of these facts, the squadron on the African station was neither large nor powerful during its entire existence and only moderately successful patrolling against the slave trade. The United States African squadron was, of course, no better than its country wanted it to be, and the nation at large, especially the South, was not much devoted to slave-trade suppression. A by-product of this national indifference . . . was a remarkable reluctance of judges and juries to convict persons charged with the crime of slave trading. In fact, the legal decisions handed down in United States courts over a period of several decades all but legitimized operations most commonly assigned to North Americans by Brazilian, Portuguese, and Spanish associates. United States citizens, for example, could "legally" sell their ships to foreign slave dealers, because there was no way to prove to a jury that they *knew* how their vessels would be used. They could "legally" sail their ships from American ports loaded with products usually traded for slaves in Africa, and they could even sell those goods at slave depots on the African coast.

The most tolerant judges recognized that actually transporting slaves was a clear legal violation, but seizure of a vessel packed from stem to stern with blacks by no means assured convictions. If the accused did not "escape" from prison or jump bail, which often happened, he might still avoid imprisonment by claiming foreign citizenship or by having the good fortune to encounter a jury who looked upon slave-trade trials as an oblique attack on the American way of life. Or he might be saved by a witness willing to swear that the ship involved was foreign property, or by asserting that he had unknowingly joined a slaving voyage or had been coerced into participation. As a result of such legal dodges, of the more than two hundred persons arrested by United States authorities for involvement in the traffic between 1837 and 1862, almost half were never brought to trial, about a third were tried but acquitted, and less than two dozen were convicted and sent to prison, most for short terms that were quickly ended by presidential pardons . . . . the vehement quality of American racial prejudice, the existence of slavery in a large part of the United States, and the notorious practice of transporting slaves across state lines and coastwise to destinations in the Deep South blunted the nation's sensitivity to the suffering of black people and perhaps intensified widespread disrespect for the laws that prohibited the participation of American citizens in the international slave trade.

TERMS AND DEFINITIONS

asiento: the Spanish practice of granting to particular individuals or companies the right to transport and sell slaves in its American colonies.

SERGE DAGET

ABOLITION OF THE SLAVE TRADE

Serge Daget, a professor of history at the University of Nantes in France, has written extensively about the African slave trade, particularly with regard to French traders and abolitionists. The following selection comes from a chapter he wrote, "The Abolition of the Slave Trade," for volume VI of UNESCO's General History of Africa, edited by J. F. Ade Ajayi. In this 1989 publication, Daget discusses the slave trade as an aspect of the shared historical experience of the Western world, identifying various of the factors that promoted governments of many nations, including the United States, to outlaw the trade. At the same time, he identifies some of the practical political issues that promoted the continuation of an illegal trade, including the difficulties created by tensions between England and the United States.

At the end of the Middle Passage the slave-traders exchanged the 6 million Africans who had survived the voyage—40 per cent of them women and children—against the produce of slave labor, which sold increasingly well on the European side of the Atlantic. Nevertheless some European intellectuals, their principles and finer feelings outraged, condemned the eating of sugar dyed with the blood of the "forgotten men of the universe," and called for the abolition of the trade.

Throughout the eighteenth century, as they polished up their definition of the universal human right to liberty and the pursuit of happiness, anthropologists, philosophers, and theologians came up against the case of the African and his condition in the world. Their thinking led them to modify the ideas commonly accepted until then about the African black and the American slave, and they transformed the brute beast of burden into a moral and social being. Their slogan, "'The Negro is a man'", implicitly impugned the generally held view about the propriety, legality, and usefulness of selling black Africans. Their humanitarian arguments led to a demand for abolition, since the balance sheet of the trade consisted, as they saw it, entirely of debits.

While denouncing the scourge, abolitionists did not seek or expect to convert back traders or white pro-slavers straightaway. They put forward a program for the regeneration of Africa through Christianity, civilization, and normal trade, and proposed rational stages for its implementation: public opinion in the Christian world to be changed, the so-called "'civilized'" governments to be persuaded to adopt official positions, and the Atlantic trade to be legally abolished.

In France in the eighteenth century, the **Grande Encyclopèdie** . . . taught bourgeois revolutionaries a disgust for slavery. There, revolutionaries were sensitive neither to the realities of the slave trade nor to the need for popular support for their new ideology. In Britain, on the other hand, ordinary folk were educated in philanthropy through theological exposition based on a vigorous revival. The American Quakers, having themselves forsworn dealing in slaves, had already persuaded British Quakers to join the British movement for abolition. The fight against the array of obstacles set up by slave owners and traders lasted twenty years, but on 25 March 1807, Britain abolished the trade. This was the second official abolition, following that of Denmark in 1802. In 1808 the USA gave general effect to the Quakers' individual decisions. This movement by governments to adopt the humanitarian cause was championed by Britain, whose slave traders had shipped some 1,600,000 Africans to its American colonies during the previous century.

With the ending of the Napoleonic wars a world was crumbling in ruins. The peace of 1815 opened the Mediterranean, the Indian Ocean, and the Atlantic to maritime trade; and to the transport of slaves. At the **Congress of Vienna,** British diplomacy sought an explicit condemnation of the trade, but all it obtained was an empty, procrastinatory declaration. . . . this pretence of official abolitionist morality gave the British Foreign Office all the authority they needed for their combined strategies in regard to the international trade. This was a radical three-point plan of action: domestic legislation making it illegal for nationals of the country concerned to engage in the traffic; bilateral treaties giving navies the reciprocal right to search and seize at sea merchant vessels of either contracting nation caught in the illegal trade; and collaboration through mixed commissions, empowered to adjudicate on captured slave ships and set free the slaves found on board.

. . . the English plan was bound to attract opposition from interests likely to be damaged by forcible suppression. States opposed it in the name of their national sovereignty, for the right of search and joint commissions presupposed a partial surrender of that sovereignty. They saw abolition as an aspect of the wicked machinations of the British in their bid for world hegemony, backed by the absolute superiority of the Royal Navy. They opposed it on the grounds of the damage that would be done to navies, colonies, and national trading interests. Portugal, Spain, and the USA and France used and distributed cotton, sugar, coffee, and tobacco produced on slave plantations dependent on the import of Africans into Brazil, Cuba, the Southern States of the USA, and the West Indies. Shipping agents were directly concerned: they also attracted investment, and provided employment for small local sectors of the economy that made a profit out of the trade.

Denmark, the Netherlands, and Sweden, which still practised slavery in some of their smaller colonies, subscribed to reciprocal suppression. In return for substantial indemnities, Spain and Portugal agreed to it in 1817. Politically stronger states reacted differently to British pressure. France, eager for prestige, maintained its freedom of action by a pretence at legislation and by naval suppression patrols which remained innocuous in home waters for as long as they did on the coast. Between 1815 and 1830, the French illicit trade fitted out 729 slaving expeditions for the west and east coasts of Africa. But when it became clear such operations no longer benefitted French ports either financially or socially, the government signed a reciprocal search agreement. Britain took the opportunity to renew its attempts to internationalize the issue, and extended its naval suppression to cover the whole of the Atlantic and Indian oceans. An "equipment" clause in the treaties allowed the seizure of ships obviously equipped for the slave traffic, even though not carrying human cargoes.

But the slave ships of the USA remained exempt. For forty years American diplomacy managed to evade any serious commitment. In 1820 the trade was legally equated with piracy; in 1842 came the compromise of "checking the flag," which protected the Americans from British suppressive actions; and the 80-gun suppression squadrons served to safeguard national pride whilst at the same time remaining mere formalities. In the 1840s the southern planters called for the legal reopening of the trade, and meanwhile took to breeding slaves for the home market on special ranches. During the Civil War the Lincoln administration committed itself to the right of search which had been in abeyance since 1820. The American trade then stopped.

Thus for half a century the proliferation and accumulation of documents testify mainly to the emptiness of the undertakings entered into. Throughout all this avalanche of words, Africa and the Africans were hardly ever mentioned, just as though they did not exist. Shipping agents benefitted from the illicit trade, making bigger profits than during the period of legally protected trade, while the slave plantations stockpiled manpower.

The effectiveness of the [mixed] commissions on the American side of the Atlantic depended on the attitude prevailing in the slave plantations. In Cuba, out of 714 slave ships captured between 1819 and 1845, the Hispano-British Commission condemned only 45. When bounties for ships seized were awarded to the sailors of the Spanish local squadron, fifty vessels were arrested during the last ten years of the trade. Only one out of every five slave-trading vessels was captured in American waters, despite the fact that around 1840 nearly seventy warships of different nationalities were assigned to suppression duties there.

On the West African coast the numbers were smaller. The Dutch, Portuguese, and American naval squadrons operated spasmodically; the American squadron was often under the command of Southerners, and it was based on **Cape Verde,** a long way from the centre of the traffic. Such were the conditions at the time of the founding of Liberia and, so far as the fleeting appearance of cruisers was concerned, they remained so until 1842. The treaty with the British stipulated the presence of four or five warships, but that remained purely theoretical. Between 1839 and 1859 two American slave ships were seized with their cargoes. In 1860 there were seven arrests, the slaves from which helped to populate Liberia.

Effective suppression depended on the human factor. The British sailors, indoctrinated from London, were for abolition heart and soul. They also had a power complex which on occasion led the Royal Navy to disobey Admiralty orders in the name of humanity and treat international maritime law with contempt. The navy illegally searched and seized French and American vessels in advance of the bilateral treaties, thus setting in train a chain of protests and diplomatic reparations.

The slave ships took shrewd advantage of the confusion that prevailed in the international field so far as suppression was concerned. On the coast their intelligence about the movement of cruisers was good and they managed to evade them perhaps four times out of five. They behaved like pirates, flying false flags and using forged ships' papers. Once the suppression treaties were strengthened they threw off their disguise: French papers were no protection after 1831, nor Portuguese after 1842. But the maintenance of American sovereignty effectively protected slave-trading under the US flag until 1862.

Between 1787 and 1807, i.e. in the period immediately preceding abolition by the West, more than a million Africans were transported to the Americas. To this figure must be added about 15 per cent who died during the Atlantic passage, and an unknown number of deaths caused by the journey to the coast and during local slave-producing operations . . . . Estimates of the volume of the slave trade during the sixty years of the abolitionist period can only be in terms of orders of magnitude. From 1807 to 1867, between Senegal and Mozambique 4000 European and American ships carried out perhaps five thousand slaving expeditions, representing a displacement of one million metric tons. Goods to the value of roughly sixty million piastres or dollars were bartered for a total of 1,900,000 Africans actually put on board at the export points. Of these, most probably 80 per cent were loaded south of the Equator.

TERMS AND DEFINITIONS

Cape Verde: Atlantic Ocean islands that belonged to Portugal.

Congress of Vienna: In 1814–15, the various European nations met to hammer out territorial settlements in the wake of the Napoleonic wars.

Grande Encyclopèdie: Compiled over the years from 1751 to 1780 by various members of the French Enlightenment, its thirty-five volumes represented an attempt to organize all knowledge in a logical fashion.

THINKING THINGS THROUGH

1. What factors prompted the beginning of the Atlantic slave trade?

2. Why did the trade continue for so long a period of time?

3. Compare John Wesley's arguments against the trade with those in the anonymous pamphlet of 1763.

4. In what ways did the United States participate in the illegal slave trade?

5. In what respects did the United States' participation in the Atlantic trade differ from that of the various European nations?

4

The Colonial Matrix

A. The International Context

During the century and a half before the American Revolution, Great Britain's North American colonies generally experienced remarkable growth in number, population, economic prosperity, social complexity, and political sophistication. Beginning as pioneer settlements of a few hundred people on the Massachusetts and Chesapeake Bays in the early seventeenth century, they transformed themselves into thirteen flourishing colonies whose nearly three million inhabitants occupied the vast expanse from New Hampshire to Georgia and from the Atlantic seaboard to the Appalachian Mountains by 1763. Much of their success derived from the abundance and opportunity that the environment supplied to settlers from a variety of European backgrounds. Much of it flowed from the colonists' willingness and ability to wrest control of vast tracts of land from Native Americans, and to exploit the labor of African slaves and European indentured servants. Much of it, too, resulted from the British policy of "benign neglect", necessitated by the great distance separating the home country from its colonial outposts. That policy was reinforced by Britain's need to attend to more pressing domestic and international problems. Equally important to the colonies' remarkable progress, however, was the fact that these thirteen European outposts were enmeshed in complex international networks of trade and commerce, migration, kinship, religion, ideas, and continuous political and military conflict.

In their haste to celebrate the emergence of the United States, modern-day Americans frequently lose sight of the fact that the thirteen original colonies were but one segment of a vast seaborne empire ruled from London, which eventually also included the British Isles, Canada, the Mississippi Valley, significant portions of the West Indies, India, and West Africa, and the gateway to the Mediterranean Sea. Although the British Parliament, of necessity, permitted the colonists a significant degree of self-government in many matters of purely local concern, it also attempted to enforce a vast body of legislation that applied to the empire as a whole, and to the American colonies in particular. Acting largely through its appointed commission, the Board of Trade, the British Parliament exercised the right of review over every single act passed by the elected colonial legislatures, although they declared only a very small number unconstitutional. The British government also appointed nearly all colonial governors and invested them with the royal "prerogative" (the kingly right to proclaim laws), making them, at least in constitutional terms, superior to the colonial assemblies. It took 150 years of ongoing conflict before the colonial assemblies achieved parity with the appointed governors, even a bit longer before they declared their equality with Parliament as lawgivers. While the thirteen colonies were not actually represented by voting members in Parliament, they were actively involved in policy making through the efforts of colonial agents, who regularly lobbied, testified, and advised, and who acted as conduits between the individual colonies and the seat of imperial power in Westminster. Some colonial agents even commanded a great deal of respect, and wielded a considerable amount of influence. Even so, the thirteen American colonies rarely occupied center stage. Their interests and concerns were frequently subordinated to those of other British outposts, and always to those of the parent country itself.

Nowhere was that reality more obvious than in the seemingly endless imperial wars engaged in by Great Britain during the seventeenth and eighteenth centuries, conflicts that frequently resembled the warfare of the twentieth century in geographical scope, because they were fought simultaneously in Europe, North America, India, West Africa, and the Caribbean. During the course of those wars, the British followed a pragmatic, totally self-interested, course, allying with and opposing other European powers as expediency dictated. Whatever the military alignment, the American colonies were usually required to provide the British with men and money. They all too often found that their interests and welfare were sacrificed to those of the empire. The colonists' substantial contribution in men and money seemed to earn them only increased taxes, stricter regulation, and a lessened status in the imperial scheme of things. Nevertheless, there can be no doubt that the American colonies were both participants and pawns in the great international wars for empire.

The American colonies were also thoroughly involved in international trade and commerce that carried their products, ships, and crews far beyond the boundaries of North America. Under the prevailing philosophy of mercantilism, the European great powers looked to colonies as sources of raw materials and precious metals, and as markets for manufactured products. Since Britain's greatest desire was for raw materials not available in the homeland, it valued its tropical possessions in the Caribbean and the near-tropical southern American colonies above more northerly ones. They rewarded their southern American colonies with generous bounties, subsidies, and credit arrangements. Because the chief value of the more northern colonies was as sources of semiprocessed materials and revenue, and as markets for British manufactured goods, Parliament enacted the complex body of regulations, subsidies, bounties, and prohibitions, commonly known as the Navigation Acts, which guaranteed them a clearly subordinate role in the imperial economic system. Under their provisions, American colonists regularly exchanged goods and products among themselves, and with Great Britain, the European continent, the West Indies, and West Africa. American colonial ships touched in at ports all over the Atlantic basin distributing products, while its own harbors frequently welcomed vessels from various European nations, whose cargoes made colonial life considerably more cosmopolitan. Although the American colonists frequently resented the restrictions, they took fullest possible advantage of the opportunities presented for thriving international trade.

Also significant, but harder to measure, was the traffic in ideas and culture that connected the American colonies to Europe. Far and away the largest flow came from Great Britain to the colonies, but France, Spain, and other European countries also made a contribution. By the mid-eighteenth century, colonial American influences even occasionally reversed the direction across the Atlantic. There can be no doubt that English religious and political ideas had the greatest single impact upon the American colonies, concepts that endured even as they were modified by New World conditions and experience. Colonial and British religious and social thinkers reinforced one another's convictions regarding the evils of slavery, fueling growing abolitionist and anti-slave-trade sentiments on both sides of the Atlantic. The com-

mentaries of English jurists had a profound influence on the development of colonial legal systems, while the experience of the colonists altered English conceptions of common law. Educated Americans regularly imbibed the works of the European Enlightenment, French, Italian, German, and Swiss, as well as British. By the 1770s, the writings of several prominent Americans were gaining significant readership in those countries.

The international orientation of the American colonies was also fostered by the steady influx of immigrants who continued to increase their population and enrich their culture. While the Spanish and French generally prohibited the settlement of other ethnocultural groups, the British actually promoted the immigration of a significant variety of northwestern Europeans. As a result, the American colonies were remarkable in their ethnocultural diversity by the early eighteenth century. By the end of the 1640s, the non-Native American population of the colonies was only about twenty-five thousand, most of these fairly recent arrivals from England. By 1700, that number had increased tenfold, with a growing admixture of West African slaves altering the still overwhelmingly English character of the population. During the next ninety years, the population exploded to just under four million, about one-fifth of whom were of African ancestry. Although the vast majority of the latter were slaves, they still exerted a powerful effect on colonial American language, food habits, agricultural practices, music, religion and other cultural mores. Among non-African arrivals, the largest contingents consisted of Scots-Irish Presbyterians and German Pietists, leavened with Sephardic Jews, French Huguenots, Irish Catholics, and Swedish, Swiss, and Dutch newcomers. While the American environment and the predominant English culture had a profound effect on the various immigrant groups during the eighteenth century, the substantial presence of non-English settlers also changed what it meant to be American in many subtle, but no less significant, ways. Gradually, almost imperceptibly, they—together with the Native Americans and Africans—enlarged and enriched colonial diets, vocabularies, religions, customs, celebrations, and recreational activities, transforming Englishmen into Americans.

The thirteen colonies, then, were a matrix, a "womb," in which the United States originated, took form, and developed. They were also a matrix in which British imperial policy was constantly challenged and deflected by the aspirations and actions of their inhabitants. In the view of the home country, each colony and every individual settler existed primarily to contribute whatever was required to enhance the wealth and power of the world's greatest empire. The success of such a policy, however, depended heavily upon the cooperation of settlers who saw no important conflict between their own self-interest and well-being and those of the empire. The more ethnically and culturally diverse, and the more prosperous the colonies became, the harder it was to maintain that perception. Religious dissenters, such as Congregationalists, Presbyterians, Quakers, Baptists, and German Pietists, were predisposed to reject British authority. Colonials of Dutch, Scots-Irish, German, French, or Swedish ancestry had no hereditary or emotional ties to England. Perhaps most of all, the combination of distance, environment, and ideology afforded such freedom and opportunity for individual achievement and advancement that more and more colonists came to regard British policy as an impediment to personal success.

B. International Views

During the long gestation period of this colonial matrix, hundreds of Europeans visited one or more of the thirteen colonies and recorded their impressions for contemporaries and posterity alike. Their collective commentaries spanned the century from the 1670s to the eve of the American Revolution, and focused upon such a diverse array of colonies as Massachusetts, New York, Pennsylvania, Virginia, and South Carolina. Included in their number was Sir William Berkeley, an English aristocrat and government official who strongly indicted his country's policy toward Virginia for its failure to develop that colony's full potential and for inhibiting its economic development.

By way of contrast, a prominent English literary figure, John Dunton, severely criticized the Puritans of Massachusetts for their intolerance and sense of moral superiority, qualities that brought them into constant conflict with other colonists and with British authorities. Along the same lines, Peter Kalm, a visiting Swedish naturalist roundly denounced the Dutch inhabitants of Albany, New York, whose allegedly insatiable avarice motivated them to cheat other colonists, defy British laws, and even aid its enemies during wartime. Moved by the sad plight of his fellow Germans who labored as indentured servants in Pennsylvania, Gottlieb Mittelberger, an articulate and humanitarian observer charged that an exaggerated sense of freedom had caused that colony's residents to glorify their personal economic pursuits at the expense of religious piety and education. Finally, an aristocratic Scottish woman, Janet Schaw, lambasted the male inhabitants of North Carolina, on the eve of the American Revolution, for their supposed ignorance and barbarity, which she believed was leading them to revolt against British authority.

Taken as a whole, these independent assessments demonstrate that the thirteen colonial British outposts differed significantly among themselves in economic and political development, as well as in social and cultural sophistication. They also suggest strongly that, for all of their remarkable progress in these areas, the American colonists still lagged far behind their European cousins in cultural and intellectual development. Finally, they provide a variety of perspectives on the process that was relentlessly transforming colonials into Americans.

SIR WILLIAM BERKELEY

VIRGINIA'S TRIALS AND TRIBULATIONS

One of the earliest, most astute and articulate observers of colonial Virginia was Sir William Berkeley, an English aristocrat who lived from 1606 to 1677. By his mid-thirties, Berkeley had achieved some reputation as a playwright, served on the royal privy council, and been knighted by Charles I. As governor of Virginia, from 1642 to 1649 and from 1660 to 1677, he tried to break the colony's dependence on tobacco and to achieve better relations with Native Americans, thereby helping to promote Bacon's Rebellion in 1676. While still governor, he wrote A Discourse and View of Virginia, in which he recorded his impressions of the colony's status in the international economy and polity. Berkeley proved to be especially perceptive in his assessment of Virginia's unrealized potential within the imperial system, as well as of the manner in which it was regarded by Great Britain and its commercial and political rivals.

Had the Dutch Virginia, they would make it the **Fortress, Mart and Magazine** of all the West Indies, (as I first intimated) for the Rivers will securely harbor twenty thousand Ships at once; the Country produces all things necessary for those Ships and the men that sail in them, nothing wanting for the supplies of war or peace, but it was ever our misery not to pursue that goal for a sufficient length of time. In half that time it has taken us to establish this colony, and to enrich this Kingdom by our labours, I can with assurance affirm, that, with resolute instructions and indulgent encouragements for just seven years, we shall not need the Northern nor Southern East Countries to supply us with Silk, Flax, Hemp, Pitch, Tar, Iron, Malts, Timber, and **Pot-ashes.** For all of these but Iron, we want only skillful men to teach us to produce them the cheapest and readiest way; but the making of Iron will require abler purses than we are yet masters of.

It must be confessed that Barbados sends a better commodity to England than Virginia yet does, but still it must be acknowledged that one Ship from Virginia brings more Money to the Crown than five Ships of the same burthen do from the Barbados. But had we ability or skill to set forward those staple commodities I mentioned, of Silk, Flax, Hemp, Pitch, Pot-ashes and Iron, a few years would make us able to send more Ships laden with these than now the Barbados do with Sugar.

Among other weighty Reasons why Virginia has not all this while made any progression into staple Commodities, this is the chief: that our Governours, by reason of the corruption of those times they lived in, laid the Foundation of our wealth and industry on the vices of men. About the time of our first seating of the Country, this vicious habit of taking Tobacco did possess the English Nation, and from them has diffused itself into most parts of the World. When Spain brought tobacco to us at great prices, it made our Governour suppose great wealth might be raised for individuals by this universal vice, and indeed, for many years, he was not deceived until, increasing in numbers and many other Plantations following the same design, tobacco has at last brought it as now it is to that lowness of price, that the **Customs** doubles the first purchase. The Merchant buys it for one penny the pound, and we pay two pence for the Custom of that which they are not pleased to take from us.

This was the first and fundamental hindrance that made the Planters neglect all other accessions to wealth and happiness, and fix their hopes only on this vicious weed of Tobacco, which at length has brought them to that extremity that they can neither handsomely subsist with it, nor without it. Another hindrance has been that there was never yet any public encouragement to assist the Planters in those more chargeable undertakings, as Iron-mines and shipping.

Another impediment, and an important one too, has been the dismembering of the Colony by giving away and erecting divers **Principalities** of it, such as Maryland to my Lord Baltimore, and part of Florida to my Lord of Arundell, these grants will in the next Age be found more disadvantageous to the Crown than is perceptible in this one; and therefore I shall not touch it (uncommanded) as to the political aspect, but only the Economic. I shall affirm that we can never make any Laws for the production of Staple Commodities, and setting a stop to our unlimited planting of Tobacco, whilst these Governments are distinct and independent, for on frequent trials when we begin to make provision for these, our people fly to Maryland, and by this means heighten our public charges, and weaken our defences against our perpetual enemies, the Indians. Nor is this all, for by reason of these interposing Grants, we have suffered the Dutch to enrich themselves on our discoveries, who have in our precincts settled a Trade of beaver with the Indians, amounting to two hundred thousand skins a year, and supply our enemies with Ammunition and Guns in greater proportion than we have them ourselves. But, god be thanked, as yet, they, their Towns and trade are in the King's power, whenever he shall command them to quit their Usurpations, or to acknowledge their Subjection to him in those parts.

Another great impediment has been confining the Planters to trade only with the English. This no good Subject or Englishman will oppose, if it be found either beneficial to the Crown or our Mother-Nation, but if it shall appear that neither of these are advantaged by it, then we cannot but resent that forty thousand people should be impoverished to enrich little more than forty Merchants, who, being the only buyers of our tobacco, give us what they please for it and, after it is here, sell it how they please. Indeed, they have forty thousand servants in us, at cheaper rates, than any other men have slaves, for they supply slaves with Meat, Drink and Clothes, while all our sweat and labour, as they order us, will hardly procure us coarse clothes to keep us from the extremities of heat and cold. Yet, if these pressures on us did advance the Customs, or benefit the Nation, we should not object. That it does contrary to both, I shall easily evidence when commanded.

Another hinderance has been the want of a **public stock** to enable us to procure able men for the finding all sorts of mines, making iron of those mines that are found, ship carpenters, men skillful in hemp, flax and silk, for the last of which no country in the world is more naturally provided than Virginia is. As by the feet we guess at the proportions of men, so we can experimentally say that, within seven years if we are affixed and commanded, we shall bring in yearly as much silk into England as now costs the nation two hundred thousand pounds sterling at least. Flax, hemp and pitch would always be according to the numbers and possibility of the labours of the planters.

On the whole matter, let it be conceded, that if the English plantations are not proportioned in a short time to supply us with all those commodities, which now we have at great charge and hazard from Turkey, Persia, Germany, Poland, and Russia, as well as the wines, oils, and fruits of France and Spain, our distance will ever hinder us from introducing at the same rates we have it now from them. It has, as I intimated, been highly imputed to us by diverse wise men, who only contemplate the natural richness of our soil, and by that weight and measure our faults and neglects, that we have not employed our cares and industry in producing more staple commodities then hitherto we have attempted. This none can more severely resent than the poor planter himself in frequent consultations has done, who, by many trials, have found their case to be like those architects who can design excellent buildings, but have not skill to square their timber, or lay their bricks, and, for want of money to procure men for these labours, their models remain only in their imaginations or papers. This is our cause, because without a public assistance we can neither survive our poverty, nor find the remedies of it. Without universal, immediate pressure from the inhabitants of the colony, men of manufacture will not be procured, but on great wages, to leave their country, and hazard (as they style it) their lives. This the poor planter cannot do, whose sweat and labours amount to no more, than to clothe and provide for the ordinary necessities of his indigent family.

To remedy this, and to procure us able men to set us in a way of staple commodities, at my departure from Virginia I was asked by the Assembly to make this proposal to His Sacred Majesty and his council: to add one penny more to the customs of our tobacco, and give it to the country. If granted, it will pay all the public charges of the country, furnish us with magazines to resist the Indians, build mills for iron and planks, procure us good salaries for able men for silk, cordage, mines and flax. All this will be done at the expence only of an indulgent grant: for who pays this but the poor planter, whose tobacco must sell for less the more is imposed on it? But a nearer way to a public contribution they cannot find, having this axiom firmly fixed in them: that never any community of people has good done except against their wills.

In order to prove this, we shall here declare what we have been necessitated to do these last two years, when war and other emergencies had involved the plantation into debts inextricable in an ordinary levy; which was to lay a tax of two shillings the **hogshead** on every one exported. Though the merchant made us pay this tax, yet we found it an easier and readier way to defray the public charges. If the propositions of the customs be not granted, we desire His Majesty's council will advance to three or four shillings the hogshead, from which will pay all public officers, and be able to make iron, and other necessary works, for the enriching our native kingdom and ourselves. And another proposal they desired me to make, which is this: that such ships as were built in the country, might carry their goods to what port they pleased. This they hoped would be easily granted, because, by this means, the excellency of their timber and masts, of both which there is now a visible scarcity in England, would be known and, when known, the timber of England might be spared for many years. Ships of the greatest magnitude can be built in Virginia cheaper than possibly they can be in England. If the first petition be granted, we shall leave this one to the wisdom, exigence and care of those His Majesty employs in those affairs.

To conclude and animate the care, providence and indulgence the nation ought to have of foreign plantations, let these few considerations be duly poised. First, it is not yet forty years when there was not one Englishman in any plantation of America, save only four or five hundred left in 1622 after the massacre in Virginia. Now there are in the West Indies at least three hundred thousand English, and of English extraction. Secondly, if we examine the customs, we shall find the fourth part of them arise from the plantations in America. This is a wealth our fathers never knew and, in human probability, will increase on us every year. Thirdly, those commodities we were wont to purchase at great rates and hazards, we now purchase at half the usual prices. Nor is this all, but we buy them with our own manufactures, which here at home employ thousands of poor people. Fourthly, when in the past ages we wanted to unburden the kingdom of indigent younger brothers, whom the peculiar policy of this nation condemned to poverty or war, [because of the law of primogeniture] we were forced to undertake the assistance of rebels, which God of late has revenged on our own bowels. Now there can be no necessity of that sin or misery, for a small sum of money will enable a younger brother to erect a flourishing family in a new world; and add more strength, wealth, and honour, to his native country, than thousands did before, that died forgotten and unrewarded in an unjust war.

I should now have ended, but I think that it is expected from me, who has lived twenty years in America, that I should declare the power, interest, and wealth we have due to our plantations in the West Indies. To do this, I shall first propose to the consideration of the reader that during the few years that we have had any footing in America, (the eldest plantation, Virginia excepted, not exceeding forty years), so many difficulties we have happily overcome. Our numbers there are now at least two hundred thousand English, and if (as in human probability they will) our numbers but double every twenty years, how great will our power, strength, and reputation be in this new Western World in only one age more? Secondly, let it be considered what sums of money was in the last age exhausted from us for sugar, cotton, drugs, dyings, and tobacco, and how easily now we supply our selves with these, and also bring home enough to balance many other foreign necessities. Thirdly, let us contemplate the respect we have from most of the princes and states of Europe, by our power and strength in America. The Dutch, I know, would not willingly quit their interest in the Indies for ten millions of money, yet all they have here is in the King's power, when any just occasion shall provoke his displeasure. The French, it is true, have not many considerable places here, but yet the Indies, as they term it, are so profitable that they would not willingly quit their holds in it, nor their pretentions to it. But it is the Spaniards, whose interest is most jealous of our power here, and we most formidable to him by it.

TERMS AND DEFINITIONS

Customs: taxes levied on imports and exports.
Fortress, Mart and Magazine: military and commercial capital.
Hogshead: large cask holding from 63 to 140 gallons.
Pot-ashes: potassium compounds found in the ashes from burned wood and used in the making of fertilizers and glass.
Principalities: proprietary colonies
Public Stock: investment capital provided or guaranteed by the government.

JOHN DUNTON

"HOLIER THAN THOU" BOSTONIANS

By the 1680s, Boston was the foremost city in the American colonies, and had a reputation for material prosperity, religious piety, and political independence. It was regarded with suspicion and hostility by many of its neighboring colonies, some of which had been founded by exiles from Massachusetts. Its persistent refusal to comply with British rules and regulations caused

Parliament to revoke the charter of the Massachusetts Bay Company in 1689 and to make it a royal colony. Boston's contentious reputation was strongly reinforced in England with the publication of Letters Written From New England A.D. 1686 *by famed London bookseller John Dunton (1659–1733). The son, grandson, and great-grandson of Anglican ministers, Dunton forsook that vocation for a career in writing and publishing. Visiting Boston in 1685, Dunton developed a powerful aversion to its inhabitants and to their system of values.*

But I need give you no further a Description of Boston, for I remember you have been at Bristol [England], which bears a very near Resemblance to Boston. But I shall say something of the Inhabitants, as 10 months of my Life was spent amongst them. There is no Trading for a stranger with them but with a **Grecian Faith,** which is, not to part with your Ware without ready Money, for they are generally very backward in their Payments, great Censors of other Men's Manners, but extremely careless of their own, yet they have a ready correction for every vice. As to their Religion, I cannot perfectly distinguish it; but it is such that nothing keeps them friends but only the fear of exposing one another's knavery. As for the Rabble, their Religion lies in cheating all they deal with. When you are dealing with them, you must look upon them as at cross purposes, and read them, like Hebrew, backward; for they seldom speak and mean the same thing, but like Water-men, Look one Way, and Row another. The Quakers here have been a suffering Generation; and there's hardly any of the **Yea-and-Nay Persuasion** but will give you a severe Account of it; for the Bostonians, though their Forefathers fled thither to enjoy Liberty of Conscience, are very unwilling any should enjoy it but themselves: But they are now grown more moderate. Those were the Heats of some Persons among them whose zeal outran their knowledge, and was the effect of their Ignorance; For you and I, **Mr. Larkin,** are, I am sure, both of this Opinion, as our sufferings for it sufficiently Testify, That Liberty of Conscience is the Birth-Right of all Men by a Charter Divine.

The Government both Civil and Ecclesiastical is in the hands of the **Independents** and Presbyterians, or at least of those that pretend to be such. On Sundays in the Afternoon, after Sermon is ended, the People in the Galleries come down and march two abreast, up one Isle and down the other, until they come before the Desk, for Pulpit they have none: Before the Desk is a long Pew, where the Elders and Deacons sit, one of them with a Money-Box in his hand, into which the People as they pass put their Offerings, some a shilling, some two shillings, and some half a Crown, or five shillings, according to the Ability or Liberality of the Person giving. This I look upon to be a Praise-worthy Practice. This Money is distributed to supply the Necessities of the Poor, according to their several wants, for they have no Beggars there. Every Church (for so they call their particular Congregations) have one Pastor, one Teacher, Ruling Elders and Deacons.

. . . As to their Laws, This Colony is a Body Corporate and Politic in Fact, by the Name of The Governour and Company of the Massachusetts Bay in New England. Their Constitution is that there shall be one Governour and Deputy-Governour, and eighteen Assistants of the same Company, from time to time. That the Governour and Deputy Governour, Assistants and all other Officers, to be chosen from among the **Freemen** the last Wednesday in Easter Term, yearly, in the General Court. . . .

Their Laws for Reformation of Manners, are very severe, yet but little regarded by the People, so at least as to make them better, or cause them to mend their manners. For being drunk, they either Whip or impose a fine of Five shillings; And yet notwithstanding this Law, there are several of them so addicted to it that they begin to doubt whether it be a Sin or no; and seldom go to Bed without Muddy Brains. For Cursing and Swearing, they bore through the Tongue with a hot Iron. For kissing a woman in the Street, though but in way of Civil Salute, Whipping or a Fine. (Their way of Whipping Criminals is by Tying them to a Gun at the Town-House, and when so Tied whipping them at the pleasure of the Magistrate, and according to the Nature of the Offence.) For Single Fornication, whipping or a Fine. And yet for all this Law, the Chastity of some of them, for I do not Condemn all the People, may be guessed at by the Number of Delinquents in this kind; For there hardly passes a Court Day but some are convened for Fornication and Convictions of this Nature are very frequent: One instance, lately told me, will make this matter yet more plain. There happened to be a Murdered Infant found in the Town Dock; The Infant being taken up by the Magistrate's Command, orders were immediately given by them for the search of all the Women of the Town, to see if thereby they could find out the Murdress: Now in this Search, though the Murdress could not be found out, yet several of the Bostonian Young Women, that went under the Denomination of Maids, were found with Child. For Adultery they are put to Death, and so for Witchcraft; For that there are a great many Witches in this Country, the late Trials of 20 New England Witches is a sufficient Proof. An English Woman, suffering an Indian to have carnal knowledge of her, had an Indian cut out exactly in red cloth and sewed upon her right Arm, and enjoined to wear it Twelve Months. **Scolds** they gag, and set them at their own Doors, for certain hours together, for all comers and goers to gaze at. Were this a Law in England, and well Executed, it would in a little Time prove an Effectual Remedy to cure the Noise that is in many Women's heads.

Stealing is punished with Restoring four-fold, if able; if not, they are sold for some years, and so are poor Debtors. I have not heard of many Criminals of this sort. But for Lying and Cheating, they out-vie Judas, and all the false other cheats in Hell. Nay, they make a Sport of it: Looking upon Cheating as a commendable Piece of Ingenuity, commending him that has the most skill to commit a piece of Roguery; which in their Dialect (like those of our Yea-and-Nay-Friends in England) they call by the genteel Name of Out-Witting a Man, and won't own it to be cheating. As an Instance of what I have said, I was shown a Man of such a **Kidney** as I have been speaking on, in Boston, who agreed with a Country-man who could not read, makes the Bill payable under his hand, at the Day of the Resurrection of the Magistrates; willing alike to take Time enough to pay his Debts; or else possibly in good hopes that the

Magistrates had no share in that Day. But he carried the Jest a little too far, for the Country-man sued him and, though with much Trouble and Charge recovered his Money. In short, these Bostonians enrich themselves by the ruin of Strangers; and like ravenous Birds of Prey, strive who shall fasten his Talons first upon them. For my own share, I have already trusted out 400 pounds, and know not where to get in 2 shillings of it. But all these things pass under the Notion of Self-Preservation and Christian-Policy.

I had not given you the Trouble of so large an Account of the manners of the Bostonians, nor raked in such a Dunghill of Filth, but that this sort of People are so apt to say, Stand off, for I am holier than Thou.

TERMS AND DEFINITIONS

Freemen: property owners and taxpayers.
Grecian Faith: belief in selling goods for cash only.
Independents: dissenting congregations of the Church of England who insisted upon self-governance.
Kidney: disposition or persuasion.

Mr. Larkin: Dunton's correspondent in England.
Scolds: women with sharp tongues who nagged and criticized.
Yea-and-Nay Persuasion: The Society of Friends, or Quakers, allowed individual adherents to accept or reject specific religious ideas.

PETER KALM

THE DUTCH YANKEES OF ALBANY

Scarcely less enamored of the Dutch in Albany was thirty-one-year-old Peter Kalm (1716–1779), professor of natural history and economy at the University of Abo, Sweden. A former pupil of famed Swedish botanist Carl Linnaeus, who developed the classification system of genus and species for plants and animals, Kalm was selected by the Swedish Academy of Sciences to do research in the middle colonies and southern Canada in 1748. During his two and a half year sojourn, Kalm proved himself to be not only a superb botanist, but also a candid and sometimes acerbic social critic of colonial life, particularly where the Dutch inhabitants of upstate New York were concerned.

The greater part of the merchants at Albany have extensive estates in the country and a large property in forests. If their estates have a little brook, they do not fail to erect a sawmill upon it for sawing boards and planks, which many boats take during the summer to New York, having scarcely any other cargo. Many people at Albany make **wampum** for the Indians, which is their ornament and money, by grinding and finishing certain kinds of shells and mussels. This is of considerable profit to the inhabitants. I shall speak of this kind of money later. The extensive trade which the inhabitants of Albany carry on, and their sparing manner of living, in the Dutch way, contribute to the considerable wealth which many of them have acquired.

The inhabitants of Albany and its environs are almost all Dutchmen. They speak Dutch, have Dutch preachers, and the divine service is performed in that language. Their manners are likewise quite Dutch; their dress is, however, like that of the English. It is well known that the first Europeans who settled in the province of New York were Dutchmen. During the time that they were the masters of this province, they seized **New Sweden** of which they were jealous. However, the pleasure of possessing this conquered land and their own was but of short duration for, towards the end of 1664, Sir Robert Carr, by order of King Charles II, went to New York, then New Amsterdam, and took it. Soon after Colonel Nicolls went to Albany, which then bore the name of Fort Orange, and upon taking it, named it Albany, from the Duke of York's Scotch title. The Dutch inhabitants were allowed either to continue where they were and, under the protection of the English, to enjoy all their former privileges, or to leave the country. The greater part of them chose to stay, and from them the Dutchmen are descended who now live in the province of New York, and who possess the greatest and best estates in that province.

The avarice, selfishness and immeasurable love of money of the inhabitants of Albany are very well known throughout all North America, by the French and even by the Dutch, in the lower part of New York province. If anyone ever intends to go to Albany it is said in jest that he is about to go to the land of Canaan, since Canaan and the land of the Jews mean one and the same thing, and that Albany is a fatherland and proper home for arch-Jews, since the inhabitants of Albany are even worse. If a real Jew, who understands the art of getting forward perfectly well, should settle amongst them, they would not fail to ruin him. For this reason nobody comes to this place without the most pressing necessity; and therefore I was asked in several places, both this and the following year, what induced me to make the pilgrimage to this New Canaan.

I likewise found that the judgment which people formed of them was not without foundation. For though they seldom see any strangers, (except those who go from the British colonies to Canada and back again) and one might therefore expect to find victuals and accommodation for travelers cheaper than in places where they always resort, yet I experienced the contrary. I was here obliged to pay for everything twice, thrice and four times as much as in any part of North America which I have passed through. If I wanted their assistance, I obliged to pay them very well for it, and when I wanted to purchase anything or be helped in some case or other, I could at once see what kind of blood ran in their veins, for they either fixed exorbitant prices for their services or were very reluctant to assist me. Such was this people in general. However, there were some among them who equaled any in North America or anywhere else, in politeness, equity, goodness, and readiness to serve and to oblige; but their number fell far short of that of the former.

If I may be allowed to declare my conjectures, the origin of the inhabitants of Albany and its neighborhood seems to me to be as follows. While the Dutch possessed this country, and intended to people it, the government sent a pack of vagabonds of which they intended to clear their native country, and sent them along with a number of other settlers to this province. The vagabonds were sent far from the other colonists, upon the borders towards the Indians and other enemies, and a few honest families were persuaded to go with them, in order to keep them in bounds. I cannot in any other way account for the difference between the inhabitants of Albany and the other descendants of so respectable a nation as the Dutch, who are settled in the lower part of New York province. The latter are civil, obliging, just in prices, and sincere; and though they are not ceremonious, yet they are well meaning and honest and their promises may be relied on.

The behavior of the inhabitants of Albany during the war between England and France, which ended with the **Peace of Aix la Chapelle,** has, among several other causes, contributed to make them the object of hatred in all the British colonies, but more especially in New England. For, at the beginning of that war when the Indians of both parties had received orders to commence hostilities, the French engaged theirs to attack the inhabitants of New England, which they faithfully executed, killing everybody they met with, and carrying off whatever they found. During this time, the people of Albany remained neutral, and carried on a great trade with the very Indians who murdered the inhabitants of New England. Articles such as silver spoons, bowls, cups, etc. of which the Indians robbed the houses in New England, were carried to Albany, for sale. The people of that town bought up these silver vessels, though the names of the owners were engraved on many of them, and encouraged the Indians to get more of them, promising to pay them well, and whatever they would demand. This was afterwards interpreted by the inhabitants of New England to mean that the colonists of Albany encouraged the Indians to kill more of the New England people, who were in a manner their brothers, and who were subjects of the same crown. Upon the first news of this behavior, which the Indians themselves spread in New England, the inhabitants of the latter province were greatly incensed, and threatened that the first step they would take in another war would be to burn Albany and the adjacent parts. In the present war, it will sufficiently appear how backward the other British provinces in America are in assisting Albany, and the neighboring places, in case of an attack from the French or Indians. The hatred which the English bear against the people at Albany is very great, but that of the Albanians against the English is carried to a ten times higher degree. This hatred has subsisted ever since the time when the English conquered this section, and is not yet extinguished, though they could never have gotten larger advantages under the Dutch government than they have obtained under that of the English. For, in a manner, their privileges are greater than those of Englishmen themselves.

In their homes the inhabitants of Albany are much more sparing than the English and are stingier with their food. Generally what they serve is just enough for the meal and sometimes hardly that. The punch bowl is much more rarely seen than among the English. The women are perfectly well acquainted with economy; they rise early, go to sleep very late, and are almost superstitiously clean in regard to the floor, which is frequently scoured several times in the week. Inside the homes the women are neatly but not lavishly dressed. The children are taught both English and Dutch. The servants in the town are chiefly negroes. Some of the inhabitants wear their own hair very short, without a **bag or queue,** because these are looked upon as the characteristics of Frenchmen. As I wore my hair in a bag the first day I came here from Canada, I was surrounded with children, who called me a Frenchman, and some of the boldest offered to pull at my French head dress, so I was glad to get rid of it. Their food and its preparation is very different from that of the English. . . .

The governor of New York often confers at Albany with the Indians of the **Five Nations, or the Iroquois,** especially when they intend either to make war upon, or to continue a war against, the French. Sometimes, also, their deliberations turn upon their conversion to the Christian religion, and it appears by the answer of one of the Indian chiefs or **sachems** to Governor Hunter, at a conference in this town, that the English do not pay so much attention to a work of so much consequence as the French do, and that they do not send such able men to instruct the Indians, as they ought to do. For after Governor Hunter had presented these Indians, by order of **Queen Anne,** with many clothes and other presents, of which they were fond, he intended to convince them still more of her Majesty's good-will and care for them, by adding *that their good mother, the Queen, had not only generously provided them with fine clothes for their bodies, but likewise intended to adorn their souls by the preaching of the gospel; and that to this purpose some ministers should be sent to them to instruct them.* The governor had scarce ended when one of the oldest sachems got up and answered *that in the name of all the Indians; he thanked their gracious good queen and mother for the fine clothes she had sent them; but that in regard to the ministers, they had already had some among them* (whom he also named) *who instead of preaching the holy gospel to them had taught them to drink to excess, to cheat, and to quarrel among themselves because in order to get furs they had brought brandy along with which they filled the Indians and deceived them.* He then entreated the governor to take from them these preachers, and a number of other Europeans who resided amongst them, for, before they came among them the Indians had been an honest, sober, and innocent people, but now most of them had become rogues. He pointed out that they formerly had the fear of God, but that they hardly believed his existence at present; that if he [the governor] would do them any favor, he should send two or three blacksmiths amongst them, to teach them to forge iron, in which they were inexperienced. The governor could not forbear laughing at this extraordinary speech. I think the words of **St. Paul** not wholly unapplicable on this occasion: For your sake the name of God is blasphemed among the heathens. (Gentiles)

TERMS AND DEFINITIONS

Bag or Queue: long hair pulled together and tied at the back of the head.

Five Nations or the Iroquois: the Mohawks, Senecas, Cayugas, Onondagas, and Oneidas, who formed a confederacy that was later a model for the Articles of Confederation.

New Sweden: Swedish colonies located in modern-day Delaware and New Jersey.

Peace of Aix la Chapelle: treaty ending the War of the Austrian Succession (King George's War) in 1748 in which Great Britain returned

to France North American territory that had been captured largely by New England forces.

Queen Anne: ruler of Great Britain from 1702 to 1714, last of the Stuart Dynasty; succeeded by George I, Elector of Hanover.

sachems: leaders of Native American nations or confederacies.

St. Paul: author of several epistles in the New Testament.

wampum: shells and beads strung together and used as currency by Native Americans.

GOTTLIEB MITTELBERGER

PENNSYLVANIA AS HEAVEN AND HELL

A sizable share of Pennsylvania's remarkable growth in the eighteenth century was provided by immigrants from the German states, many of whom were religious dissenters and "redemptioners," a special form of indentured servant whose prospective employer paid the debts of this impoverished person in exchange for his or her labor for a specified period of years. One of the most complete accounts of their situation was provided by a German visitor named Gottlieb Mittelberger in his Journey To Pennsylvania. *Mittelberger spent four years, from 1750 to 1754, in that colony as an organist and schoolmaster, and the book published upon his return to his homeland was his only published work. In it, he wrote passionately but accurately about the harsh treatment of redemptioners and other impoverished immigrants. He also was sharply critical of what he regarded as the excesses resulting from too much individual freedom and disdain for authority.*

To come back to Pennsylvania again. It offers people more freedom than the other English colonies, since all religious sects are tolerated there. One can encounter Lutherans, members of the Reformed Church, Catholics, Quakers, **Mennonites or Anabaptists, Herrenbiiter** or **Moravian Brothers, Pietists,** Seventh-Day Adventists, **Dunkers,** Presbyterians, **New-born,** Freemasons, Separatists, Freethinkers, Jews, Mohammedans, Pagans, Negroes, and Indians. But the Evangelicals and the Reformed constitute the majority. There are several hundred unbaptized people who don't even wish to be baptized. Many pray neither in the morning nor in the evening, nor before or after meals. In the homes of such people are not to be found any devotional books, much less a Bible. It is possible to meet in one house, among one family, members of four or five or six different sects.

Freedom in Pennsylvania extends so far that everyone's property—commercial, real estate and personal possessions—is exempt from any interference or taxation. For owning a hundred **MORGEN** of land one is assessed an annual tax of not more than one English shilling. This is called **ground-rent or quit-rent.** One shilling is worth approximately eighteen **kreuzer** in German money. What is peculiar is that single men and women must pay two to five shillings annually, in proportion to their earnings, the reason for this being that they have none but themselves to look after. In Philadelphia, the money raised in this way is used to purchase lights by which the streets of the city are illuminated every night.

This province was granted by the King of England to a distinguished Quaker named Penn. That is how it got its name. The young lords, the Penns, are still alive, residing not in America but in London, in Old England. In 1754 a young Lord Penn visited the country. He renewed and confirmed all previously granted privileges with his signature, and also made many grants to the Indians or savages.

In Pennsylvania no profession or craft needs to constitute itself into a **guild.** Everyone may engage in any commercial or speculative ventures, according to choice and ability. And if someone wishes or is able to carry on ten occupations at one and the same time, then nobody is allowed to prevent it. And if, for example, a lad learns his skill or craft as an apprentice or even on his own, he can then pass for a master and may marry whenever he chooses. It is an admirable thing that young people born in this new country are easily taught, clever, and skillful. For many of them have only to look at and examine a work of skill or art a few times before being able to imitate it perfectly. Whereas, in Germany, it would take most people several years of study to do the same. But in America, many have the ability to produce even the most elaborate objects in a short span of time. When these young people have attended school for half a year, they are generally able to read anything.

The province of Pennsylvania is a healthy one; for the most part it has good soil, good air and water, lots of high mountains, and lots of flat land. There are many woods, and where these are not inhabited, there is natural forest through which flow many small and large rivers. The land is also very fertile, and all kinds of grain flourish.

The province is well populated, inhabited far and wide, and various new towns have been founded here and there, namely Philadelphia, Germantown, Lancaster, Reading, Bethlehem, and New Frankfort. Many churches have also been built in this region, but it takes a great many people up to ten hours to get to church. But everyone, men and women, rides to church on horseback, even though they could walk the distance in half an hour. This is also customary at weddings and funerals. At times at such formal country weddings or funerals, it is possible to count up to four hundred or five hundred persons on horseback. One can easily imagine that on such occasions, just as at Holy Communion, nobody appears in black crepe or in a black cloak. I should like to describe the funeral customs in greater detail. When someone has died, especially in the country, where people live far apart from one another, separated by plantations and forests, the actual time of burial is first announced only to the four closest neighbors of the deceased, each of whom in turn passes the information along to his closest neighbor. In such a manner, the news of that kind of a funeral spreads through a radius of more than fifty English miles within twenty-four hours. Then, whenever possible, each family sends at least one representative, riding on horseback, to the funeral at the proper time. While these people are assembling, those present are handed pieces of good cake on a large tin platter. Aside from that, everyone gets a goblet of well-warmed West Indian rum, to which are added lemons, sugar, and juniper berries, which makes a good combination. After this the guests are also offered warmed sweet cider.

This particular American funeral custom is just like the European wedding custom. When almost all the people are there and the time of the funeral approaches, the corpse is carried to the general burial ground. When that is too far away, burial takes place in the dead person's own field. Those people who have previously assembled ride silently behind the coffin. Sometimes one may count from one to four hundred persons in such a procession. The coffins are all made out of beautiful walnut wood, stained quite brown, and shiny with varnish. Wealthy people attach four beautifully worked brass handles to the coffin. By these, one can take hold of the coffins to carry them to the grave. If the deceased has been a young man his coffin is carried by four maidens; if a young girl, by four unmarried youths.

In this country, it is no rarity to find many totally unlearned men preaching in the open fields. For the sectaries say, and believe, that today's scholars are no longer apostles and have turned their learning into a mere trade. Nevertheless, there are, at present, many fine preachers in Pennsylvania who through God's mercy and their own indefatigable zeal have converted many to the Christian faith. I can myself testify to the manner in which our Evangelical ministers have baptized and confirmed many adults, both white and Black. Many people come to watch such ceremonies when they take place.

Alas, among the preachers there are also several quite irritating ones who offend many people, besides causing much annoyance to our ministers. I will cite one example of such an objectionable preacher. His name was Alexander. At a gathering of young farmers from the township of Oley with whom he had been carousing he announced that with his sermon he would so move the people standing in front of him that all of them would begin to cry, but at the very same time all of those standing behind him would start laughing. He wagered these same young farmers a considerable sum that he would be able to do this. And on a certain agreed day he appeared at a church meeting, stationed himself in the midst of the assemblage, and began to preach with a great deal of power and emotion. When he saw that his listeners had become so moved that they began to cry, he put his hands behind him, pulled his coat-tails apart, and revealed through a pair of badly torn breeches his bare behind, which he scratched with one hand during this demonstration. At this those who were standing behind him could not help roaring with laughter; and so he won his bet. An account of this disgusting incident appeared both in the German and English newspapers of Philadelphia.

The sectarians often said to the people of our faith: such men are false prophets who go around in sheep's clothing, but are ravenous wolves underneath. They are a great source of difficulty and annoyance for all the upstanding teachers and for all good pastors and ministers in this country. Apart from these, there are at present many good English, Swedish, Dutch, and German ministers of the Lutheran and Reformed churches in Pennsylvania, of whom I knew the following very well. [Here Mittenberger lists the names of about two dozen ministers of various nationalities and denominations.]

In Pennsylvania, preachers receive no salary or tithes. Their total income is what they get annually from their church members, and that sum varies a good deal. For some heads of households annually contribute according to their means, and of their own free will, from two to six **florins**. Others, however, contribute very little. For baptisms, funerals, and weddings the contribution is generally a whole **thaler**. Preachers do not receive free lodging or other similar emoluments, but they are given many presents by penitents who confess to them.

Schoolteachers are in the same situation. Since the year 1754, however, England and Holland have annually contributed a large sum of money for the general benefit of the many poor in Pennsylvania and for the maintenance of six Reformed English churches and an equal number of Reformed English free schools. Many hundreds of children, however, are unable to go to school partly because the distances are too great and partly because of the extent of forest land they would have to traverse. Thus many planters lead a rather wild and heathenish life. The situation of rural churches and rural schools is similar. In general, churches and school houses are located only in those places where several neighbors or church members live close together.

Throughout Pennsylvania the preachers do not have the power to punish anyone, or to force anyone to go to church. Nor can they give orders to each other, there being no consistory to impose discipline among them. Most preachers are engaged for the year, like cowherds in Germany; and when any one fails to please his congregation, he is given notice and must put up with it. So it is very difficult to be a conscientious minister, especially since one has to tolerate and suffer a great deal from so many hostile, and to some extent vile, sects. Even the most exemplary preachers, especially in rural districts, are often reviled, laughed at and mocked by young and old, like Jews. I, myself, would therefore rather be the humblest cowherd at home than be a preacher in Pennsylvania. Such outrageous coarseness and rudeness result from the excessive freedom in that country, and from the blind zeal of the many sects. Liberty in Pennsylvania does more harm than good to many people, both in soul and in body. They have a saying there: Pennsylvania is heaven for farmers, paradise for artisans, and hell for officials and preachers.

TERMS AND DEFINITIONS

Florins: an Italian coin or English silver one worth two shillings.
Ground-rent or Quit-rent: annual property tax assessed by the colonial proprietor.
Guild: organization of craftsmen, artisans, or professionals in Europe that set standards quality and controlled the right of entry.
Kreuzer: German coin worth somewhere between a pence and a shilling.

Mennonites, et al. and the Sectarians: a variety of dissenting religious groups who split off from the established churches in European states and immigrated to the colonies in order to be able to practice their particular religions.
MORGEN: an area of land equal to about nine-tenths of an acre.
Thaler: a German silver coin of the period.

JANET SCHAW

A SCOTTISH "LADY OF QUALITY" IN "LUBBERLAND"

On the eve of the American Revolution, few places in the colonies were farther removed from the action taking place in Boston, New York, and Philadelphia than were the plantations in the Carolinas. Yet, as the following excerpt from Journal of a Lady of Quality *by Janet Schaw (1731–1801) illustrates, they were both well informed and anxious to duplicate the activities of their more urban compatriots. A native of Edinburgh, Schaw combined a deeply felt Presbyterian religiosity with an intellectual grasp of the tenets of the Scottish Enlightenment that produced Adam Smith and David Hume, among others; yet she was fiercely loyal to king and country. She spent much of 1774 and 1775 in North Carolina, which was sarcastically called "Lubberland" by its more sophisticated neighbors in Virginia and South Carolina. Schaw was greatly incensed by what she regarded as the efforts of self-styled "patriots" to push the colonists to rebellion when they had no legitimate grievances against the government in Great Britain.*

I think I have read all the descriptions that have been published of America, yet meet every moment with something I never read or heard of. I must particularly observe that the trees everywhere are covered over with a black veil of a most uncommon substance, which I am however at a loss to describe. . . . The trees that keep clear from this black moss (as it is called) are crowned with the Mistletoe in much higher perfection than ever you saw it, and as it is just now in berry looks beautiful. Indeed all the trees do so at this Season. The wild fruits are in blossom and have a fine effect among the forest trees. . . . But though I may say of this place what I formerly did of the West Indian Islands, that nature holds out to them every thing that can contribute to conveniency, or tempt to luxury, yet the inhabitants resist both, and if they can raise as much corn and pork, as to subsist them in the most slovenly manner, they ask no more; and as a very small proportion of their time serves for that purpose, the rest is spent in sauntering through the woods with a gun or sitting under a rustic shade, drinking New England rum made into **grog,** the most shocking liquor you can imagine. By this manner of living, their blood is spoiled and rendered thin beyond all proportion, so that it is constantly on the fret, like bad small beer, and hence the constant slow fevers that wear down their constitutions, relax their nerves and enfeeble the whole frame. Their appearance is in every respect the reverse of that which gives the idea of strength and vigor, and for which the British peasantry are so remarkable. They are tall and lean, with short waists and long limbs, sallow complexions and languid eyes, when not inflamed by spirits. Their feet are flat, their joints loose and their walk uneven. These I speak of are only the peasantry of this country, as hitherto I have seen nothing else, but I make no doubt when I come to see the better sort, they will be far from this description. For though there is a most disgusting equality, yet I hope to find an American Gentleman a very different creature from an American clown. Heaven forefend else.

. . . I have been in town a few days, and have had an opportunity to make some little observations on the manners of a people so new to me. The ball I mentioned was intended as a civility, therefore I will not criticize it, and though I have not the same reason to spare the company, yet I will not fatigue you with a description, which however lively or just, would at best resemble a **Dutch picture,** where the injudicious choice of the subject destroys the merit of the painting. Let it suffice to say that a ball we had, where were dresses, dancing and ceremonies laughable enough, but there was no object on which my own ridicule fixed equal to myself and the figure I made, dressed out in all my British airs with a high head and a hoop and trudging through the unpaved streets in embroidered shoes by the light of a fathom carried by a black wench half naked. No chair, no carriage—good leather shoes need none. The ridicule was the silk shoes in such a place. I have, however, gained some most amiable and agreeable acquaintances amongst the Ladies; many of whom would make a figure in any part of the world, and I will not fail to cultivate their esteem, as they appear worthy of mine.

I am sorry to say, however, that I have met with few of the men who are natives of the country, who rise much above my former description, and as their natural ferocity is now inflamed by the fury of an ignorant zeal, they are of that sort of figure, that I cannot look at them without connecting the idea of tar and feather. Though they have fine women and such as might inspire any man with sentiments that do honour to humanity, yet they know no such nice distinctions, and in this at least are real patriots. As the population of the country is all the view they have in what they call love, and, though they often honour their black wenches with their attention, I sincerely believe they are excited to that crime by no other desire or motive but that of adding to the number of their slaves.

The difference between the men and the women surprised me, but a sensible man, who long resided here, in some degrees accounted for it. In the infancy of this province, said he, many families from Britain came over, and of these the wives and daughters were people of education. The mothers took the care of the girls, they were trained up under them, and not only instructed in the family duties necessary to the sex, but in those accomplishments and genteel manners that are still so visible amongst them, and this descended from Mother to daughter. As the father found the labours of his boys necessary to him, he led them therefore to the woods, and taught the sturdy lad to glory in the stroke he could give with his Ax, in the trees he felled, and the deer he shot; to conjure the wolf, the bear and the Alligator; and to guard his habitation from Indian inroads was most justly his pride, and he had reason to boast of it. But a few generations this way lost every art or science, which their fathers might have brought out, and, though necessity no longer prescribed these severe occupations, custom has established it as still necessary for the men to spend their time abroad in the fields; and to be a good marksman is the highest ambition of the youth, while to those enervated by age or infirmity drinking grog remained a last consolation.

The Ladies have **burnt their tea in a solemn procession,** but they had delayed, however, till the sacrifice was not very considerable, as I do not think any one offered [to pay] above a quarter of a pound [for it]. The people in town live decently, and though their houses are not spacious, they are in general very commodious and well furnished. All the merchants of any note are British and Irish, and many of them very genteel people. They all disapprove of the present proceedings. Many of them intend quitting the country as fast as their affairs will permit them, but are yet uncertain what steps to take. This town lies low, but is not disagreeable. There is at each end of it an ascent, which is dignified with the title of the hills; on them are some very good houses and there, almost all my acquaintances are. They have very good Physicians, the best of whom is a Scotchman, at whose house I have seen many of the first planters. I do not wish, however, to be much in their company, for, as you know, my tongue is not always under my command; I fear I might say something to give offence, in which case I would not fail to have the most shocking retort at least, if it went no further.

The ports are soon to be shut up, but this severity is voluntarily imposed by themselves, for they were indulged by parliament and allowed the exclusive privilege of still carrying on their trade with Europe, by which means they would not only have made great fortunes themselves by being the mart for the whole continent, but they would have had the power to serve the other colonies by providing them in those commodities, the want of which they will ill brook, and which is a distress they themselves must soon suffer, as European goods begin to be very scarce and will daily be more so, as the merchants are shipping off their properties, either to Britain or the West Indies. I know not what my brother proposes to do with himself or me; for if he stays much longer, he will find himself in a very disagreeable situation. He is just now up the country at a town called Newbern, where Governor Martin resides, whose situation is most terrible. He is a worthy man by all accounts, but gentle methods will fail with these rustics, and he has not the power to use more spirited means. I wish to God those mistaken notions of moderation to which you adhere at home may not in the end prove the greatest cruelty to the mother country as well as to these infatuated people; but I am no politician, as yet least, though I believe I will grow one in time, as I am beginning to pay a good deal of attention to what is going on about me.

TERMS AND DEFINITIONS

Burnt their tea in a solemn procession: a reference to the North Carolina version of the Boston and other "tea parties".

Dutch picture: a snide reference to the allegedly poor quality of Dutch art, from a British perspective.

Grog: watered-down rum mixed with sugar, lemon, and spices and usually served to lower class people.

THINKING THINGS THROUGH

1. Compare and contrast the criticisms made of British policy with those made of colonial behavior. On the whole, which side receives more favorable treatment?

2. What specific issues caused the most tension between the home country and the various colonies?

3. What seemed to be the overall impact of European religious conflict upon the American colonies?

4. Did Janet Schaw's observations about the superiority of North Carolina women to its men apply as well to the situation in the other four colonies?

5. All things considered, which posed the greatest threat to colonial peace and prosperity: British policy? the other Great Powers? Native American hostility? the ambitions of the colonists?

5

THE AMERICAN REVOLUTION

A. The International Context

In the poetic language of Henry Wadsworth Longfellow, the Minute Men who confronted the British Regulars at Lexington and Concord on the nineteenth of April 1775 "fired the shot heard round the world." That shot, and the revolution that it began, have continued to reverberate around the globe and down through the ages, serving as the partial inspiration for a wide range of social and political movements in a variety of settings. Each revolution has reinterpreted the ideology of the American Revolution to fit circumstances of time and place, and to serve its own particular needs. None have followed exactly the same course or arrived at the same destination. Few modern-day Americans, however, recognize that underneath these apparent differences lay many of the same beliefs and aspirations that motivated the colonists to gain their independence by force of arms, regardless of the opinion of other nations and no matter the cost in lives, fortunes, and sacred honor.

One of the major reasons for the widespread and continuing significance of the American Revolution is the fact that the authors of the Declaration of Independence justified their course in the rhetoric of the Enlightenment, stated in universal terms that transcended boundaries of time, space, and culture. The authors also explicitly addressed their appeal to "posterity", i.e., future generations. Jefferson and his colleagues began with such fundamental Enlightenment premises as the essential rationality of all human beings, the fundamental equality of all human beings under natural law, and the unalienable character of the natural rights conferred upon them by the creator of the universe. From those fundamental beliefs, they derived three truly revolutionary propositions concerning the origins and purpose of government: (1) that the primary reason why human beings founded governments was to protect them in the exercise of their natural rights; (2) that all governments "derive their just powers from the consent of the governed"; and (3) that citizens, therefore, have a "right," indeed an "obligation," to abolish their government and form a new one whenever it failed to protect the rights of its citizens. So commonplace have these ideas become by the end of the twentieth century that it is difficult to appreciate how truly radical they were in the age of despotism, enlightened or otherwise, and how far from realization they still remain in much of the world. The authors of the Declaration proclaimed a national purpose far more exalted than that of any other nation, thereby holding themselves and their posterity to a far higher standard.

The truly revolutionary character and power of the American Revolution was almost immediately obvious from the outraged cries of European elites. They instinctively recognized its direct challenge to the belief that monarchs and aristocrats owed their station to divine sanction or hereditary privilege, that human beings were fundamentally unequal and arranged by God or Nature into elaborate systems of hierarchy and deference, that rights were granted by all-powerful governments and could be withdrawn at will, and that people were "subjects" rather than "citizens". The first nation to feel its effect, ironically, was France, the primary seat of the Enlightenment. France was also a country on the verge of financial ruin, in part because of its aid to the American revolutionaries. The first half of the nineteenth century witnessed an epidemic of liberal national revolutions in Latin America and Europe, many of whose leaders proclaimed the American Revolution a partial model and inspiration. The leaders of the March 1917 revolution in Russia and the 1911 revolution in China, Alexander Kerensky and Sun Yat-Sen, repectively, both openly professed their desire to emulate the United States. The millions of eastern Europeans who embraced the Wilsonian doctrine of "self-determination" after World War I also frequently invoked the philosophy of the Declaration, as did Irish and Israeli nationalists. So did, and have, spokesmen for the myriad "wars of national liberation" that have erupted throughout Asia, Africa, and Latin America since the end of World War II.

So many peoples over the years and miles have looked to the American Revolution as a model and inspiration, because it produced such a favorable result within a relatively brief time. Not only did the thirteen colonies gain their complete independence from Great Britain in just eight years of fighting, they also managed to secure substantial additional territory and generous fishing rights, in exchange for vague promises regarding the payment of British debts and the treatment of Loyalists. Moreover, they quickly formed a viable national government out of thirteen sovereign states, drafted a constitution and a bill of rights that have endured longer than any other comparable documents, held peaceful elections, settled major policy disputes in a constitutional manner, and established the standard for orderly political transitions. Even though the reality frequently conflicted with the new nation's professed ideals, no other country born of revolution ever achieved political stability so quickly or so completely. However, it is also clear that no other people ever embarked upon a revolution with circumstances more in their favor.

Unlike their French and Spanish counterparts, the British deliberately attempted to recruit tens of thousands of non-English immigrants to their North American colonies. They promoted settlement by providing generous land grants, bounties, and subsidies to free white males, and by guaranteeing them markets throughout the British Empire. Within the restrictive provisions of the Navigation Acts, the colonists were relatively free to experiment with the best methods of production and distribution among themselves. The Triangular, Coastwise, and other legitimate trades, along with smuggling, black marketeering, privateering, and counterfeiting brought the colonists a wealth of practical economic experience at operating an economy in an international setting, as well as providing them with steadily increasing levels of prosperity. Although both parties harbored suspicions that they could do even better under a more favorable set of circumstances, each would undoubtedly have continued to prosper indefinitely, if the British had not embarked on their "New Imperialism" after the French and Indian War. By that point, the colonists were sufficiently skilled and affluent to make a go of it themselves. Even two decades filled with political and military strife failed to do lasting damage to what the new Americans had carefully constructed over a century and a half.

To further encourage European settlement of their colonies, the British also granted property-owning settlers a liberal degree of self-government within the context of the times, something that the Spanish, French, Portuguese, and Dutch empires chose not to do. Beginning with the first meeting of the Virginia House of Burgesses in 1619, nearly all the British colonies enjoyed a measure of representative, consti-

tutional government well above that allowed in any of the other colonial regimes. At the outset, these colonial assemblies existed primarily to vote taxes and to authorize spending, and were at the beck and call of the colonial governors. Over the course of more than a century, however, colonial assemblymen learned to negotiate with their governors, winning such concessions as the right to elect a speaker, determine their own membership, apportion representative districts, set voting qualifications, call themselves into being and adjourn their sessions, and initiate legislation on a wide range of subjects. They fought continually, and often fiercely, with the representatives of the British government over the printing and coining of money, the provision of men and arms during imperial wars, the prohibition of manufacturing, the enforcement of the Navigation Acts, and the raising and spending of money.

Through their colonial agents, the colonists also gained experience at dealing with Parliament, the Board of Trade, and other agencies of the British imperium. They successfully resisted the imposition of the Dominion of New England in the 1680s, and experimented with the Albany Plan of Union in the early 1750s. When the Stamp Act crisis hit in 1765, they had sufficient experience and sophistication to call a national convention, organize a successful boycott of English goods, frustrate the activities of the tax collectors, and successfully lobby Parliament for repeal. In response to the Coercive Acts, experienced and knowledgeable colonial politicians called and managed the First Continental Congress that issued a coherent Declaration and Resolves, engineered another successful boycott, and proclaimed the Declaration of the Necessity of Taking Up Arms. A year later, they were sufficiently confident to call a Second Continental Congress, adopt the Declaration of Independence, prepare to fight a war against the most powerful nation in the world, and conduct foreign relations with the other Great Powers. Whatever else the leaders of the American Revolution were, they were definitely not amateurs in the arena of politics and government.

Adding to their arsenal of unique advantages was the fact that the American colonials also benefited a great deal from conditions within Great Britain itself. King George III had become increasingly unpopular, despite the country's sweeping victories in the struggle with France. George's attempt to reestablish monarchical authority in alliance with a coalition of "the King"s Friends," held together by patronage and *bribery, resulted in a succession of unstable and unpopular governments. George also suffered from a rare disease that manifested itself in periodic bouts of insanity; even in the best of times, he tended to be dangerously immature and insecure. As if that were not enough, the war with France left the country with a crushing burden of debt and high taxes that finally persuaded the king and his ministers to resort to the unprecedented device of taxing the American colonists directly. These levies proved to be unpopular with the powerful merchant classes, who vehemently opposed any measure that might interrupt their lucrative trade with America. Pushed to the wall by the success of the various colonial boycotts, merchants besieged Parliament with petitions for repeal.*

Their cause was swiftly embraced by such influential Whig politicians as William Pitt, Charles James Fox, and Edmund Burke, who were determined to restore Parliamentary supremacy and return their party to power. As a result, the American colonists began their revolt with powerful allies in the mother country determined to use the issue of "no taxation without representation" to put the king and his cronies in their proper place. It was primarily to them that the authors of the Declaration of Independence made their appeal to their "British brethren." Throughout the course of the war, the Whigs continued to harass its prosecution, until their efforts finally paid off with the inauguration of peace negotiations in 1781. Had the Whigs been in power during the crisis period, it is at least conceivable that the two sides might have arrived at a mutually acceptable settlement.

Finally, the American revolutionaries profited greatly from an international situation in which Britain's dominance stirred fear, envy, and hostility among the rulers of the other Great Powers. Russia, Spain, the Netherlands, and others seriously hindered British efforts to stifle American trade with Europe, while France increasingly became a cobelligerent. Pressured by a British initiative offering the Americans home rule in exchange for cessation of hostilities, the French eventually agreed to a formal treaty of alliance, diplomatic recognition of the United States as a sovereign nation, and direct military intervention on 6 February 1778. In exchange, the United States pledged not to sign a separate peace treaty with Great Britain. From that moment, the American Revolution became an international conflict, and the British were forced to concentrate much of their effort on the European phase of the war against France, Spain, and the Netherlands. It was a French fleet that played a decisive role in the final British defeat at Yorktown. In addition, the American cause was aided significantly by the contributions of Europeans and Latin Americans who volunteered their military services. The final American victory would have been impossible without substantial international involvement.

In "the revolution that worked," then, the American cause profited immeasurably from 150 years of managing its own economic and political systems, powerful opposition within Great Britain to its government's colonial policies, and substantial international support—conditions that no other revolution since that time has been able to replicate.

B. International Views

The turmoil that swirled in the American colonies for almost two decades was widely discussed in Europe, especially in Great Britain and France. For the first several years, the controversy mainly revolved around the subject of taxation and representation. The debate over the passage and repeal of the Stamp Act was hotly debated in Parliament, with one side asserting the absolute right of that body to levy taxes upon the colonies and the other insisting that taxes were a voluntary contribution that could only be given with the expressed consent of representatives elected for that purpose. Perhaps the most articulate spokesman for the former position was Dr. Samuel Johnson, England's most celebrated man of letters. He vigorously attacked what he considered to be the inner contradictions, and even the occasional hypocrisy, of the colonials' contentions. The most powerful British voice supporting those arguments was that of former prime minister William Pitt, who had led the government to victory in the Seven Years War and established British supremacy on the North American continent. While yielding to no one in his assertion of Parliamentary authority or British power, he saw taxation as a special case that required the explicit consent of those who were being assessed. Although the repeal of the Stamp Act seemed to indicate that the latter interpretation had majority support, events soon proved otherwise. With the enactment of the Declaratory Act, Parliament seemed to embrace at least the spirit of the former position.

By 1774, the debate had escalated to the point where the entire right of Parliament to legislate for the colonies was now seriously disputed by the American colonists. While that view was certainly less popular in Great Britain than the denial of the right of taxation had been, there were those, especially among the kingdom's non-English peoples, who

*identified with the position of the American colonists. One of
the most prominent was Catharine Macaulay, a Scottish
devotee of the Enlightenment. She saw clear parallels with
the situation of the Scots, Irish, Welsh, and other non-
English Britons. In praising the Americans, she also challenged the British people to follow their example.*

*Once the dispute between Britain and the American
colonists erupted into all-out war, the focus of European
speculation turned to the subjects of whether the latter could
make good its claims of independence in a test of fire and
blood, and whether, even if victorious in battle, the newly
proclaimed United States of America could survive and prosper in a largely hostile world. One of the earliest contributions to that debate was an anonymous Frenchman who
visited the country in 1777, the crucial year in which his own
nation eventually decided to enter the conflict openly, as a
full-fledged ally of the Americans. While candidly acknowl-
edging the obstacles to an American victory, he clearly reflected French confidence in the eventual outcome. Writing
just after the Peace of Paris had granted the United States its
independence, John Ferdinand Dalziel Smith, a British loyalist, strongly expressed the bitterness felt by the large number
of colonials who had remained faithful to the British cause—
and paid dearly for their actions. His views were typical of
those who felt that the Americans would have been better off
remaining within the protective confines of the British Empire and who predicted a dire future for the fledgling nation.*

DR. SAMUEL JOHNSON

TAXATION IS NOT TYRANNY

*One of the most famous and articulate critics of the American assertion of "no taxation without
representation" was Dr. Samuel Johnson (1709–1784), the English literary giant so highly regarded that the second half of the eighteenth century in the English-speaking world is often referred to as the "Age of Johnson." Immortalized by James Boswell's* Life Of Samuel Johnson
*(1791), he compiled a major English dictionary, produced a classic edited compilation of Shake-
speare, wrote several plays and works of poetry, and is regarded as one of the foremost literary
critics of all time. An English chauvinist who insisted that the London of his day was the epitome
of all human civilization, Johnson was so incensed by colonial protests against taxation that he
penned an acerbic pamphlet entitled* Taxation No Tyrany: An Answer to the Resolutions
and Address of the American Congress. *In it, he strongly proclaims the absolute sovereignty of
Great Britain and points out what he sees as the obvious contradiction in colonial claims that
their rights are both "natural" and the result of their privileged status as Englishmen. He also
staunchly defends the concept of "virtual representation." The pamphlet was reprinted in*
The Works of Samuel Johnson, *published in Troy, New York, in 1903.*

That the Americans are able to bear taxation, is indubitable; that their refusal may be overruled, is highly probable; but power is no sufficient evidence of truth. Let us examine our own claim, and the objections of the **recusants** with caution proportioned to the event of the decision, which must convict one part of robbery, or the other of rebellion.

A tax is a payment, exacted by authority from part of the community, for the benefit of the whole. From whom, and in what proportion such payment shall be required, and to what uses it shall be applied, those only are to judge to whom government is intrusted. In the British dominions taxes are apportioned, levied, and appropriated by the states assembled in Parliament. In every empire, all the subordinate communities are liable to taxation, because they all share the benefits of government, and, therefore, ought all to furnish their proportion of the expense.

This the Americans have never openly denied. That it is their duty to pay the costs of their own safety, they seem to admit; nor do they refuse their contribution to the exigencies, whatever they may be, of the British empire; but they make this participation of a public burden a debt, an obligation, a duty temporary, occasional, and elective, of which they reserve to themselves the right of settling the degree, the time, and the duration; of judging when it may be required, and when it has been performed.

They allow to the supreme power nothing more than the liberty of notifying to them its demands or its necessities. Of this notification they profess to think for themselves, how far it shall influence their counsels; and of the necessities alleged, how far they shall endeavor to relieve them. They assume the exclusive power of settling not only the mode, but the quantity, of this payment. They are ready to cooperate with all the other dominions of the king; but they will cooperate by no means with that which they do not like, and at no greater charge than they are willing to bear. This claim, wild as it may seem, which supposes dominion without authority, and subjects without subordination, has found among the libertines of policy, many clamorous and hardy vindicators. The laws of nature, the rights of humanity, the faith of charters, the danger of liberty, the encroachments of usurpation, have been thundered in our ears, sometimes by interested faction, and sometimes by honest stupidity. . . .

All government is ultimately and essentially absolute, but subordinate societies may have more immunities, or individuals greater liberty, as the operations of government are differently conducted. The colonies of England differ no otherwise from those of other nations, save as the English constitution differs from theirs. An Englishman in the common course of life and action feels no restraint. An English colony has very liberal powers of regulating its own manners, and adjusting its own affairs. But an English individual may, by the supreme authority, be deprived of liberty, and a colony divested of its powers, for reasons of which that authority is the only judge.

In sovereignty there are no gradations. There may be limited royalty, there may be consulship, but there can be no limited government. There must, in every society, be some power or other, from which there is no appeal, which admits no restrictions, which pervades the whole mass of the community, regulates and adjusts all subordination, enacts laws or repeals them, erects or annuls judicatures, extends or contracts privileges, exempts itself from question or control, and is bounded only by physical necessity.

An English colony is a number of persons, to whom the king grants a charter, permitting them to settle in some distant country, and enabling them to constitute a corporation enjoying such powers as the charter grants, to be administered in such forms as the charter prescribes. As a corporation, they make laws for themselves; but as a corporation, subsisting by a grant from higher authority, to the control of that authority they continue subject. . . .

Our colonies, . . . however distant, have been hitherto, treated as constituent parts of the British empire. The inhabitants incorporated by English charters are entitled to all the rights of Englishmen. They are governed by English laws, entitled to English dignities, regulated by English counsels, and protected by English arms; and it seems to follow, by consequence not easily avoided, that they are subject to English government, and chargeable by English taxation. But hear, ye sons and daughters of liberty, the sounds which the winds are wafting from the western continent. The Americans are telling one another, what, if we may judge from their noisy triumph, they have but lately discovered, and what yet is a very important truth: "That they are entitled to life, liberty, and property; and that they have never ceded to any sovereign power whatever a right to dispose of either without their consent."

While this resolution stands alone, the Americans are free from singularity of opinion; their wit has not yet betrayed them to heresy. While they speak as the **naked sons of nature,** they claim but what is claimed by other men, and have withheld nothing but what all withheld. They are here upon firm ground, behind entrenchments which can never be forced.

Humanity is very uniform. The Americans have this resemblance to Europeans, that they do not always know when they are well. They soon quit the fortress, that could neither have been mined by **sophistry,** nor battered by **declamation.** Their next resolution declares, that "Their ancestors, who first settled the colonies, were, at the time of their emigration from the mother-country, entitled to all the rights, liberties, and immunities of free and natural-born subjects within the realm of England."

This, likewise, is true; but when this is granted, their boast of original rights is at an end; they are no longer in a state of nature. These lords of themselves, these kings of ME, these demigods of independence sink down to colonists, governed by a charter. If their ancestors were subjects, they acknowledged a sovereign; if they had a right to English privileges, they were accountable to English laws; and, what must grieve the lover of liberty to discover, had ceded to the king and parliament, whether the right or not, at least, the power of disposing, "without their consent, of their lives, liberties, and properties." It, therefore, is required of them to prove, that the parliament ever ceded to them a dispensation from that obedience, which they owe as natural-born subjects, or any degree of independence or immunity, not en-joyed by other Englishmen. . . .

We are told, that the subjection of Americans may tend to the diminution of our own liberties; an event, which none but very perspicacious politicians are able to foresee. If slavery be thus fatally contagious, how is it that we hear the loudest yelps for liberty among the **drivers of negroes?**

TERMS AND DEFINITIONS

Declamation: bombastic oratory.
Drivers of negroes: slaveholders.
Naked sons of nature: refers to the colonial claims that their rights were given to them by God in a "state of nature," before there were any governments.

Recusants: persons who refuse to conform to established authority.
Sophistry: arguments that appear valid but are intended to deceive.

WILLIAM PITT, THE ELDER

THE AMERICANS HAVE BEEN DRIVEN TO MADNESS BY INJUSTICE

Directly challenging Johnson's contentions were those of William Pitt, the Elder (1708–1778), the first Earl of Chatham, the "Great Commoner" and champion of the Whigs, the King's "loyal opposition." He remains perhaps the most eulogized of all British prime ministers. Absent due to illness during the passage of the Stamp Act, Pitt quickly condemned the taxation policy of Lord Grenville's government as "the making good by force there, preposterous and infatuated errors here." Upon his return to Parliament, he led the fight to repeal the Stamp Act, basing his argument on the Enlightenment doctrine of the "natural rights" of life, liberty, and prosperity, over which no government has power. He also ridicules the notion of "virtual representation" advocated by the government and by Dr. Johnson. His "Address to the Throne, House of Commons" was recorded in the Correspondence of William Pitt, Earl of Chatham, *edited by William S. Taylor and John Henry Pringle in 1840.*

It is my opinion that this kingdom has no right to lay a tax upon the colonies. At the same time, I assert the authority of this kingdom over the colonies to be sovereign and supreme in every circumstance of government and legislation whatsoever. They [the colonists] are the subjects of this kingdom, equally entitled with yourselves to all the natural rights of mankind and the peculiar privileges of Englishmen: equally bound by its laws, and equally participating of the constitution of this free country. The Americans are the sons, not the bastards of England. Taxation is no part of the governing or legislative power. The taxes are voluntary gift and grant of the Commons alone. In legislation, the three estates of the realm are alike concerned; but the concurrency of the Peers and the Crown to a tax is only necessary to close [clothe] it with the form of a law. . . .

There is an idea in some that the colonies are virtually represented in this House. I would fain know by whom an American is represented here? Is he represented by any knight of the shire in any county in this kingdom? Would to God that respectable representation was augmented to a greater number! or will you tell him that he is represented by any representative of a borough— a borough which perhaps its own representatives never saw? The idea of a virtual representation of America in this House, is the most contemptible that ever entered into the head of man. It does not deserve a serious refutation.

The **Commons of America,** represented in their several assemblies, have ever been in possession of the exercise of this, their constitutional right, of giving and granting their own money. They would have been slaves if they had not enjoyed it. At the same time, this kingdom, as the supreme governing and legislative power, has always bound the colonies by her laws, by her regulations, and restrictions in trade, in navigation, in manufacturing—in every thing, except that of taking their money out of their pockets without their consent. Here I would draw the line. . . .

The gentleman tells us America is obstinate; America is almost in open rebellion. I rejoice that America has resisted. Three millions of people so dead to all the feelings of liberty as voluntarily to submit to be slaves would have been fit instruments to make slaves of all the rest. I come not here armed at all points with law cases and Acts of Parliament, with the statute book doubled down in dog's ears, to defend the cause of liberty; if I had, I myself would have cited the two cases of **Chester and Durham;** I would have cited them, to have shown that even under the most arbitrary reigns, Parliaments were ashamed of taxing people without their consent, and allowed them representatives. . . . The gentleman tells us of many who are taxed, and are not represented—the **India Company,** merchants, stock-holders, manufacturers. Surely many of these are represented in other capacities, as owners of land, or as freemen of boroughs. It is a misfortune that more are not equally represented: but they are all inhabitants, and, as such, are they not virtually represented? Many have it in their option to be actually represented: they have connections with those that elect, and they have influence over them. Since the accession of **King William,** many ministers, some of great, others of more moderate abilities, have taken the lead of government. . . .

None of these thought or ever dreamed of robbing the colonies of their constitutional rights. That was reserved to mark the era of the late administration: not that there were wanting some, when I had the honour to serve his Majesty, to propose to me to burn my fingers with an American stamp act. With the enemy at their back, with our bayonets at their breasts in the day of their distress, perhaps the Americans would have submitted to the imposition; but it would have been taking an ungenerous, an unjust advantage. The gentleman boasts of his bounties to America. Are not these bounties intended finally for the benefit of this kingdom? If they are not, he has misapplied the national treasures. . . . Our legislative power over the colonies is sovereign and supreme. When it ceases to be sovereign and supreme, I would advise every gentleman to sell his lands, if he can, and embark for that country. Where two countries are connected together like England and her colonies, without being incorporated, the one must necessarily govern; the greater must rule the less; but so rule it as not to contradict the fundamental principles that are common to both. . . .

. . . In a good cause, on a sound bottom, the force of this country can crush America to atoms. I know the valour of your troops. I know the skill of your officers. There is not a company of foot that has served in America out of which you may not pick a man of sufficient knowledge and experience to make a governor of a colony there. But on this ground, on the Stamp Act, which so many here will think a crying injustice, I am one who will lift up my hands against it.

In such a cause, your success would be hazardous. America, if she fell, would fall like the strong man **Samson;** she would embrace the pillars of the state, and pull down the constitution along with her. Is this your boasted peace? Not to sheathe the sword in its scabbard, but to sheathe it in the bowels of your countrymen? Will you quarrel with yourselves, now that the whole **House of Bourbon** is united against you? While France disturbs your fisheries in Newfoundland, embarrasses your slave trade to Africa, and withholds from your subjects in Canada their property stipulated by treaty. . . .

The Americans have not acted in all things with prudence and temper; they have been wronged; they have been driven to madness by injustice. Will you punish them for the madness you have occasioned? Rather let prudence and temper come first from this side. . . .

Upon the whole, I will beg leave to tell the House what is really my opinion. It is, that the Stamp Act be repealed absolutely, totally, and immediately; that the reason for the repeal be assigned because it was founded on an erroneous principle. At the same time, let the sovereign authority of this country over the colonies be asserted in as strong terms as can be devised, and be made to extend to every point of legislation whatsoever; that we may bind their trade, confine their manufactures, and exercise every power whatsoever—except that of taking money out of their pockets without their consent.

TERMS AND DEFINITIONS

Chester and Durham: two English boroughs that had no actual representation in Parliament for several decades. Grenville argued that this was a precedent for the colonial situation, but Pitt stressed the fact that the government eventually gave the two boroughs representation.
Commons of America: colonial legislatures.
The gentleman: Lord George Grenville, prime minister and leader

of the Tories or "King's Friends," whose government enacted the Stamp Act.

House of Bourbon: the royal family whose branches ruled both France and Spain.

The India Company: the British East India Company, which was controlled by several prominent Tories and had a monopoly on the colonial tea trade.

King William: ruler of the Netherlands who, along with his wife Mary Stuart, served as the English monarchy from 1689 to 1701.

Samson: powerful biblical hero who pulled the entire temple down with him after the Philistines had captured and blinded him and Delilah had cut his hair.

CATHARINE MACAULAY

THE AMERICANS ARE FIGHTING FOR BRITISH RIGHTS

As Parliament, in response to the Boston Tea Party, punished the colonists with the Coercive or Intolerable Acts, closing the port of Boston, shutting down the government and courts of Massachusetts, and quartering soldiers in private homes, internal criticism of British colonial policy grew even more harsh. One of the fieriest opponents of coercion was Catharine Macaulay (1731–1791), daughter of a prominent Scottish family and a firm believer in the philosophy of the Enlightenment. She was the author of the eight-volume The History of England From the Accession of James I to That of the Brunswick Lines, *designed to prove the claims of the Scottish Stuart family to the throne of Great Britain. Macaulay was also a political activist and cofounder of the Supporters of the Bill of Rights, an organization dedicated to Parliamentary reform. Incensed by the passage of the Coercive Acts in 1774, she penned the rousing* Address to the People of England, Ireland, and Scotland. *She corresponded with George Washington and came to America to meet with him in 1785.*

It can be no secret to any of you, my friends and fellow citizens, that the ministry, after having exhausted all those ample sources of corruption which your own tameness under oppressive taxes has afforded, either fearing the unbiased judgment of the people, or impatient at the slow, but steady progress of despotism, have attempted to wrest from our American Colonists every privilege necessary to freemen—privileges which they hold from the authority of their charters, and the principles of the constitution.

With an entire supineness, England, Scotland, and Ireland have seen the Americans, every year by year, stripped of the most valuable of their rights: and, to the eternal shame of this country, the stamp act, by which they were to be taxed in an arbitrary manner, met with no opposition [in England], except from those who are particularly concerned, that the commercial intercourse between Great-Britain and her Colonies should meet with no interruption.

With the same guilty acquiescence, my countrymen, you have seen the last parliament finish their venal course, with passing **two acts** for shutting up the Port of Boston, for indemnifying the murderers of the inhabitants of the Massachusetts Bay, and changing their chartered constitution of government: And to shew that none of the fundamental principles of our boasted constitution are held sacred by the government, the same Parliament, without any interruption either by petition or remonstrance, passed **another act** for changing the government of Quebec: in which the **Popish religion,** instead of being tolerated as stipulated by the treaty of peace, is established; in which the Canadians are deprived of the right to an assembly, and of trial by jury; in which the English laws in civil cases are abolished, the French laws established, and the crown empowered to erect arbitrary courts of judicature; and in which, for the purpose of enlarging the bounds where despotism is to have its full sway, the limits of that province are extended so as to comprehend those vast regions that lie adjoining to the northerly and westerly bounds of our colonies.

The anxious desire of preserving that harmony which had so long and so happily existed between the Parent State and her Colonies, occasioned the Americans to bear, with an almost blamable patience, the innovations which were continually made on their liberty, till the ministry, who imagined their moderation proceeded from ignorance and cowardice, by depriving them of almost every part of their rights which remained unviolated, have raised a spirit beyond the Atlantic, which may either recover the opportunities we have lost of restoring the breaches which for near a century have been making in our constitution, or of sinking us into the lowest abyss of national misery.

In these times of general discontent, when almost every act of our Governors excites a jealousy and apprehension in all those who make the interests of the community their care, there are several among us who, dazzled with the sunshine of a court, or fattening on the spoils of the people, have used their utmost endeavors to darken your understandings on those subjects, which, at this time, it is particularly your business to be acquainted with. There are others who, whilst they have the words Freedom, Constitution, and Privileges, continually in their mouths, are using every means in their power to render those limitations useless, which have from time to time been erected by our ancestors, as mitigation of that barbarous system of despotism imposed by the **Norman tyrant,** on the inhabitants of this island. . . .

To all the restrictions laid on their trade, the Americans declare they will ever readily submit; and this on the generous consideration that they are supposed to be for the benefit and advantage of the whole empire. . . . That they will be ever ready to contribute all in their power towards the welfare of the empire; and they will consider your enemies as their enemies, and hold your interests as dear to them as their own.

They exhort you for the sake of that honour and justice for which this nation was once renowned, they entreat you by all those ties of common interest which are inseparable from the subjects of free states, not to suffer our enemies to effect your slavery, in their ruin. They set before you, in the strongest colours, all those disadvantages which must attend that large independent power the sovereigns of Great-Britain will gain by the means of taxing, in an arbitrary manner, the Americans; and they invite you, for these cogent reasons, to join with them in every legal method to disappoint the designs of our common foes. It is not impossible, that after having tamely suffered the government, by a yearly increase of taxes, to beggar yourselves and your posterity, you may be led away with the delusive hope, that the **Ministry,** when they have the power to pick the pockets of your American brethren, will have the moderation to save those of their countrymen.

If these are your thoughts, my fellow citizens, little have you studied your own natures, and the experience of all ages, which must have convinced you that the want of power is the only limitation to the exertion of human selfishness; but should you be contented to bid defiance to the warnings of common policy, should you be contented to be slaves on the hope that the Americans will bear the greater part of the burden of your enormous taxes, be assured, that such an alternative will never be in your power. No, if a civil war commences between Great-Britain and her Colonies, either the mother country, by one great exertion, may ruin both herself and America, or the Americans, by a lingering contest, will gain an independence; and in this case, all those advantages which you for some time have enjoyed by our colonies, and advantages which have hitherto preserved you from a national bankruptcy, must for ever have an end; and whilst a new, a flourishing, and an extensive empire of freemen is established on the other side the Atlantic you, with the loss of all those blessings you have received by the unrivaled state of your commerce, will be left to the bare possession of your foggy islands; and this under the sway of a domestic despot, or you will become the provinces of some powerful European state. . . .

Suffer me again to remind you of the imminent danger of your situation. Your **Ministers,** by attacking the rights of all America, have effected that which the malicious policy of more judicious minds would have avoided. Your colonists, convinced that their safety depends on their harmony, are now united in one strong bond of union; nor will it be in the power of a **Machiavel** to take any advantage of those feuds and jealousies which formerly subsisted among them, and which exposed their liberties to more real danger than all the fleets and armies we are able to send against them. Your Ministers also, deceived by present appearances, vainly imagine, because our rivals in Europe are encouraging us to engage beyond the possibility of a retreat, that they will reject the opportunity when it offers, of putting a final end to the greatness and the glory of our empire; but if, by the imprudent measures of the government, the public expenses increase, or the public income decrease to such a degree that the public revenue fail, and you be rendered unable to pay the interest of your debt, then will no longer be delayed the day and the hour of your destruction; then will you become an easy prey to the courts of France and Spain, who, you may depend upon as soon as they see you fairly engaged in a war with your Colonists; and, according to what is foretold you in a late publication, that conjuncture will prove the latest and the uttermost of your prosperity, your peace, and, in all probability, of your existence, as an independent state and nation.

Rouse, my countrymen! rouse from the state of guilty dissipation in which you have too long remained, and in which, if you longer continue, you are lost for ever. Rouse! and unite in one general effort: till, by your unanimous and repeated addresses to the throne, and to both houses of parliament, you draw the attention of every part of the government to their own interests, and to the dangerous state of the British empire.

TERMS AND DEFINITIONS

Another act: the Quebec Act that guaranteed political and religious rights to French Canadian Catholics.
Machiavel: follower of the principles of Nicolo Machiavelli, the fifteenth-century Florentine author of *The Prince* and *The Discourses,* notorious for his advocacy of amoral political behavior.

Ministry/Ministers: the British cabinet that made policy for the empire.
Norman tyrant: William the Conqueror, who invaded England in 1066 and overthrew the existing government, society, and culture.
Popish religion: Roman Catholicism.
Two acts: the Coercive or Intolerable Acts.

ANONYMOUS

THE CHANCES OF AMERICAN VICTORY

In the midst of the American Revolution, an anonymous French visitor spent five months traveling through the war-torn countryside, keeping a journal of his experiences and observations. Although he apparently intended the work for publication, it was not translated into English and published until 1959. In it, he enumerated the alleged strengths and weaknesses of the American colonials and assessed their chances of winning a military and political victory. Like many French intellectuals of the Enlightenment era, he regarded the American colonies as the new Garden of Eden where perfect liberty could prevail and the human race could begin anew. The following excerpt from On the Threshold of Liberty: Journal Of A Frenchman's Tour Of The American Colonies In 1777, *he expressed his faith in the power of human liberty to triumph over all obstacles.*

The Americans believe that they have so little real need of European goods, that they patriotically extol as true marvels their recent products such as corn spirits and corn sugar, which appeared this very year. It may be that they will put rather high import duties on European goods, so that prices that are naturally high and proportional to the risks involved will go so much higher that the prestige of European commerce will be irrevocably lost, and, with an about-face with respect to their own needs, they will force us, in our turn, to come and exchange our goods for theirs and to their profit.

When prices become lower, with easier times or with the coming of peace, the volume of paper money will also decrease for the same reason that public expenditures will stop accumulating; and since the people make the laws regulating monetary matters, they will prefer to extend terms of final payment three- or fourfold rather than cancel assets that represent payment for their trouble and labors, and which alone constitute their resources and become more valuable as the time approaches for conversion into actual specie.

When will the present troubles be settled? How far will the Americans, in the end, carry their conquests, and what will be the nature of their views and their gratitude toward the powers that have given them protection? We shall know in time, and not through conjectures. I gather this from certain persons fanatically attached to their country and to the notion that the population of the colony will probably double every twenty years: the Americans believe that they will soon take over the Newfoundland banks and Bermuda; they are casting fond glances at the **Antilles** and becoming quite used to the idea of possessing them; and of all those notions of **aggrandizement** with which they love to delude themselves, none flatters them more (and with reason) than do their designs on the Mississippi region and Mexico.

This superficial but accurate description of the Americans' projects, to follow their complete victory over the Royalists, might be interpreted to their disadvantage. Such would be the case if the history of nations were like that of an individual who, with an **epicurean** point of view and complete detachment in everything save himself, was to behave in a republic according to his peculiar principles, and break the bonds or conventions of his own society. But the history of nations is quite another matter; and without misjudging those patriotic virtues which sustain the Americans and elevate them in a powerful body, one cannot deny that, in view of the Europeans' seizure of the Antilles, Mexico, and their own land, the Americans have a better right to retaliate than do any other people with the exception of the **Caribs**, Peruvians, and Mexicans. But the population of these has shrunk, as the result of avarice, so far below that of their dispossessors, that there is no fear or hope that they will revolt. Moreover, such a revolution is so remote and would depend upon so many previous occurrences that, glorious as it appears to the Americans and even to European statesmen, it can be regarded as both a physical and moral impossibility.

Consider, first of all, the small population of the country compared with an equal ground area in Europe. Consider also the wars that the colonists are obliged to wage against the neighboring Indians, as they have to push them back in order to clear new land and harvest new crops; the delays and ravages that land clearing and agriculture suffer because of these minor conflicts and, especially, the present war with England; and America's need of Europe for the perfection of the arts of warfare, agriculture, and manufactures, already recognized and felt as a necessity for maintaining luxury and easy living. Consider also the lack of vineyards, mulberry trees, silkworms, and olive trees; the present shortage of manpower to exploit their mines, and the further retarding of population that these mines will occasion; and, finally, the demonstrated superiority of the European powers in the arts, in ability to get things done, in wealth and strength: one will then see that the projected conquests of the future against those powers are still very remote, and that they can be conceived as events possible in themselves, but depending, as demonstrated possibilities, upon so many circumstances as to be regarded as **chimerical**. It would be quite otherwise if those countries which are already sharing the speculations of the Americans, would come to their aid and offer themselves in order to participate in their independence, avenge the massacre of their own early inhabitants, and punish the atrocious crimes of the first Europeans who appeared in their midst carrying the torch of destruction. These are issues which will depend more on the discontent of the ex-European colonists than on the projects, troops, and conquests meditated by these people who more recently fled from despotism and tyranny.

The present successes of the Americans proceed from certain events, for example, the English generals' lack of familiarity with the land in which they are waging war; their difficulty in getting aid once they have advanced into the country; the steadily increasing number of the enemy and the daily diminishing of their own troops; the necessarily inevitable weakening of their soldiers who live constantly in the woods and who are deprived of hospitals and asylums where they can recover from the harm wrought on their constitutions by their change of place, climate, and manner of living; and, finally, the progress of a relentless war fought in a hilly or unwholesome land where roads must be cleared continually in order to make contact with the enemy. To these impediments may be added the discontent of expatriated men who have been beguiled with assurances of easy and sure success, and who are granted citizenship and productive land whenever they voluntarily desert to the American side. It will, then, be no surprise if fortune has favored the insurgents in the face of the bravery and intrepidity of the **Hessian** and **Royalist** troops, and in spite of their own lack of experienced soldiers: they are superior in number and more skillful in destructive fusillades; they are in their own country and are there being attacked; they lack nothing, and they are demoralizing their foe through favors and gratitude.

The one thing capable of destroying once and for all the Americans and their hope of independence is the possible capture and abolishment of the Congress, for in this body alone lies the strength of the dominion. Created and chosen by the united provinces, it is the sole agency which makes the laws, prints paper money, and gives the insurgents a modicum of legislative power. Once abolished, and before the colonies could be apprised, their choice of a president elected, and the site of a capital selected, one would soon witness—but let me suppress any proofs that I might bring forward to convince those of contrary views: the damage would be too severe, it would occasion the loss of so many good men, that I had rather be accused of negligence or presumption in my treatment of this subject, than to repent for suggesting an idea which the English themselves have never had, and which might have been so easily realized.

Permit me to make one final remark with respect to these colonies. In the northern provinces the toil and care demanded by cultivation are in the hands of white men, to about the same degree as in Europe and in France. How, then, does it happen that men and women of both the very wealthy and the very poor classes exhibit an almost identical delicacy of English features, slenderness, elegance in dress, noble bearing, and easy manner? Why does wealth not breed arrogance, as it does in France? Why do the indigent and the laborer not grovel before those who provide their work and sustenance? Why are the women of the farms or villages not embarrassed or awed at the sight of an influential or well-dressed man? Why do we not find, in the manner of living, mutual greetings, and conversation of rich and poor, common soldier and general, merchant and artisan, that difference existing in Europe where the lower classes remain in a state of servile dependency which is voluntary and demonstrated by the slight esteem accorded them by society—or, if you will, by a tacit and humiliating acceptance of the importance of condition, rank, fortune, and birth?

These reflections, which will be considered novel in France, should astonish neither the sage nor anyone who examines the ways of men and governments. If one meditates simply on the single word *liberty,* the basis and foundation of the English colonies, one will soon recognize the origin of the noticeable distinctions between the manners of their inhabitants and those of a land where liberty does not reign. Where there is liberty, there man is ennobled, becomes more esteemed; he feels and believes that he is constrained only by his needs, not by the caprices of arbitrary and inconsistent conventions of greatness, birth, pomp, and luxury; he sees in his fellow man no difference other than that of wealth. He consequently becomes, in his manners, freedom of mind, nobility of feeling, behavior, and outlook, both the equal and the friend of rich and poor, of the most opulent and of him who must work daily for his food and basic needs. This is the source of the charity, humaneness, mutual beneficence and aid, recognition, and gratitude which have been so favorable to agriculture, the clearing of the land, the formation of the political and civil structure of the English colonies—in short, all those undeniable patriotic virtues recognized even by their enemies. Where indeed is the man who can fail to love a country in which, though born in want, he knows no masters or tyrants other than his own needs and those sentiments, implanted through education, which bind him voluntarily to his native land and to those places where he enjoys in peace the assistance and demands of society and of everyday living? What man can fail to love a country in which, with modest means, he reaps the fruit of his own labor, where his judges, neighbors, and compatriots are his equals and his friends, where the laws, dictated solely by reason and justice, proscribe selfishness, render all men mutually free and dependent, and forcefully oppose any who would disturb the harmonious order and equality created by these laws and upheld with enthusiasm and fervor?

It is a demonstrable truth that liberty is a **rampart** against the natural and inevitable deterioration of men living in society, for in a region of uniform climate one can easily distinguish between the free and the enslaved: the noticeable alteration that takes place in the one, and the advantages of the other, cannot honestly be denied. Now the human species is not degenerating among the poorest families in the American colonies. In the humblest homes, even those farthest removed from the great cities, are discovered simple villagers whose clothing, in keeping with their economic situation, neither mars nor alters their appearance and bearing. Their faces do not reflect their poverty, continual want of necessities, or the conviction of their almost negligible status and importance in society. Far from shunning wealthy or powerful men, or trembling in their presence, they eagerly welcome such persons, overwhelm them with questions, familiarities, and any service they can offer. Their only interest and motive in so doing is to oblige and to be sociable. This privilege is bestowed only by liberty and the conviction of perfect equality not encountered in countries where liberty does not reign except as it degenerates into turmoil and license.

TERMS AND DEFINITIONS

Aggrandizement: increasing or enlarging its possessions.

Antilles: the islands of the West Indies, except for the Bahamas.

Caribs: native inhabitants of the Caribbean Islands who were largely displaced by Europeans.

Chimerical: imaginary, fanciful, or fantastic.

Epicurean: a life of pleasure regulated only by morality, temperance, serenity, and cultural development, with no outside coercion.

Hessian: mercenary troops sent to fight for the British by the Elector of Hesse in Germany.

Rampart: a strong defense or bulwark.

Royalists: American colonial loyalists fighting with the British in the Revolution.

JOHN FERDINAND DALZIEL SMYTH

A BRITISH LOYALIST DECRIES INDEPENDENCE

One of the earliest and most critical commentators on the new nation was John Ferdinand Dalziel Smyth (1745–1814), an English-born Loyalist fighting with the British who had been twice captured by the Americans during the Revolutionary War. Upon his return to England in 1784, he published his two-volume A Tour of the United States of America, *a work that the acerbic John Randolph of Roanoke, longtime Virginia Congressman and fierce advocate of individual liberty and states rights, said was "replete with falsehood and calumny," but containing the "truest picture of the state of society and manners in Virginia (such as it was half a century ago) that is extant." Smyth firmly believed that American independence would prove to be a disaster for both countries and that their treatment of Loyalists like himself had deprived the Americans of any moral advantage that they might try to claim.*

This unhappy and unfortunate war having terminated in a manner so peculiarly unfavourable and inauspicious to the future prosperity of both countries, particularly to that of America, in a total separation of government, interest, and connections, as far as people proceeding from the same origin, habituated to the same manners and customs, speaking the same language, and professing the same religion, can possibly admit of—, and what is still more extraordinary, and equally to be regretted, this fatal event is universally confessed to be absolutely against the known and acknowledged interest of both.

For these new formed United States of America, at the expense of real freedom and the greatest share of felicity that ever was or will be possessed by any people or community upon earth, at the expense of an increasing commerce and population, of opulence and perfect security in person, property, and laws, of a name, as British subjects, then held in the highest respect and veneration by all the powers in the known world; in short, at the expense of every blessing that could possibly be desired, possessed, and enjoyed, not only by the public at large, but by every individual thereof, have acquired what is absolutely nothing better than a shadow, "a momentary, delusive, misconceived consequence in the estimation of other powers;" which will vanish, like the phantom from whence it proceeds, upon a more intimate knowledge and experience of its deception and fallacy.

Nay, they have acquired what is worse than a shadow; they have shackled themselves in **fetters,** which every future struggle to disengage themselves from will only rivet more firmly and render more heavy and oppressive; and to the support of which every year's experience will evince them to be altogether inadequate. For when the enormous load of their debt, contracted during this war, is considered, the interest of which alone is sufficient to bear them down, added to their necessary and unavoidable expenses in supporting the dignity of thirteen different governments, with the naval, military, and civil establishments of the whole; besides the annual presents to the Indians, and the enormous expenses of ambassadors, envoys, and so forth at foreign courts, to watch over their skeleton commerce and interest, to keep up their shadow of dignity as free, independent, and sovereign states, and to procure them some small degree of respect among other powers, these vast and continued expenditures, compared with the resources from whence they all must necessarily be derived, viz. a country instead of advancing in opulence and strength, actually immersed in poverty and decreasing in population in a degree that might down the most powerful....When all this is duly attended to, what prospect is left of emancipation for this unfortunate country?

When in their intoxication of having succeeded in obtaining their boasted fatal independence has worn off, and the unavoidable pressure of taxes begins to operate and become grievous, then will they look back with inexpressible concern and regret at the happy time when they enjoyed every felicity, security, and substantial benefit, under the auspices of the free and mild government of Great Britain. They will **execrate** the destructive measure, and most sincerely lament the fatal period of separation. Nor will even hope itself, the great supporter in affliction, be left them for their comfort, to point out any method of extricating themselves from their difficulties. For entangled in French politics, enthralled by ruinous obligations to, and an unnatural alliance with, a nation totally different from themselves in habits, manners, and inclinations, in language and sentiments, in religion, in form of government, and in short, in every thing; their rulers corrupted by French gold, captivated by the tinsel parade, grandeur, and affected amity of that artful, perfidious, gaudy people, and influenced by their promises and specious affability, unequal also to that subtle nation in policy, and infinitely inferior in opulence and power, what possibility is there of the American states disengaging themselves from their control, or ever again becoming free?

From this representation, which is by no means exaggerated, every person with the least share of discernment, or even common understanding, must plainly see how undesirable, and indeed unfit, a place of residence the United States of America must be for any one whatsoever, either needy or affluent. For so far is it from being possible now to acquire a fortune in that country that merely to retain what one already possesses without diminution is a matter of difficulty, and to procure a decent and comfortable subsistence by trade or labour must be next to impossible. All the foregoing observations are evinced by the amazing depopulation of these provinces. A decrease, for the time, unexampled in history, and clearly proves every thing herein alleged. For the reasons must be weighty indeed, that would induce men to abandon their native land, their friends, fortunes, and climate, country, and soil in the world, to settle where every thing is infinitely inferior, among strangers, or in an inclement barren wilderness, and in a region of frosts and fogs. Yet this is undoubtedly the case at present, and thus it will continue. So that, instead of the numerous emigrations that formerly crowded to America, increasing her strength, population, and resources with a rapidity beyond all example, the state of things is now reversed, and multitudes of the inhabitants certainly are leaving the dominions of the American States as speedily as they possibly can. This fluctuating state of the country, and their unsettled versatile government, will likewise prevent a possibility of any exact account of the United States of America being given for many years to come, as during that time they will be perpetually liable to changes so that what might have been a just representation in one year, may be found totally different in the next, the inevitable consequence of their present situation.

These observations naturally lead to a reflection on the situation of the American loyalists of every description, among whom I include all who have been true to their sovereign in principle, whether they have publicly declared it or not, as well as those who have openly avowed their allegiance and taken up arms in favour of Great Britain and the old established government. Of both these, I consider the condition of those such as have remained at their homes, and are now subject to the domination of the Congress, as in reality the most deplorable. The rest depend upon Great Britain for protection and it would be an indelible stain upon her honour, policy, and her most sacred engagements, were she to abandon them.

But the other poor unfortunate men, whose hearts were as true as loyalty and virtue itself, and who have been constantly requested to remain in peace at their homes, and were always promised never to be given up or forsaken, and who, to my knowledge, would not have hesitated to shed the last drop of their blood, had they been called forth in support of their king and country, have now no power on earth to look up to for protection from the insults and barbarity of their illiberal, vindictive, implacable foes. Even hope itself is withheld them, and they must be reduced to absolute desperation. Few have had such opportunities as I of knowing and being witness to the ardent zeal, loyalty, and great desire, of these most unfortunate people, and my heart really bleeds for their distresses. How hard has been the fate of all those truly meritorious but unhappy men, the American Loyalists of every denomination. True to their king, faithful to their country, attached to the laws and constitution, they have continued firm and inflexible in the midst of persecutions, torments, and death. Many of them have abandoned their homes, their friends, their nearest and most tender connections, and encountered all the toils of war, want, and misery; solely actuated by motives the most disinterested and virtuous. In short, they have undergone trials and sufferings, with a determined resolution and fortitude unparalleled in history, and have submitted even to death sooner than stain their integrity, honour, and principled loyalty with the odious guilt of rebellion against their king. Yet these very men, whose virtues and **deserts** are above estimation, have been publicly **traduced**, vilified, and defamed, with every species of **obloquy** and **opprobrious epithet** applied to them and their conduct by the partisans of a ruinous faction in this country, for which they have shed their blood and sacrificed their all.

There cannot be a doubt but the more worthy and principled part of the nation reprobated such conduct, not only as illiberal, ungenerous, and unjust, but impolitic also in the highest degree. For such subjects as the American Loyalists were highly to be prized in any government, and were certainly entitled to every protection and encouragement that this could bestow. For no compensation whatever can be adequate to the loss sustained by these deserving men, not only of their possessions and the society of their friends and relations, but of that apparently established for ages to come felicity and affluence which they themselves, and their posterity after them, had the prospect of enjoying for ages to come.

TERMS AND DEFINITIONS

Deserts: merits, worth, or claim upon rewards.
Execrate: to curse or call down evil upon someone.
Fetters: chains or bonds like those of a prisoner.

Obloquy: verbal abuse.
Opprobrious epithet: a shameful or disgraceful name or title given to someone.
Traduced: slandered or maligned.

THINKING THINGS THROUGH

1. What points of agreement and disagreement regarding the nature of the relationship between Great Britain and the American colonies can you identify in the pieces by Johnson and Pitt?

2. Compare the language and ideas found in the Declaratory Act with those in the selections from Pitt and Johnson. Could Pitt have supported the Declaratory Act?

3. On what grounds does Macaulay claim that the people of Great Britain should support the American position? Do you think that her argument was persuasive?

4. Can you find any points of agreement between the anonymous Frenchman and J. F. D. Smyth regarding the reasons for an American victory and its prospects for future success?

5. How do you think that Johnson and Pitt would react to Macaulay's criticism of the Coercive Acts and her call for British support of colonial rebellion?

6

THE PROSPECTS OF THE NEW NATION

A. The International Context

Looking at the matter from a vantage point of more than two centuries later, it seems almost inconceivable that the United States, the most powerful nation in the world, was ever regarded as little more than an experiment in constitutional republican government. Moreover, it seems impossible to imagine that intelligent, well-informed people could ever have entertained the slightest doubt regarding the inevitability of its success, or that there were even those who vociferously predicted, and earnestly desired, its failure. However, any careful reading of the history of other new nations brought into being by revolution over the past two centuries reveals that the odds are heavily weighted on the side of failure—of descent into anarchy and chaos, on the one hand, or degeneration into authoritarian government, on the other. Such has surely been the fate of numerous Latin American nations in the nineteenth century, of erstwhile European colonies in Africa and Asia since World War II, and of the Soviet Union, China, and the former Yugoslavia. The happier fate of the United States owes itself to a complex set of environmental and historical circumstances that various observers, foreign and domestic, have attempted to discern over the years. None of these have ever provided any compelling evidence that the success of the United States can be explained by any theories of racial superiority or divine intervention.

The years between 1783 and 1815 were extremely precarious ones for the fledgling country, as it struggled to establish an effective national government, build a viable economic system, forge a widespread and deep-seated sense of national identity, and gain recognition and respect in the international arena. As an upstart republic in a world of authoritarian monarchies, the United States elicited praise and hope from much of Europe's "enlightened" intelligentsia, but inspired fear and loathing among many of those with a powerful stake in the existing order. During the first decade after independence, the new nation exchanged the Articles of Confederation for a constitution that established a workable federal system of government. It also developed a plan for settlement and development of its western territories, began to admit new states, and inaugurated a serious debate about the future direction of its economic, social, and political development. Despite those impressive gains, however, foreign observers continued to disagree significantly about the wisdom and worth of the American experiment. Some waxed ecstatic over its achievements and prospects, while others happily forecast its ultimate failure. For the most part, such observers were highly impressed with the rapid geographical expansion and economic development of the new nation. They were, however, much more critical and skeptical about the operation of its political system, especially as it evolved in the direction of "universal" white male suffrage.

The Peace of Paris, which officially concluded the American Revolutionary War in 1783, formally recognized the United States as a sovereign nation, independent of foreign control. However, it did not disengage the fledgling country from the various international systems of which it had been an integral part during the colonial period. Still effectively confined east of the Allegheny and Appalachian mountain ranges, Americans needed only to look to Canada on the north and to the upper Great Lakes region on the west to realize that Great Britain still maintained a formidable presence. Moreover, the extensive Spanish Empire extended into Florida on the southeast and Texas on the southwest, barring American access to the Caribbean and the Gulf of Mexico. Even though France and Spain were nominally friendly nations, that condition was always subject to change upon short notice in the fast-moving, self-interested world of Great Power conflicts. Together, Britain, France, and Spain still controlled almost the entire Western Hemisphere, rendering the infant nation's future highly dependent upon the vagaries of European politics.

When Britain and France renewed their centuries-old military struggle in the wake of the French Revolution of 1789, President George Washington immediately proclaimed America's official neutrality, thereby inaugurating a quarter century of fluctuation between the new nation's frequently naive

pursuit of independent action and the often harsh realities of
international conflict. Undeterred by the niceties of international law, both belligerents violated America's proclaimed
rights as neutrals with impunity. Only with the signing of the
Treaty of Ghent ending the War of 1812 on Christmas Eve,
1814, did the United States redefine its position in the international system. Even so, it still remained a relatively minor
power.

Having gained some measure of respect and security in
its dealings with Europe's two greatest powers, the United
States soon found its position in the Western Hemisphere
threatened by turmoil within the extensive Spanish Empire.
Beginning with Mexico in 1820, most of the countries in Central and South America mounted liberal, national revolutions,
at least in partial emulation of the Americans and the French.
This revolutionary outburst was initially encouraging to the
United States, which had already demonstrated a chronic yen
for Cuba and other Spanish possessions in the Caribbean. In-
dications that Spain might unite with other European powers
to put down Latin American independence movements by
military force galvanized the new nation to proclaim that the
Western Hemisphere was closed to further colonization.

Nor did American political independence do much to
sever the other sinews of connection to the rest of the world,
especially trade and immigration. As early as 1784, the first
American ship, the Empress of China, laid anchor off the
coast of Canton, setting off a fascination with things Chinese
that has continued unabated. By 1810, an expedition outfit-
ted by New York merchant John Jacob Astor established the
American Fur Company at the mouth of the Columbia River
in Oregon, bringing Americans into contact—and conflict—
with Great Britain, Spain, and Russia and propelling it ever
closer to the huge expanse of the Pacific Ocean. By 1812,
New England ships were engaging in regular commercial traffic with the Hawaiian Islands, the Dutch East Indies, and
British India. Led by New York City's famous Black Ball
Line, the American merchant marine also established regular
trade channels with the Middle East, the Baltic states, Africa,
the West Indies, South America, and western Europe. Even
in 1801, Jefferson considered American trade with the North
African states important enough to wage a four-year unde-
clared "Barbary War."

Although immigration to the new United States between
1790 and 1830 was relatively slight compared to that which

would characterize the century following, it still constituted a vital link with the outside world. One of the first important acts of the first Congress was a measure providing for fast and easy naturalization of European male immigrants, a certain sign that the new nation hoped to serve as a magnet for such people in a mutually beneficial arrangement. By the same token, persons not of the white race were denied naturalization, a condition that persisted until the 1950s. The 1790s also produced the first of those periodic anti-immigration waves that have alternately waxed and waned, thus firmly establishing the country's enduring "love-hate relationship" with immigration. With the ending of the Napoleonic Wars in 1815, the rapid growth and expansion of the United States, and the continuance of socioeconomic and political turmoil in Europe, the groundwork for the century of mass immigration from Europe that was to erupt after 1830 was soon laid.

During those same years, the United States continued to experience impressive domestic growth. The number of states rose to twenty-four, while the country's population soared to thirteen million, more than triple what it had been in 1790. The eastern half of the nation was linked by a system of canals and natural waterways, and many cities in that region were already linked by rail. Already one of the most bountiful and prosperous agricultural countries in the world, the United States was also industrializing at a breathtaking pace in lower New England and the Middle Atlantic states. Although still overwhelmingly rural in settlement, it already boasted nearly a dozen cities of over twenty-five thousand population. By 1830, the question was no longer if the United States would succeed, but how much and how quickly would it grow.

B. International Views

The progress of the United States was of particular interest to two groups of foreign observers—Europeans and Latin Americans. The former were primarily concerned with the question of whether this experiment in constitutional republican government and relatively classless society was a preview of things to come in their own countries. Depending upon whether they found the American situation to be positive or negative, they portrayed it to their countrymen either as a dire warning or a shining vision of the future. Latin

American observers, on the other hand, had already embraced the United States as the model that they hoped to emulate. Their major purpose was to study its actual operation in detail, assess its strengths and weaknesses, and discover ways in which its best features could be adapted to their own societies and cultures. What claimed the primary attention of both groups was the way in which the egalitarian philosophy of the Declaration of Independence and the Bill of Rights translated into day-to-day operation in the new nation's society and polity. Although they arrived at varying answers to that crucial question, their universal concentration upon it gave powerful implicit testimony to the long-term significance of that query, both for the United States and for much of the rest of the world.

The three European observers included in this chapter—all British by birth—differed significantly in their assessments of the past, present, and future of the new nation. One, Basil Hall, a British naval officer of Scottish ancestry, clearly regarded the very independence of the United States from Great Britain as a terrible mistake for both countries. He flatly detailed the reasons for his convictions that Canada was far more valuable to Britain than the former American colonies ever would be, and that Canada was much better off as part of the British Empire than it would be as part of the United States. Another, Henry Bradshaw Fearon, a visiting London physician, was openly disdainful of the quality of governance in the new nation, a condition that he attributed largely to the proliferation of lawyers. The third, Frances Wright D'Arusmont, a young Scottish woman destined to become an important antislavery crusader, chastised Europeans for underestimating the United States, largely out of ignorance of its accomplishments. She boldly hailed its achievements in the "science of government," and challenged Europeans to study and copy its accomplishments. Her views were remarkably similar to those of Lorenzo de Zavala, a celebrated Mexican patriot excited by his own country's successful revolt against Spanish rule. He profusely praised the United States for its achievement of material prosperity, lauded it for translating its lofty political principles into practical operation, and proposed it as a model for his own and other Latin American new nations. Far more skeptical were the views of Francisco de Miranda, a Venezuelan "freedom fighter" who participated in the American, French, and several Latin American revolutions. While deeply committed to the philosophy of the American Revolution, he detected a fatal contra-

diction between the maintenance of "republican simplicity"
and the seemingly unregulated pursuit of individual, and na-
tional, wealth and power.

FRANCISCO DE MIRANDA

A LATIN AMERICAN REVOLUTIONARY IN THE CRADLE OF LIBERTY

Highly discriminating in his assessment of the new nation, and particularly of conditions in Boston, the cradle of American liberty, was Francisco de Miranda (1750–1816), the knight-errant of Spanish-American liberty. The first cultured South American to visit the United States, and one of the few people to be involved in the American, French, and Latin American revolutions, the Venezuelan-born author and patriot visited Boston and numerous other locales in 1783–1784, and recorded his impressions in The Diary of Francisco de Miranda: A Tour of the United States. *In that work, he boldly identifies the love of property and material prosperity as "poison" to the realization of republican ideals. He also criticizes the young country for its celebration of the practical and material at the expense of respect for learning and the arts.*

The women here have very little education, and their diversions are confined to games of circumspection in which society hardly has a place. The married women have a club that meets every Saturday, at which six or eight families gather to eat (often seven miles from the city); when the meal is over, each goes to her home. The unmarried women have tea parties with each other as their only school for manners, customs, elegance, etc., and therefore they are highly deficient in these respects and have a self-preoccupation such as I have never seen. In the winter, there is a badly directed Assembly (the hall, although somewhat small, is made with taste and the ornaments are elegant), at which the old and the young dance together, grossly as a rule. It is a very peculiar thing that the list of subscribers has not been offered to any officer of the American army, with the result that not one of them can attend. See here the envy of the mercantile corps and the ingratitude of the people in general!

The men are not better off in point of society. A club that meets on Monday evenings, at which they play cards and partake a little of cold meats from seven to ten o'clock, is all they have been able to invent in behalf of society. In a word, society is not known yet. Extravagance, ostentation, and a bit of vanity are the predominant features in the character of those that are rich today. A young man who, ten years ago, wore silk stockings and satin breeches or powdered his hair needed nothing more to ruin his character forever. Today, not only do they wear all this, but they wear it even when booted and riding horseback. The women as follows: silks, ribbons, muslins, pomades, and perfumes every day. (The schools of French dance are on a par with this and are so numerous that even the Negroes have theirs, which they attend twice a week from seven miles away.) There is not a mechanic who does not send his daughters with predilection to this important branch of democratic-American education, paying four or five pesos monthly. Since the region does not have a single manufactory of the above-mentioned, and by necessity must pay foreign countries for it all, it follows that ruin is unavoidable. If we consider that the only products with which the region can pay its debts are potash, tar, and codfish, we will not be surprised when the businessman says all the wealth in this capital today can barely pay Europe half the current debts! And if this happens in so short a period of time, what will it be in twenty years? Commerce will always be the principal downfall of democratic virtue. This stems from the simplicity and equality of the people!

I have had the pleasure of communicating with the famous republican and very prominent actor in the recent revolution, **Mr. Samuel Adams.** He is a man of talents and extensive accomplishments in legislation. We had some drawn-out conversations regarding the constitution of this Republic. As for two objections which I raised about this subject, he declared he would meet with me after he had chewed them well. The first was, how is it that in a democracy the foundation of which was virtue no position whatever was indicated for it, and, on the contrary, all the dignities and the power were given to property, which is precisely the poison of a similar republic? The other was the contradiction I observed between admitting as one of the rights of mankind the worship of the Supreme Being in the manner and form one chooses without giving predominance by law to any sect, and later excluding from every legislative or representative office the man who does not swear he is of the Christian religion. Weighty **solecisms** without doubt. He gave me much interesting information on the origin, beginnings, and occurrences of the past revolution, favoring me with his conversation familiarly.

On all the avenues and the environs of Boston one encounters fortified works, made by the British and Americans during the siege of this place. Likewise there is an infinity of the most advantageous heights for views and for locating country houses I have ever seen in so short an extension of land; Milton Hill and Dorchester Point are very remarkable. Last Sunday morning I went for a ride in the chaise to the castle a little below Dorchester Point and, since it is necessary to cross a small inlet, I asked for the boat, but, as it was Sunday, they did not wish to send it. Patiently I returned over the same road, quite good and pleasant, and when I was about to cross some low ground, found that with the rising tide there was about one foot of water there. A very decent man approached at that moment on horseback with a woman on the haunches. He came up to me and asked if I could take her across in my chaise, as she was afraid. I told him yes, and with that she jumped off the horse, got into my chaise, and I carried her two miles. She then asked me to let her off and remained there in a house waiting for her husband, who came on horseback some distance behind us. Now who is there in Europe who judges so favorably of the human heart as to deliver thus to a stranger his young and beautiful wife? Nor who so crackbrained as to think it a great sin to cross a river on Sunday?

On various occasions, I attended the General Assembly of the state legislative body, where I saw clearly the defects and inconveniences to which this democracy has subjected itself by placing the legislative power in the hands of ignorance. One member recited couplets in the middle of a debate he did not understand. Another, at the end of this debate and after the matter had been discussed for two hours, asked what the motion was so he could vote. And thus it is for the most part, with the result that the most absurd and unjust points have been debated, proposed, and approved in these democratic assemblies throughout the continent. All the influence being given by the constitution to property, the leading members do not have to be the wisest, and the Senators and Assemblymen are generally people destitute of principles and education. One was a tailor four years ago; another, an innkeeper; another, a porter; another was a smith; etc.

. . . I had occasion to talk to him [the **Marquis de Lafayette**] and he seems to me a mediocre character, invested with that activity and perpetual motion of a Frenchman. This trip of the Marquis seems to me one of those **legerdemains** with which France is wont to wish to delude human nature and which, on many occasions, have had the desired effect. But to the eyes of those who see well, they are nothing but ridiculous political farces. These simple people, inexpert as yet in politics, have made excessive and absurd demonstrations as the "Hero" passes from one town to another, with the speed of a **Roland,** to receive their praises.

Dr. Waterhouse and I set aside one day to visit the **University of Cambridge.** We started out at eight o'clock in the morning and crossed the Charlestown Ferry in ten minutes. (This ferry is the best regulated I have seen. There are four boats. Two are constantly in motion taking the people who arrive across, and hardly do these touch the dock but the others depart, even if there are no passengers.) Taking a chaise on the other side, we undertook our literary excursion towards Cambridge, about four miles away. In passing by Bunker Hill, I could not do less than stop and look into this important military affair, with the aid of both an American officer who had been in the action and of the original information I had acquired. The event did not occur in the place mentioned, as is generally thought, but on a height closer to the landing place of Charlestown, called Breed's Hill. What difficulties will there not be, therefore, in posterity, when its **Polybius,** traveling in order to write with truth and prudence the history of this military action, encounters the contradiction between the name of the position and that of the event, unless a monument erected now for immortality on the very spot clears up this doubt?

We then proceeded to Cambridge and there, in the company of some tutors visited the college. The quarters of the tutors and of the students are middlingly comfortable and without taste or ornament. The library is well arranged and clean. It contains some twelve thousand volumes, English generally, although not badly selected. The room or cabinet of natural history hardly deserves the name: a few things of that sort placed there in a disorderly manner. Afterwards we went to the so-called Philosophical Hall. It is a spacious room, well proportioned and decorated with pictures of the principal benefactors of the college, some engravings by **Copley** (a native of this city), and a marble bust of **Lord Chatham,** a work of middling merit. The key to the philosophical apparatus could not be found, and, it being mealtime for the students, we descended to the refectory, where we all ate quite frugally: a piece of salt pork, potatoes, cabbages, a bit of cheese with the bread, and cider. As scholars are wont to rush through their meals, our repast was soon concluded.

We returned the following week to examine the rest of the College. With Professor Williams, a man of science and judgement, we visited the philosophical apparatus, which is without doubt very good and quite complete for its purpose. They lack, nevertheless, an observatory, for which reason the astronomical pieces are scattered in one place and another. Afterwards we climbed to the top of the building, from which there is a beautiful prospect, and, not having more to see, we went to the house of the President, who had invited us for dinner. We ate in his reverend company, and I made them a present of a silver medal engraved in Mexico by **Gil** to commemorate the founding of the Academy of National and Public Law, which they much esteemed. This establishment seems to me better calculated to form clerics than capable and educated citizens. It is certainly an extraordinary thing that in this college there is no professorship whatever of the living languages and that theology is the principal professorship. The manner of dressing, presenting oneself, being polite in company, etc., are branches to which not the least attention is paid, therefore the exterior of these scholars is the most slovenly I have ever seen in those of their sort. The President is unsociable, austere and of an unbearable circumspection.

Terms and Definitions

Mr. Samuel Adams: American patriot active in the Sons of Liberty and the Committees of Correspondence and a leader of the Boston Tea Party.

Lord Chatham: Sir William Pitt, Earl of Chatham and British prime minister (see Chapter 5).

Copley: John Singleton Copley (1738–1815), a prominent American painter.

Gil: famed Spanish sculptor and metal worker.

Legerdemains: sleights of hand practiced by magicians in order to deceive.

Marquis de Lafayette: young French nobleman and favorite of George Washington who served in the American Revolutionary War.

Polybius: ancient Greek writer considered to be the first historian.

Roland: legendary hero of the *Song of Roland,* an epic poem set in eighth-century France.

Solecisms: violations of logical reasoning, often deliberate.

University of Cambridge: Harvard University, located in Cambridge, a suburb of Boston.

Dr. Waterhouse: Miranda's host in Boston.

HENRY BRADSHAW FEARON

A COUNTRY INFESTED
WITH LAWYERS

Sounding almost like a present-day American in his disdain for lawyers and their nefarious impact on politics and government, London surgeon Henry Bradshaw Fearon (1770–?) pointedly skewered his target just after the War of 1812. He is especially critical of the members of that profession for making the law a servant of business rather than an expression of the national interest and a search for justice. Fearon is scathing in his assessment of the country's legislative institutions and of the caliber of their members. So critical was he in his book A Narrative of a Journey of 5000 Miles through the Eastern and Western States *that even British critics noted "the tone of ill-temper which this author usually manifests in speaking of the American character," and conceded that he was "a little given to exaggerate in his views of vices and prejudices."*

Congress being sitting, I have several times attended their debates. Their present place of meeting is a temporary one. It was designed, I believe, for an hotel, and is in the immediate neighbourhood of the Capitol. My first visit to congress was to the senate. This body is, at present, comprised of forty members, the States having increased from their original number of thirteen to that of twenty and each State, regardless of its population, sending two. The gallery is open to all, without orders from members or half-a-crown to the door-keeper. The only form to be observed is taking off the hat in obedience to a public notice to that effect. The chairman's seat is central, under a handsome canopy. The members are placed on rich scarlet cushions, some at double, and some at single desks. There are two large fires. The room is carpeted, as is also the gallery. The forms of business are taken from those of our parliament, with a few minor exceptions. One point of variation, at least from the British senate, is that every speech is apparently listened to and all, whether good or bad, whether marked by superior excellence or by unequaled dullness, seem regarded with equal apathy and complete lifeless endurance, neither applause nor censure being allowed. It would not be an easy task to discern which were felt, judging from the countenance. I have heard nearly all their usual speakers. **Mr. Otis** of Massachusetts is an eloquent man, but not remarkable for solidity of reasoning. **Mr. Rufus King** is a true gentleman and one whom, I should conceive, has not many superiors among the public men of any country. **Mr. Barbour,** called Governor Barbour of Virginia, is a speaker who, perhaps, violates all the rules of theoretic oratory, but who, notwithstanding, possesses an irresistible charm from his evident sincerity and the manliness of his deportment, which, while it rivets the attention of his audience, compels them to love the object of their admiration. His countenance is one of that kind which, in a few minutes, enlists in its favour all the social affections, and you insensibly feel anxious and predisposed to take that side of the argument of which so apparently kind and able a man professes himself the advocate. There are, in the senate, a great proportion of men of experience, of sound ability, and who would do credit to any nation upon earth.

The Representative chamber is in the same building, and of about twice the extent. An admission to the gallery is equally easy, and is also open to both sexes. This assembly consists of nearly two hundred. They want in appearance the age, experience, dignity, and respectability which we associate with the idea of legislators, and which are possessed by the superior branch of the congress. The interior decorations of this room are marked by an inferiority to the senate, which is rather anti-republican. The members sit on very common chairs at unpainted desks, which are placed in rows, the whole resembling a **Lancasterian school,** though without its regularity. Some two or three speakers regularly command attention; others talk on as long as they please, the members being occupied in writing letters, and in reading or folding up newspapers. This is carried to such an extreme that it appears fully to justify the charge of **Mr. Randolph** that the House of Representatives consisted only of "a large collection of printers boys." **Spitting boxes** are placed at the feet of each member and, contrary to the practice of the Upper House, at once members and visitors wear their hats. . . .

Nearly all the members of the representative chamber are young men and, out of the 190 members, 150, at the least, are lawyers, a class of men whose minds, here, as elsewhere, appear moulded and contracted by their profession, and not possessed of that general knowledge, or not taking those large and equitable views of things, which should be the distinguishing characteristics of the legislators of a great and a commercial people. Last session the member from Baltimore, who is a merchant, introduced the late "tariff." While giving the details, and necessary statements on this most important subject he perceived that nearly the whole assembly, Mr. Speaker included, were inattentive or slumbering. Stopping in the midst of his speech, he apologised for his own deficiency of ability, stating that he perceived the subject he was speaking on was not understood by the body he was addressing. The exact cause of this he could not pretend to determine, but of this he felt quite confident: that there was not a boy in his counting-rooms but would comprehend the subject perfectly. This roused the "learned gentlemen" and throughout the remainder of the subject they put on, at least, the aspect of attention.

The State legislatures are equally infested with lawyers. They occupy, in fact, eight-tenths of all the public situations in America. This is a great and a crying evil, and being one that is more likely to increase than diminish, may naturally give rise to some melancholy forebodings concerning the practical continuation of this excellent constitution.

In relation to the laws of the United States, I have remarked, on a previous occasion, the dependence of judges upon the counsel. I have been present in courts where this has been strikingly injurious to the cause of justice, though this is not to be understood as an universal feature of judicial proceedings; at least I saw no evidence of it in the Supreme Court at Washington, where **Judge**

Washington is among those who preside. He is nephew to the late General and resides at Mount Vernon. Some of the judges are, doubtless, men of superior legal knowledge and high standing in society; but there are others who certainly are not in possession of the former, though they may be of the latter qualification; as, for instance, the Chief Justice of the Common Pleas at Newark, who, I am informed, is a butcher—not a butcher retired from business and become a lawyer, but he attends to both trades, even on the same day, selling at seven o'clock in the morning a leg of mutton, and at eleven supplying his customers with a slice of **Blackstone.** Much evil must necessarily result from this heterogeneous admixture of ignorance with learning. Although we might hail the appointment of plain men of business and possessed of good solid understandings to award justice to their fellow citizens as an important benefit conferred on society, in substitution of the legal quibbling and learned oppression of the bar and bench. Yet if such men are not permitted to follow the plain dictates of their own understanding, but are tied down by legal forms, by ancient precedents, and by the laws and practice of a country with which they are entirely unacquainted, then, indeed, the appointment of such men become evil instead of a benefit to society. It would be better to place individuals on the bench who,—whatever may be their characters in other respects, their arrogance of deportment or their political subserviency,—yet, at any rate, understand the business upon which they are employed.

Although there may be, and doubtless are, many members of the legal profession who are honourable men, yet from all I have seen, or have been able to understand, the lawyers of this country do not seem to merit a particularly high character. My impression of them is, to use an American mode of estimation, at least thirty three and a third per cent lower than of their brethren in England. There are various causes which may have produced this deterioration. In the first place, deep and solid research in any occupation is neither so much wanted, so much esteemed, nor is it so marketable a commodity as in Great Britain. Further, the greater equality of society, which renders men more independent of each other, the non-classification of the profession of the law, which prevents either portion from being deeply studied, while the ease with which even legal gentlemen can and do alter their mode of obtaining a livelihood, naturally weakens the motives to exertion, and lessens, too, that strong impression of having at once a reputation, and the very means of existence at stake. These latter causes we know to be powerfully operative in England. The vast number of lawyers also, as compared with the amount of American population, divides the business into so many channels that, when a job is obtained, no means can be afforded to be left untried to render it profitable. These causes, aided by that prolific source of **chicanery,** our statute book, may account for that of which Americans complain so loudly—the expense of law proceedings, and the want of principle in their professional men.

TERMS AND DEFINITIONS

Mr. Barbour: James Barbour, U.S. senator from Virginia, 1815–1825.
Blackstone: Sir William Blackstone (1723–1780), English judge and legal authority.
Chicanery: legalistic trickery employed by some lawyers and others.
Mr. Rufus King: U.S. senator from New York, 1789–1796 and 1813–1825.
Lancasterian school: a regimented educational system introduced in late-eighteenth-century England by Joseph Lancaster.

Mr. Otis: Harrison Gray Otis, U.S. senator from Massachusetts, 1817–1822.
Mr. Randolph: John Randoph of Roanoke, Virginia, a Congressman from 1799 to 1829.
Spitting boxes: spitoons for the deposit of the residue from chewing tobacco.
Tariff: tax on imports that raised most of federal revenue at that time.
Judge Washington: Bushrod Washington, Supreme Court justice from 1798 to 1829.

FRANCES WRIGHT D'ARUSMONT

THE SINGULARLY ENLIGHTENED AMERICANS

At the opposite end of the critical pole from Fearon in her opinion of the emerging American polity was a young Englishwoman who toured the country in 1818. Recording her impressions in Views of Society and Manners in America, *published in 1821, Frances Wright D'Arusmont (1795–1852) was so laudatory that one London reviewer dismissed the book as "a most ridiculous and extravagant panegyric on the government and people of the United States; accompanied by the grossest and most detestable calumnies against this country that folly and malignity ever invented." In the book, Wright blames Europeans for willfully ignoring the remarkable achievements of the new nation, especially in the areas of economic development and self-government. She lavishly praised the Americans for their energy and for their pragmatic approach to nation building. In 1824, Wright returned to the United States to establish an antislavery utopian community in Nashoba, Tennessee, which purchased slaves and allowed them to earn their freedom.*

It was the **last war,** so little regarded in Europe but so all-important to America, that fixed the character of this country and raised it to the place which it now holds among the nations of the world. Am I mistaken in the belief that Europeans (and I speak here of the best informed) have hitherto paid but little attention to the internal history of the United States? When engaged in the Revolutionary struggle, they were regarded with a momentary sympathy; the fate of mankind hung upon the contest. It was **Tyranny's armed legions** opposed to **Liberty's untrained but consecrated band,** and the enlightened patriot of every clime felt that the issue was to decide the future destinies of the world. The battle being fought, this young and distant nation again seemed to shrink into insignificance. The whirlwind had now turned upon Europe, and all her think-ing heads were employed in poising state against state, empire against empire, or one tyrant against another tyrant, while America, removed from the uproar, was binding up her wounds and arranging her disturbed household. The people of Europe had soon well nigh forgotten her existence, and their gover-nors only occasionally remembered her, to tell her that she was not worth re-garding. Her ships were robbed upon the seas and insulted in the ports and from these at length shut out. She remonstrated to be laughed at; she resented the insults and, at last, challenged the aggressors and was stared at. The min-istry which had dared her to the quarrel drew carelessly a million from their treasury, dispatched some detachments from their fleets and armies, and sat down in quiet expectation that the American republics were once again to be transformed into British colonies. A few more generous politicians occasion-ally threw a glance across the ocean, curious to see how the **Herculean infant** would once again cope with the matured strength of a full-grown empire, and were perhaps scarcely less surprised than was the **cabinet of St. James.**

If ******** will study the history of this country, he will find it *teeming with business.* America was not asleep during the thirty years that Europe had for-gotten her. She was actively employed in her education, in framing and trying systems of government, in eradicating prejudices, in vanquishing internal ene-mies, in replenishing her treasury, in liquidating her debts, in amending her laws, in correcting her policy, in fitting herself to enjoy that liberty which she had purchased with her blood, in founding seminaries of learning, in facilitat-ing the spread of knowledge—to say nothing of the revival of commerce, the reclaiming of wilderness after wilderness, the facilitating of internal naviga-tion, the doubling and tripling of a population trained to exercise the rights of freemen, and to respect institutions adopted by the voice of their country. Such have been the occupations of America. She bears the works of her genius about her; we must not seek them in volumes piled on the shelves of a library. All her knowledge is put forth in action, lives in her institutions, in her laws, speaks in her senate, acts in her cabinet, breathes even from the walls of her cities and the sides of her ships. Look on all she has done, on that which she is; count the sum of her years, and then pronounce sentence on her genius. Her politicians are not ingenious theorists, but practical statesmen; her sol-diers have not been conquerors, but patriots; her philosophers not wise rea-soners, but wise legislators. Their country has been and is their field of action; every able head and nervous arm is pressed into its service. The foreign world hears nothing of their exploits and reads none of their lucubrations, but their country reaps the fruits of their wisdom and feels the aid of their service, and it is in the wealth, the strength, the peace, the prosperity, the good govern-ment, and the well-administered laws of that country that we must discover and admire their energy and genius.

In Europe we are apt to estimate the general cultivation of a people by the greater or less number of their literary characters. Even in that hemisphere, it is, perhaps, an unfair way of judging. No one would dispute that France is greatly advanced in knowledge since the era of the Revolution, and yet her literary fame from that period has been at a stand. The reason is obvious—that her genius was called from the closet into the senate and the field, her historians and poets were suddenly changed into soldiers and politicians, her peaceful men of letters became active citizens, known in their generation by their virtues or their crimes. Instead of tragedies, sonnets, and tomes of philosophy, they manufactured laws or martialled armies, opposed tyrants or fell their victims, or played the tyrant themselves. Engaged in the war of politics, a nation is little likely to be visited by the muses; they are loungers, who love quiet and sing in the shade. They come not upon the field until the battle is long over, and before they celebrate the actions of the dead, the moss has grown upon their graves.

The battle is now over in America, but it is no more than over, and it is doubtful, perhaps, whether her popular government must not always have something too bustling in it for the "gentle nine." A youth, conscious of talents, here sees the broad way to distinction open before him; the highest honors of the republic seem to tempt his ambition, and the first wish of his heart is to be a statesman. This secures able servants to the commonwealth and quickens the energy and intelligence of the whole people, but it causes all their talent to be put forth in the business of the day, and thus rather tends to impart dignity to the country rather than to procure immortality to individuals.

Those Americans who have been known in Europe as authors have been better known in their own country as active citizens of the republic, nor does my memory at this moment furnish me with more than two exceptions to this rule. The able political writers of the Revolution and of the busy years succeeding it were all soldiers or statesmen, who with difficulty, snatched a moment from the active duties which their country devolved upon them to enlighten their fellow citizens upon points of vital national importance. **Barlow,** known only in England as the author of *The Columbiad,* was a diplomatist, and an able political writer. The venerable Dwight was here held in honor, not as the author of *The Conquest of Canaan,* but as the patron of learning, the assiduous instructor of youth, and a popular and energetic writer of the day. I could in the same way designate many living characters whose masterly abilities have been felt in the cabinets of Europe, and which here are felt in every department of the civil government and in all the civic professions. These men, who in other countries would have enlarged the field of the national literature, here quicken the pulse of the national prosperity; eloquent in the senate, able in the cabinet, they fill the highest offices of the republic, and are repaid for their arduous and unceasing labours by the esteem of their fellow citizens and the growing strength of their country.

No nation has, perhaps, ever produced in the same term of years more high-minded patriots and able statesmen than the American. Who laid the foundation of these republics? Not robbers and bandits, as some of our ministerial journals would persuade their readers, but the wisest citizens of the wisest country then existing on the globe.

The **father of Virginia** was an English hero, who might adorn a tale of chivlary, a knight errant, who hunted honor through the world and came at last, in the pure love of liberty and daring adventure, to found a colony in the American wilderness. The **fathers of Maryland** were sages and philanthropists, who placed freedom of conscience before the privileges of birth or the enjoyments of luxury-English noblemen, whose birth was their poorest distinction, who taught religious and political equality in an age when both were unknown and, raised an asylum in this distant world for the persecuted of every sect and every clime. The fathers of New England were the **Hampdens** of Britain, who came to enjoy liberty and serve their austere God, among savage beasts and yet more savage men, bearing all things rather than the frowns of tyranny and the jurisdiction of hierarchs. Among them were men of erudition and of opinions before their age. The venerable **Roger Williams** (an advocate of religious as well as civil liberty) promulgated principles which were afterwards abetted by **Milton and Locke. Oglethorpe,** the father of Georgia, united the characters of a soldier, a legislator, a statesman, and a philanthropist. In his youth, he learned the art of war from **Prince Eugene;** in his maturer years he supported, in the British Parliament, the interests of his country and the claims of humanity. He was the leader of "the generous band, Who, touched with human woe, redressive searched Into the horrors of the gloomy jail." (a quotation from *Winter* by Thomson, Scottish poet (1700–1748), lines 359–361).

Pennsylvania wears the name of **her sage.** In fact there is not one of the colonies whose foundations were not laid by the hands of freemen and men wise in their generations. The political revolutions of England continued to throw into them many of her best and bravest citizens, many, too, of gentle birth and refined manners. The **Edict of Nantes** sent to them some of the most enlightened and virtuous sons of France; similar edicts, many of the noblest sons of Ireland. From the loins of such exiles proceeded the heroes of the Revolution. Until the very period of the quarrel which raised America to the rank of an independent nation, many of England's most distinguished families came to establish their **penates** in the New World, either from a spirit of adventure or attracted by the superior beauty of the climate and the frank and hospitable character of the people. We find, among others, the representative of the noble house of **Fairfax** foregoing the baronial honors of his native land for the liberty and simplicity of America, laying down his title and establishing himself in patriarchal magnificence in Virginia, abetting, in his old age, the cause of liberty, and wearing the simple and freely-bestowed dignities of a republic in lieu of the proud titles of an aristocracy.

But while America was thus sought by enlightened individuals, the Parliamentary speeches and pamphlets of the time show how little was known by the English community of the character and condition of the colonists.

Because the government had chosen at one time to make Virginia a **Botany Bay,** an insult which tended not a little to prepare her for the Revolution, the country of Franklin, Washington, Patrick Henry, Jefferson and a thousand other high-minded gentlemen, soldiers, orators, sages, and statesmen, was accounted a hive of pickpockets and illiterate hinds! Never was a national revolution conducted by greater men, by men more magnanimous, more self-devoted, and more maturely wise. And these men, too, were not self-elected, nor raised by chance to pilot the vessel of the state; they were called by the free voices of their fellow citizens to fill the various posts most suited to their genius. The people were as discriminating as their servants were able—not an illiterate multitude, hurried by a few popular orators or generous heroes into actions above themselves. They were a well-informed and well-organized community, animated with the feeling of liberty, but understanding the duties of citizens and the nature and end of civil government.

As colonies, the American states had, for the most part, lived under constitutions as essentially democratic as those of the present day; the chief difference, was that they were engaged in continual struggles to support them. In their first infancy, their future destiny was little foreseen. The patents, granted to the early settlers of New England, involved rights which the arbitrary monarchs who signed them had never dreamed of, but of this remissness they very speedily repented.

The colonial history of America would be alone sufficient to stamp the character of the **Stuart kings:** not content with torturing the consciences and outraging the rights of the English people in their own island, we find them hunting the patriots whom their tyranny had made exiles even in the howling wilderness of the New World, as if determined that a freeman should not live on the whole surface of the globe. One might pause to smile at the contradictory acts of Charles II, at once a thoughtless voluptuary and a rapacious tyrant, had they sported with matters of less value than the rights and happiness of mankind. This spoiled child of power carelessly set his hand to noblest charters ever accorded by a king to a people, and then waged an eternal war with the peaceful and far-distant handful of freemen who determined to abide by them.

The hard contest in which the young colonies were unceasingly engaged with the successive monarchs and varying administrations of the mother country sharpened the wits of their people. Occasionally their charters were broken down by force, but never was a fraction of their liberties yielded up by themselves or stolen from them without their knowledge: they struggled and bled for every right which fell. "To die by the hands of others rather than by their own" was the early motto of this people, nor, perhaps, could one have been imagined more calculated to render them invincible.

What is most worthy of admiration in the history of America is not merely the spirit of liberty, which has ever animated her people, but their perfect acquaintance with the science of government, which has ever saved that spirit from preying on itself. The sages who laid the foundation of her greatness possessed at once the pride of freemen and the knowledge of English freemen; in building the edifice, they knew how to lay the foundation; in preserving untouched the rights of each individual, they knew how to prevent his attacking those of his neighbour. They brought with them the experience of **the best governed nation then existing,** and, having felt in their own persons the errors inherent in that constitution, which had enlightened but only partly protected them, they knew what to shun as well as what to imitate in the new models which they here cast, leisurely and sagely, in a new and remote world. Thus possessed from the beginning of free institutions or else continually occupied in procuring or defending them, the colonies were well prepared to assume the character of independent states.

How seldom is it that history affords us the example of voluntary sacrifice on the part of separate communities to further the common good? It appears to me that the short history of America furnishes us with more examples of this kind than that of any other nation, ancient or modern.

TERMS AND DEFINITIONS

Barlow: Joel Barlow (1754–1812), American poet and patriot.

Best governed nation then existing: a reference, perhaps somewhat sarcastic, to Great Britain.

Botany Bay: famous British penal colony in Australia.

Cabinet of St. James: the seat of British government was in St. James Square, London.

Dwight: Timothy Dwight (1752–1817), American preacher and educator.

Edict of Nantes: proclamation issued by French king Henry IV in 1598 giving religious freedom to Protestants. Its revocation by Louis XIV in 1685 caused thousands of Huguenots (Protestants) to flee to the American colonies.

Fairfax: English nobleman who removed to Virginia and became a neighbor of George Washington.

father of Virginia: John Smith (1580–1631).

fathers of Maryland: The Calvert family, headed by George (1580–1632), the first Lord Baltimore.

Hampdens: prominent leaders of Parliament during the Civil War of the 1640s.

her sage: William Penn (1644–1718), Quaker founder of Pennsylvania.

Herculean infant: a reference to the United States as a young potential superpower.

Last War: The War of 1812, sometimes called the Second War for American Independence.

Liberty's untrained but consecrated band: America's amateur but highly motivated troops.

Milton and Locke: John Milton (1608–1674), English poet and John Locke (1632–1704), English philosopher and political theorist.

Oglethorpe: James Oglethorpe (1696–1785), English general and philanthropist.

Penates: new base of operations for a family.

Prince Eugene: Ruler of Savoy in Italy (1663–1736), a prominent Austrian general.

Roger Williams: religious reformer and founder of Rhode Island (1603–1683).

Stuart kings: James I (1566–1625), Charles I (1600–1649), Charles II (1630–1685), and James II (1633–1701), rulers of England and Scotland during the seventeenth century.

Tyranny's Armed Legions: the British military forces.

LORENZO DE ZAVALA

MEXICO MEASURES THE UNITED STATES

Illustrative of the great number of Latin Americans who looked to the United States as a model and inspiration for independence movements in their own countries was Lorenzo de Zavala of Mexico (1788–1836), ardent liberal, revolutionary, impresario, and government official. Erstwhile president of his country's Chamber of Deputies, signer of its 1824 constitution, governor of the state of Mexico, vice-president of the Texas Republic, and staunch foe of Mexican president Antonio López de Santa Ana, Zavala traveled in the United States as a political refugee in 1829 and compared its institutions to those in his own country in Journey in the United States of North America. *Unlike Miranda and Fearon, Zavala sees no tension between the growth of material prosperity and the realization of republican ideals. Like Wright, he regards the United States as a model to be studied and copied, especially by the newly independent nations of Latin America.*

It is true that one of the principal causes of the stability of the institutions of the United States of North America is the fortunate situation of the great majority of the people. But, side by side with those material enjoyments, the people place the sacred right of taking part in all transactions that have as their purpose the organizing of public powers, individual guarantees that assure them their laws, freedom to write and publish their opinions, freedom that they have to worship God according to their own consciences, and the deep and indestructible conviction of all the citizens that the law is equal for all, and that there are no institutions set up to favor one class, nor a hierarchy of privilege.

As he casts a rapid glance over this gigantic nation, which was born yesterday and today extends its arms from the Atlantic to the Pacific and the China Sea, the observer stands in deep thought and naturally asks himself the question, "What will be the final outcome of its greatness and prosperity?" It is not the power of conquests nor the force of arms, nor is it the illusions of a cult that unites the rules of morality with the mysteries of dogma. It is a new social order, brilliant, positive; a political system that has excluded all privilege, all distinctions consecrated by previous centuries, that has produced this prodigious creation. Standing before this political phenomenon, statesmen of all countries, philosophers, and economists have stopped to contemplate the

rapid march of this amazing people and, agreeing with one accord on the
never before seen prosperity of its inhabitants, side by side with sobriety, love
of work, unlimited liberty, domestic virtues, a creative activity, and an almost
fanatical religious feeling, they have made an effort to explain the causes of
these great results.

What have the ancient republics, the **anarchies of the Middle Ages,** or
the European confederations been in comparison with this extraordinary
nation? . . . Miserable attempts, although useful lessons, in order one day to
arrive at the establishment of the American system! Indeed, the political school
of the United States is a complete system, a classic work, unique, a discovery
such as that of printing, the compass, steam power, but a discovery that applies moral force to individual intelligences to move the great social machine,
which until our day has been dragged rather than directed, driven by **factious
springs** composed of heterogeneous combinations, a monstrous mosaic of
gathered bits of **feudalism,** superstition, **caste privilege,** legitimacies, sancti-
ties, and other elements against nature, and ruins of that flood of shadows
that inundated the world for twelve centuries.

Political experts of Europe may well turn to interpretations, prophecies,
conjectures, and doleful commentaries upon the constitutions, future, stability, and laws of the United States. What they cannot deny is that there is not,
nor ever has been, a people where the rights of the citizens were more respected, where individuals had more participation in government, where the
masses were more perfectly equal in all social pleasures. What sort of argument against its institutions is it to announce to a nation an unhappy future,
melancholy catastrophes, when the present is filled with life, happiness, and
good fortune?

Those who cannot resist the conviction of obvious facts of daily experience resort to doleful prophecies and predict now the dissolution of the great
republic. We shall answer them that the present good is better than hopes unrealized that there is, probably, no man or people who would prefer living
under oppression or in poverty to the happy and independent existence of that
republic; only because some **dyspeptic** politicians tell them that prosperous
situation will not last two hundred years. No, never will the strength of that
living and persevering example of social **Utopia** be weakened by such arguments. Be welcome to spy out their small and fleeting mob scenes; exaggerate
the heat of their public debates, the turmoil of their elections, their most curious aberrations of **Presbyterian fanaticism,** their **aversion to the black caste,**
their difficulties because of their system of slavery, their questions of tariffs,
momentary difficulties with their banks, make the most unfavorable comments concerning these political and economic crises; a positive solution, a
happy and quick insight comes forward to answer all your arguments. That
nation, full of life and movement, continues its course towards a goal and,
from the frontiers of Nova Scotia to New Mexico, the North American labors
only upon these principles: work and the rights of the citizen. His code is con-
cise, but clear, pure, and easily perceived. Complicated questions, which they

cannot decide since they are beyond the grasp of the less-educated classes, they refer entirely to that part of the people that has seemed to them to have best deserved their confidence because of a series of upright actions and decisions with beneficial results. . . .

In such a state of affairs, two hundred thousand Europeans come to the United States every year, seeking refuge in their wretchedness and recompense for their work and weariness, free from the deductions to which the taxes of the Old World subject them and from the shackles placed upon them by their systems more or less arbitrarily. With active and robust arms, they find work immediately and, within a few months, owners of land made fertile by their sweat, they found towns in spots a short time before inhabited only by wolves, bears, and other wild animals.

Populous cities spring up overnight; steamboats ply rivers and lakes thousands of leagues from the sea in lands just discovered and unknown to the civilized world; manufactured goods are transported by skillful craftsmen from Europe; flying printing presses that multiply thoughts and ideas spreading education, missionaries of sects that from Italy, Germany, France, England, and other places come to preach their gospel beliefs, each one as he understands and professes it, and that agree completely in moral principles. The love of God and of fellow man is the basis of all religions. Immigrants from Ireland, France, Mexico, Colombia, Spain, Italy, from both hemispheres, who in the political upheavals in their own countries, obliged to leave their fatherland, come to find out what the enviable tranquillity of that people consists of. Here you have the spectacle that the United States of the North presents. Add its maritime cities: that of New York, third port in the world, receiving in its bay three thousand boats each year that come loaded with products from the four corners of the world; that of New Orleans, the depot for a hundred cities that send to it their fruits by the boundless Mississippi, and by means of which a thousand communities are provided with foreign articles, remarkable cities because of the education of their inhabitants, their trade activity, the advantageous situation of their ports, the hospitality of their people, in short that openness, that assuredness, that liberty that all men enjoy, without the hindrances of passports, without the apparatus of soldiers, without the troublesome police, are circumstances that cannot fail to lead to prosperity and progress in all areas.

Those who accuse the North American people of being rude and unsociable fail to think about the elements that have gone into the makeup of that unusual nation. Persecuted families who came to seek liberty and a living in the frozen and uncivilized forests of northern America were forced to devote themselves to harsh and difficult tasks, to suffer painful privations, and to accustom themselves to a monotony of foods, words, and communication, to which the needs of their continual work condemned them. So here you have the forefathers of the North Americans. To these have been added the farmers and artists that have come later from Holland, Germany, and Ireland, people who are generally hard working, economical, **taciturn**, dedicated exclusively to their undertakings; and think then how there have come; the Washingtons, the Jeffersons, the Franklins, the Adams, the Clintons, the Madisons, the Clays, the Websters, the Livingstons, the Hamiltons, the Monroes, the Jacksons, the Van Burens, the Dwights, and many other statesmen, famous writers, profound sages, distinguished literary men, economists, and illustrious generals who have lifted the country to its high degree of prosperity and glory.

The people of the United States are wise, economical, and fond of accumulating capital for the future. That is the way it should be naturally. Because, in addition to their origins from which they inherit these qualities, in a climate like that, where man is obliged to work half the year for a severe season that confines him to his hearth and home, he cannot abandon himself to chance, confident in the fertility of the land and the cooperation of the seasons. The progress of primary education, to which Americans give a great deal of interest, and the ease of their communications, will, with time, make the manners of that people better and more sociable.

. . . I must not overlook the political relations that should progressively increase between the United States of the North and the United Mexican States, and the influences that the first undoubtedly exercises over the second. There is not a more seductive example for a nation that does not enjoy complete liberty than that of a neighbor where are found in all public acts, in all writings, lessons, and practices of an unlimited liberty, and in which instead of the disastrous cataclysms that have overwhelmed some peoples in their anarchical revolutions, or in their bloody despotic systems, one sees the spectacle of the peaceful joys of a numerous segment of the human race, lifted up by the simultaneous energy of its popular intelligence to an eminently free and happy social rank. Could the legislators of the Mexican nation resist so strong an influence, when they had in their hands the arranging of the destinies of their constituents? . . . But the example of thirteen republics born at the end of the last century in the **New Continent** that have not only maintained themselves but, by growing progressively, have become twenty-four, thus forming a great confederation, produced so great and universal a sensation in minds that forthwith ancient doctrines were considered to have been destroyed by such an event. The reasoning appeared to be conclusive. English colonies with which at that time the political and commercial world little concerned itself, which with just the name of colonies were supposed to be degraded, ignorant and enslaved, suddenly elevated to the rank of free nations, in consequence of a well-written declaration of the rights of man and of peoples. "Why should we not do the same thing," said many writers, politicians and philosophers of the Old World; "we the depositories of the sciences, masters of the human race, proprietors of the commerce of nations, heirs to the glory of the Greeks and the Romans, fathers of those emancipated peoples?" Great events that have come to pass subsequently in both hemispheres have provided sufficient proof of the irresistible impulse given to the social movement by the appearance of that bright star in the firmament of nations.

What should be then the consequences of the constant example near at hand presented by the United States of the North to the young Mexican nation, young and inexperienced, full of life and desirous of shaking off the remnants of its ancient chains? . . . In America things are different: Although the monarchical principle is not proscribed, it is evident that the opinion, as it can be applied to the emerging republics, is almost exclusively democratic.

TERMS AND DEFINITIONS

Anarchies of the Middle Ages: the almost complete absence of central government during the Middle Ages.
Aversion to the black caste: strong prejudice against African Americans, resulting in a closed system of discrimination and unfair treatment.
Caste privilege: rights peculiar only to the higher social classes.
Dyspeptic: morbid or excessively negative.
Factious springs: sources promoting divisions of opinion.

Feudalism: medieval system of government in which only a privileged few had any political power or influence.
New Continent: North America.
Presbyterian fanaticism: immoderate self-righteousness attributed to members of that religion by others.
Taciturn: habitually quiet and uncomplaining.
Utopia: imaginary perfect society with no serious social problems or inequities.

CAPTAIN BASIL HALL

BRITAIN PREFERS CANADA TO THE UNITED STATES

During both the American Revolution and the War of 1812, Canada and Great Britain had succeeded in repulsing an invasion of their southern neighbor, the United States. By the end of the latter conflict, it was a settled fact that Canada would remain part of the British Empire and, therefore, a growing number of British observers began to ponder seriously the question of the relative advantage of retaining Canada as opposed to the United States. One of those who presented a powerful argument in favor of the proposition that Great Britain was very better off with Canada than it would have been keeping the United States was Captain Basil Hall (1788–1844), a Scottish officer in the Royal Navy, who toured both countries during the 1820s and reported his findings in a three volume work entitled Travels In North America, In The Years 1827 And 1828. *He also gives Canadians a strong warning of the dangers of getting too involved with the expansionist young giant to its immediate south.*

I know that it has been often urged, that the export of British goods to the United States is infinitely greater now than it was to the Colonies before they revolted—and so undoubtedly it is. But people who make a stand on this position omit two considerations. Judging from the progress made by Nova Scotia, Canada, and the other remaining provinces, since they have been admitted to a thorough commercial companionship with the Mother Country, it is no more than fair to infer, that if the old Colonies, now forming the United States, had been originally treated in the same liberal spirit, they might never have deemed it their interest to withdraw from their allegiance. At this hour, therefore, they might have been, if not equally populous, perhaps more prosperous than they now are. Such, at least, is my own deliberate opinion, after having viewed both countries. The other consideration which people are apt to forget, is, that however great the mere export of our goods to the United States may be, every art is used by that country to discourage their carriage by British shipping. In spite of the doctrine of reciprocity, I could very seldom discover an English flag in the forest of masts at New York. What is the cause, I do not exactly know—such is the fact, and the documents just quoted show the result. A similar, or rather a much greater loss, of one of the largest and best of our nurseries for seaman, would therefore inevitably be sustained by the defection of these Colonies. And I have no hesitation in expressing my belief, that this one consideration alone outweighs, by many degrees, the whole expenses incurred, by us in maintaining the provinces.

By means of our present relations with these countries, we command, under all circumstances, a great variety of useful supplies of timber, naval stores, fish, and other articles, not only for ourselves, but for the important colonies in the West Indies, most of which we might in time of war be obliged to procure at a great disadvantage elsewhere, if we no longer possessed the **North American Provinces.**

These are a few of the direct benefits arising to us from the Colonies;— but the indirect ones are still more important. It seems to be a pretty general opinion, that there are only two alternatives for the Provinces in question;— one is, to remain in connexion with the Mother Country,—the other, to merge into the **Mare Magnum of the American Confederation.** The probability of their forming themselves into a separate, independent nation, is seldom dwelt upon, and is hardly to be contemplated.

The maritime resources of the United States at present are limited, by climate and other circumstances, almost exclusively to those parts of the ocean which lie on the Atlantic coast, to the northward and eastward of the Delaware; and although these are no doubt very important, and daily increasing, they are inconsiderable in comparison with those furnished by the coasts of the British Provinces. The American maritime line does not embrace above one-third of the distance that ours occupies; it possesses, no single port or bay—not even New York—to compare, in a naval point of view, with **Halifax,** and various other harbours of British North America, into which the largest line-of-battle ships can sail at all times of the year, and at all times of tide. It must also be recollected, that the climate of the Southern States is not suited to the production of hardy seamen; while the Western Section of the country, where the population is making the greatest strides, brings forward few of the essential attributes of a navy.

The fishermen, and other thorough-bred seamen, who crowd the shores of the British Provincial line of coast, are, numerically speaking, considerably

greater than those of the American shore alluded to. And I have the best authority for stating that these men are not only eminently loyal to England, but
heartily desirous of maintaining the union inviolate. Indeed, both they, and
their superiors in riches and station in the Colonies, have abundant reason, as
I shall endeavour to show by and by, for being sincere in these professions.

The idea that the United States can obtain possession of these provinces by
conquest, against the will of the inhabitants, is totally out of the question. If
the Colonists had substantial reason to be dissatisfied with the Mother Country, such a contingency might perhaps begin to be thought of; but as long as
they are treated as they have been for some years past, they must continue to
be fully as impregnable as any part of the Parent State. Besides which, the genius and practical structure of the American Government are such, as to render that country entirely unfit to engage in offensive hostile enterprises. The
militia of the provinces, even putting the assistance of regular troops out of the
question, is in every respect as good as that of their neighbours; and when fighting their own soil, they would be equally difficult to subdue. With a small additional assistance, therefore, from us, and supposing the Colonists to be
thoroughly loyal, which I believe they are, and am certain they have good reason to be, any chance of foreign conquest is altogether visionary. Every day
that the present friendly Colonial policy is persevered in, they will find more
and more reason to be staunch and true to themselves, and to us, besides dis-
covering more reason to rejoice that they are not what is called Independent—
a term which, if we analyze it closely, we shall commonly find a great misnomer.

If, however, we suppose the British Colonies added to the American
Union, the whole face of maritime affairs in that Republic would at once be
changed. I do not now ask whether such a change would, or would not, be
for the better, as respects either of the parties concerned on that side of the
water; but there can be little doubt it would be a matter of serious consequence
to England, to find the naval resources of the United States trebled, if not
quadrupled, at a blow,—while our own would be diminished, if not exactly in
the same ratio, certainly to an amount which, I am sure, if stated fairly would
induce many persons, who at present think lightly of the Colonies, to consider
them as much more important possessions than they are now supposed to be.

We must never forget that the "**cheap defence of nations**" is not to be balanced like a merchant's accounts—so many pounds debtor, and so many
pounds creditor. We must look deeper into our transactions, and not think
alone of what we expend, but of what we keep. And who is bold enough
today, that if, for the sake of a comparatively trivial saving of money, we relinquish these noble colonies, we shall not essentially weaken the foundations
of the wooden wall which is proverbially the safeguard of our island? Besides
all these considerations, I may just hint in passing, that the tenure by which
we hold the West India Islands, which employ nearly three hundred thousand
tons of British shipping, and fifteen thousand seamen, annually, would be
greatly weakened by the abstraction of these northern Provinces, from which
their chief supplies are derived. Neither do I say any thing of the Newfoundland or Labrador fisheries, those prolific nurseries of seamen, because their

advantages are now shared by the Americans and by the French. Yet it should not be forgotten, that, if the British Provinces were to become members of the American Union, it is more than doubtful whether these important maritime advantages would be any longer shared by foreign nations. . . .

When the British Provinces are compared with the United States, it is by no means too much to say, that the laws, which, in fact, are those of England, are out of all sight more steady; and, from that circumstance besides many others, better administered. The independence of the Colonial judiciary is much greater, not, indeed, nonminally, but in practice, for reasons which I shall have occasion to go into minutely in treating of this branch of the American government. As to personal freedom and the protection of property, therefore, the Colonists are, at least, equal to the Americans, and, I fully believe, much more secure. The foundations of those powers which preserve social order, are certainly more stable and better organized in the Provinces than in the United States. Their rulers do not derive their authority from those over whom their power is to be exercised; they look up, and not down, for approbation, and can, therefore, use that authority with more genuine independence. This doctrine, of course, is **scouted** in the United States as altogether **heterodox;** but the Colonies, when prompted to compare their condition with that of their neighbours, I am quite certain, will never find cause to regret the distinctions which arise from this source; and that they feel this as they ought to do, I know by ample experience.

In the United States, places of power and eminence depend entirely upon popular caprice; and, consequently, the candidate must often submit, per force, to much that is repugnant to the best feelings of his nature. Where station depends for its continuance upon the fluctuating will of a giddy populace, it must be frequently bestowed without merit, and still more frequently bestowed without crime.

In the British Provinces, all situations of honor or profit are derived from the crown. They are no doubt sometimes bestowed on improper persons, and are obtained by improper means. But can this be prevented by any human devices yet invented? Are such things prevented by the democratical institutions of the United States? After all, it is perhaps better to be subservient to a monarch than to a mob. If a man must condescend to smile in order to obtain a selfish end, it is probable his character will suffer less by bowing to one man above him, than by cringing to a thousand below.

In the Colonies, men are content to insist upon equality of rights, and their protection, without ever dreaming of the visionary doctrine of universal equality amongst persons or property. In looking about also for preferments suited to their station and capacity, they are not obliged to stoop before they attempt to soar. Their flights, it may be said, are of no great elevation; but those who sincerely desire to reach the comparative eminence which the Provincial offices bestow, may, generally speaking, be convinced, that respectability of conduct, united with sufficient talent and industry for the due performance of public duties, will seldom fail to attract the attention of government; and when such men once gain the station to which they aspire, and which their knowledge and talents enable them to fill with utility, they are sure to retain their place, under a system of mutual confidence and proper responsibility, as long as they comply conscientiously and diligently with the obligations imposed upon them.

Thus all that influential class of men in the Colonies who are actuated by ambition, whether on the great or on the small scale, have little reason to wish an exchange of their present constitutions for those of the stormy democracy in their neigbourhood. On the other hand, by means of the **elective franchise,** which is very generally enjoyed, the great bulk of the people retain in their own hands sufficient political influence to make them feel quite free and truly independent in the situation where nature has placed them. Happily, also, the exercise of their political rights does not interfere to any hurtful degree with their social duties, nor carry them at all out of their proper sphere of life.

Thus the community at large possess fully much, if not more, freedom than their neighbours, while the best informed and ablest members of it have better, and incomparably more permanent and definite, stimulants to honest ambition than the same class of men in the United States. Neither is the peace of society disturbed by incessant contentions for temporary power, and, the inhabitants of the Colonies are enabled to manage their internal affairs upon more uniform principles, because they are confided to the hands of experienced and able men. All this is arranged in direct defiance and ridicule, I admit, of the doctrine of universal equality; but, nevertheless, in a manner strictly conformable to the decrees of Providence, as far as they are made known to us by the lights of experience and plain common sense.

These advantages, and many others of a similar character, would immediately be lost to the Colonies, if their connexion with England were dissolved; and the conviction that this is true, has so firm a hold on every reflecting mind in those countries, that I feel confident of their not only confirming it more and more every day, but that they will seize every possible opportunity of assimilating their condition, and intertwining their fortunes still more with a nation, whose constitution has at all events the merit of working well, and whose prosperity seems to be at least equal to that of any other.

The colonists should bear in mind that, as they are really and truly British Subjects, they enjoy in common with the natives of England, the privilege of trading from port to port anywhere in the Empire at large, which no other countries possess. Nor is this fair title to equal rights with ourselves any longer counterbalanced, as it was a few years ago, by impolitic restrictions upon their intercourse with foreigners. Wherever they now choose to go they carry along with them the very same privileges which are allowed to the natives of the Old Country, and like them reap all the benefit of treaties made between foreign nations and England. Thus they are as truly members of this powerful empire as we in Scotland are, and they can no more be oppressed or molested by any other nation than we can be. Meanwhile, they enjoy all the other advantages of Englishmen, without being called upon to share almost any of their burdens. The weight of taxation in every one of the British Colonies, is less than in any of the United States; while the whole expense of the general defence, and especially that of creating, and maintaining a navy, and keeping up a se-ries of powerful fortresses, is paid by England without our demanding any contribution from them.

The revenues which the Colonies derive from foreign trade are applied by their own legislatures to the internal improvement of the respective provinces;—whereas, were they to become members of the American Confed-eracy, all such duties would be subjected to the control of the Congress at Washington—and every improvement then made, would be at the expense of direct taxation, from which they are now exempt. They should recollect, also, that in the event of a separation, they would lose the enormous benefit they now derive from the duties on their timber and corn being much lower in Eng-land than those levied on the same, or even better commodities, coming from other countries. That we benefit by this, in the long run, even more than the Colonies do, I fully believe; but still the loss to them of such sources of profit would be immense, in case of the connexion being broken.

TERMS AND DEFINITIONS

"Cheap defence of nations": achieving the best defense system for the least cost.
Elective franchise: right to vote.
Halifax: chief port city of Nova Scotia.

Heterodox: heretical or unpatriotic.
Mare Magnum of the American Confederation: union of Canada and the United States.
North American Provinces: Canada.
Scouted: scorned or ridiculed.

THINKING THINGS THROUGH

1. What effects, if any, do you think that the later American annexation of Texas and American–Mexican War might have had on Zavala's impressions of the United States?

2. In what ways do Miranda and Fearon agree and disagree on the direction being taken by the United States?

3. Do you feel that Wright and Zavala were overly optimistic in their assess-ments of the new nation? In what ways? Why?

4. Do you think that Hall really believed that Britain was better off with Canada instead of the United States or was he just trying to make the best of a bad situation? If you were a Canadian, would his analysis of the dangers of union with the United States have been convincing?

5. What overall impressions of the prospects of the United States would a contemporary reader have gotten from reading all five of these selections?

7

DISCOVERING AN AMERICAN CHARACTER

A. The International Context

During the three decades preceding the outbreak of the Civil War, the United States experienced tremendous growth in size, population, technological innovation, agricultural and industrial development, urbanization, and ethnocultural diversity. The changes wrought by this rapid and massive transformation gave rise to the first widespread reform movements in the nation's history. At the same time, most American states took important steps toward democratizing the political process through a number of structural changes. Permeating and transcending all of these developments and movements was the escalating debate over the place of slavery in American society and culture, a conflict that increasingly polarized the country. Caught up in these swirling currents, the nation experienced the 1850s as a decade of perpetual crisis that constituted a fitting prelude to the bloody armed conflict soon to ravage it.

Although most Americans fixed their gaze resolutely inward during those fateful years, the country itself steadily strengthened its connections to the outside world in a variety of areas. Moreover, the historical processes of industrialization, urbanization, and modernization that underlay American development differed only in degree and detail, not in kind, from those that transformed much of western and central Europe during the same period. In addition, its phenomenal development and growing importance significantly heightened the interest of other nations toward almost all things American.

Thanks to its territorial expansion between 1803 and 1853, the United States increased its geographical area by nearly 240 percent. Settlers flocked to the Pacific and Gulf coasts, leapfrogging over the Great Plains and the Rocky Mountains to Oregon and California. By the eve of the Civil War, migrants were already beginning to pour into the newly organized territories of Nebraska, Kansas, Washington, Utah, and New Mexico. During that same period, the number of states in the Union rose from twenty-four to thirty-three, with the addition of Michigan, Wisconsin, Iowa, Minnesota, Texas, California, Oregon, Florida, and Arkansas.

Fed by natural increase and immigration, the population of the United States soared from just under thirteen million in 1830 to well over thirty-one million in 1860, a staggering growth rate of 146 percent. While the United States remained a predominantly rural country in 1860, nearly one American in five lived in what the Census Bureau designated as "urban places," compared to just over one in twelve thirty years earlier. This urban growth was heavily concentrated in the northeastern quadrant, where the population of the New York City–Brooklyn metropolitan area increased eightfold between 1830 and 1860, while that of Philadelphia quintupled, that of Baltimore tripled, and that of Boston quadrupled. Rapid urbanization also began to transform the Mississippi and Ohio River valleys and the upper Great Lakes region, where New Orleans, Cincinnati, St. Louis, Buffalo, Cleveland, Detroit, Louisville, and Milwaukee all enjoyed phenomenal growth rates. Chicago, nonexistent in 1830, had already achieved a population of 109,260 by 1860. Those figures far outstripped any that the world had thus far witnessed, even surpassing that of Manchester and other English industrial cities. America's urban network, linked by strands of transportation and communication, was beginning to rival that of northwestern Europe. Its proliferation of urban places was in direct contrast to the pattern in most other countries, where one or two large cities burgeoned in a predominantly rural landscape. While this urban explosion was unquestionably a sign of the country's fundamental strength, it also produced the first of the nation's periodic "urban crises," as residents found themselves plagued by overwhelming problems of overcrowding, poverty, vice, crime, epidemic disease, noise, air, and water pollution, and inadequate housing, and an appalling lack of municipal services with which to combat them.

The economic engine that drove this tremendous expansion became tremendously larger and more powerful in the thirty years before the Civil War. The invention of the steel plow, the automatic reaper, and the threshing machine, combined with new varieties of seeds, revolutionized cereal grain agriculture and transformed the American Midwest into the world's breadbasket. The opening of the Great Plains in the 1850s guaranteed that the country's agricultural hegemony would become even more impressive. The processing of nature's abundance to produce food, textiles, lumber, farm implements, and rudimentary machinery paved the way for the country's industrial future. The era from 1830 to 1880 was unquestionably America's Age of Iron, with the railroad and shipping industries providing a rapidly expanding market, and new discoveries in heating and manufacturing techniques steadily improving the quality of the product. The invention and proliferation of the railroad and the telegraph relentlessly shrank the distances between raw materials and manufacturers, facilitating the construction of extensive marketing networks. In this rapid and massive industrialization, the United States largely emulated Great Britain, which had pioneered that development in the mid-eighteenth century. Along with the nations of northwestern Europe, the United States benefited substantially from the exportation, intentional or otherwise, of British technology, entrepreneurship, and capital. By the time of its Civil War, the United States had already begun to contest Great Britain, Prussia, and France for industrial supremacy.

To service those burgeoning demands, Americans once again relied upon Great Britain to provide them with what one historian has called "perhaps the most profound economic development in mid-nineteenth century America: the rise of the factory." By the first decades of the next century, European nations would be hastening to copy American methods of mass production, the assembly line, vertical integration, and marketing networks. Fueled by water and steam power, manufacturing machinery became increasingly larger and more productive, demanding an ever bigger workforce under a single roof. The development of that machinery resulted from a dramatic increase in inventions between 1830 and 1860, as the number of patents issued per year leaped from 544 to 4,778. The country's remarkable economic expansion during these years greatly augmented national wealth and earned it the admiration and envy of the rest of the world, but it also resulted in a permanent loss of economic independence for millions of people, as well as a potentially

*dangerous gap in wealth and income for a nation that adver-
tised itself as the bastion of equal opportunity.*

*Much of the workforce and market that sustained this
economic spurt was supplied by a substantial increase in
European immigration. A relative trickle prior to 1840, immigration quickly swelled to a flood tide over the next two
decades. Between 1844 and 1854 alone, some three million
people entered the country to become permanent residents,
nearly one-quarter of its total population in 1830. While the
United States was the leading receiver of European immigrants during this time period, it was by no means the only
one. Immigration to the United States was an important segment of a general European diaspora, which was primarily a
response to the dislocations forced by the agricultural and industrial revolutions. Millions more were "voting with their
feet" by migrating from countryside to city, from one European country to another, and to other such New World destinations as Canada, Brazil, Argentina, Australia, and New
Zealand. The vast majority of immigrants to the United
States settled in the Northeast and upper Great Lakes regions, and found work in industry and agriculture, usually
near the lower rungs of the socioeconomic ladder. The
tremendous influx of immigrants gave rise to a virulent nativist or "Know-Nothing" movement that also appealed to
many who were seeking scapegoats for economic dislocations
and diversion from the increasingly ominous debate over
slavery. Despite these manifestations of hostility, however,
the United States continued to be a favorite destination for
the growing number of European immigrants over the next
several decades.*

*To some extent, the nativist movement of the 1840s and
1850s was symptomatic of a people struggling to find its national identity, and to differentiate itself more sharply from
Europe. That quest also manifested itself in the development
of a distinctive American culture. Although borrowing liber-
ally from the romantic movement that was permeating European arts and letters, American artists and intellectuals
infused it with heavy doses of egalitarianism, democracy, social mobility, and pietism. A legion of literary giants laid the
foundations of a distinctively American literature, while the
Transcendentalists evolved the principles of the first truly
American philosophy. The establishment of a public school
system, the rise of the "penny press," and the spread of the
lyceum movement all bespoke a growing commitment to*

widespread popular education. The proliferation of "revivalism" signaled the maturation of an American religious tradition that was more emotional, assertive, and socially activist than its European antecedents. Although still lagging far behind Europe, the United States had taken great strides towards finding its own cultural niche by 1860. Its finest products were beginning to gain attention, and even some respect, in other parts of the world.

Meanwhile, the country's remarkable growth was reflected in its increasing involvement in international trade and diplomacy. Between 1843 and 1860, the combined value of American imports and exports more than quintupled. For all its economic development, however, the United States consistently suffered from an unfavorable balance of trade during the period. Only its sizeable exports of wheat, flour, and California gold, and Southern cotton prevented the trade deficit from reaching catastrophic proportions. To offset its European losses, the country looked increasingly to Asia and Latin America—what would later be called "the Pacific Rim." First by clipper ship, and then by steamship, Americans plied the seas in search of expanding markets. In the 1844 Treaty of Wanghai, the United States secured permission to operate in five Chinese port cities, opening the way for a trade that would fire the imagination of Americans to the present day. A decade later, Commodore Matthew Perry used "gunboat diplomacy" to secure the first outside access to Japanese ports, which had been closed to the West for nearly three centuries. Two years later, the modernizing nation of Siam significantly increased the trading privileges that it had granted to the United States twenty years earlier. Sitting astride these Pacific trade routes, Hawaii, too, became a favorite economic partner for Yankee merchants. "Pacific fever" also fueled growing interest in constructing a route across Central America to link the two great oceans, an ambition that almost triggered war with Great Britain, before the Clayton-Bulwer Treaty of 1850 cooled tempers. The growing volume of trade with Latin America also lay at least partially behind American efforts to purchase Cuba, before the furor over the Ostend Manifesto in 1854 forced a halt. Intensifying commercial rivalry with Great Britain in the Pacific and North Atlantic, as well as the Caribbean, also spawned several crises between the two countries, before the signing of the Webster-Ashburton Treaty of 1842 and the peaceful settlement of the Oregon dispute in 1846 lessened tensions considerably.

B. International Views

The remarkable development of the United States during this brief thirty year span engendered tremendous interest in other parts of the world. One result of this celebrity was a substantial outpouring of books penned by foreign visitors attempting to understand, interpret, and explain almost every aspect of the country's society, economy, polity, and culture. Despite differences in detail, emphasis, and interpretation, these various accounts manifested a fairly universal consensus on several major points. Americans, the writers agreed, had a sense of personal liberty so highly developed and intensely felt that it led to an abiding suspicion of, and hostility toward, authority—particularly where government was concerned. Americans were absolutely convinced of their own newness and uniqueness, yet highly sensitive to charges that they were out of touch with European culture. They worshiped the practical and the commercial—and disdained the intrinsic value of the purely intellectual and aesthetic. They were intensely future-oriented and adapted to change far more readily than did Europeans. They were fascinated with technology and believed that it would allow them to master their environment and overcome any obstacle, natural or otherwise. Most of all, foreign observers, even those inclined to be hostile or condescending toward American society and culture, were favorably impressed with how quickly and effectively the American experiment in self-government matured and adapted to the forces of democratization.

Among the most perceptive and articulate foreign observers of the United States between 1830 and 1860 were a French economist, Michel Chevalier, an Austrian-born writer, Francis Grund, South American educator-statesman Domingo Faustino Sarmiento, German journalist Julius Moritz Busch, and a British military officer, George Warburton. The first was generally lavish in his praise of the ordinary American, but disdainful of the country's lack of an educated and cultured upper class dedicated to the finer things of life. The second explored the roots of American patriotism, compared it to the European variety, and speculated on the relationship between political freedom and the opportunities for social mobility. The third criticized "North Americans" for their "moral defects," allegedly magnified by excessive liberty and equality, but also acknowledged the existence of powerful social forces working to civilize what might otherwise degenerate into a nation of barbarians. The fourth candidly discussed the growing conflict between the

*American people's dominant striving for individual liberty
and the disturbing "subordinate characteristics" that threatened to prevent the ultimate realization of that ideal. The fifth
saw not one nation, but three, each with its own distinctive
society and culture, a condition that would eventually lead to
the dissolution of the precarious federal political union. In
the process, all five foreign observers gave eloquent testimony
to tension between the forces of unity and diversity that were
shaping the American character.*

MICHEL CHEVALIER

The "Initiated" American Multitudes

*Plainly "bullish on America" was Michel Chevalier (1806–1879), a French economist who was
once a follower of socialist theoretician Claude-Henri de Rouvroy, Comte de Saint-Simon, and
later became a powerful advocate of free trade. Imprisoned during his country's Revolution of
1830, he recanted many of his radical views and later joined the Liberal government of Adolphe
Thiers, who sent him to the United States in 1832 in order to study American water and rail-
way systems. During his stay of eighteen months, Chevalier traveled widely, later recounting his
observations and conclusions in Society, Manners, and Politics in the United States: Letters on
North America. In it, he argued that the American masses were far more energetic and receptive
to innovation, and far less superstitious, than were their French counterparts. However, he
found very little to admire in those who constituted the "upper classes" of the young nation,
and faulted American culture for its lack of spiritual or aesthetic values.*

An eminent philosopher, . . . who is an honor to the French name, defines the
progress of the human race in its slow and majestic pilgrimage round our
globe by the term "initiation". Following out this thought, we may pronounce
North America, at least the nonslaveholding States, to be already in advance
of us, for in many respects what among us is accessible only to a small number of the elect has become common property in the United States and is
familiar to the vulgar. The conquests of the human mind to which the Reformation gave the signal, and the impulse and the great discoveries of science
and art which in Europe are yet concealed from the general eye by the ban-
dage of ignorance and the mists of theory, are in America exposed to the vulgar gaze and placed within the reach of all. There the multitude touches and
handles them at will. Examine the population of our rural districts, sound the
brains of our peasants, and you will find that the spring of all their actions is
a confused medley of biblical parables with the legends of gross superstition.
Try the same operation on an American farmer and you will find that the great
scriptural traditions are harmoniously combined in his mind with the principles of modern science as taught by **Bacon** and **Descartes,** with the doctrine of

moral and religious independence proclaimed by Luther, and with the still more recent notions of political freedom. He is one of the initiated.

Among us the powerful instruments and machinery of science and art, the steam engine, the balloon, the **voltaic pile,** the lightning rod, inspire the multitude with a religious dread. In France, out of a hundred peasants in the back areas of our provinces you will not find one who, having witnessed their effects, would dare to lay his hand upon them; they would fear to be struck dead like the sacriligious wretch who touched the **ark of the Lord.** But to the American, on the contrary, these are all familiar objects; he knows them all by name, at least, and he feels that they are his. To the French peasant they are mysterious and terrible beings, like the Negro's **fetish** or the Indian's **manitou,** but to the cultivator of the western wilds they are what they are to a member of the **Institute,** tools, instruments of labor, or science. He is one of the initiated.

There is no **profanum vulgus** in the United States, at least among the whites. This is true not only in regard to steam engines and electrical phenomena, but the American multitude is also much more completely initiated than the European mass in all that concerns domestic relations and the household. The marriage tie is held more sacred among the lowest classes of American society than among the middle class of Europe. Although the marriage ceremony has fewer forms than among us and the connection is more easily dissolved, cases of adultery are extremely rare. The unfaithful wife would be a lost woman; the man who should seduce a woman or be known to have an illicit connection would be excommunicated by the popular clamor. In the United States, even the man of the laboring class is more completely initiated in the obligations of the stronger sex toward the weaker than most men of the middle class in France. Not only does the American mechanic and farmer spare his wife as much as possible all the hard work and employment unsuitable to the sex, but he exhibits toward her and every other woman a degree of attention and respect which is unknown to many persons among us who pride themselves on their education and refinement. In public places and in public conveyances in the United States, no man, whatever may be his talents and his services, is treated with any particular attention; no precedence or privilege is allowed him; for all men are equal. But a woman, whatever may be the condition and fortune of her husband, is sure of commanding universal respect and attention.

In political affairs, the American mass has reached a much higher degree of initiation than the European mass, for it does not need to be governed. Every man here has in himself the principle of self-government in a much higher degree and is more fit to take a part in public affairs. It is also more fully initiated in another order of things which is closely connected with politics and morals, that is, in all that relates to labor. The American mechanic is a better workman; he loves his work more than the European. He is initiated not merely in the hardships, but also in the rewards of industry. He dresses like a member of Congress; his wife and daughters are dressed like the wife and daughters of a rich New York merchant and, like them, follow the Paris fashions. His house is warm, neat, and comfortable; his table is almost as plentifully provided as that of the wealthiest of his fellow citizens. In this country, articles of the first necessity for whites embrace several objects which among us are articles of luxury, not merely among the lower middle classes.

The American mass is more deeply initiated in what belongs to the dignity of man, or at least to its own dignity, than the corresponding classes in Europe. The American worker is full of self-respect; and he shows it not only by an extreme sensibility, by pretensions which to the European bourgeoisie would appear extraordinary, and by his reluctance to make use of the term *master,* for which he substitutes that of *employer,* but also by good faith and scrupulous exactness in his engagements. He is above those vices of slavery, such as theft and lying, which are so prevalent among hirelings with us, particularly among those of the towns and their factories. The French worker is more respectful and submissive in his manners, but, hard-pressed by poverty and surrounded by temptations, he rarely neglects a chance of cheating his bourgeois when he can do it with impunity. The worker of **Lyons** secretly steals silk, that of **Rheims** gold lace. There are, doubtless, frauds committed in America; more than one smart fellow has his conscience oppressed with numerous **peccadilloes.** How many strolling Yankee peddlers have sold charcoal for indigo and **soapstone** for soap to the rural housewives? But, in the United States, these petty frauds are rare exceptions. The character of the American workman is, to a high degree, honorable and excites the envy of the European, when the latter compares the prospect here with the aspect of things in his own country. What I have said about the worker applies still more strongly to the farmer; not being obliged like the worker to argue every day with an employer over the price of his labor, surrounded by equals, and a stranger to the seductions of the city, the American farmer possesses the good qualities of the worker in at least an equal degree, and has his faults in a much less degree. He is less unjust toward, and less jealous of, the richer or more cultivated classes.

If, then, we examine the condition of the American multitude, we find it on the whole much superior to that of the mass in Europe. It is true that it appears to be almost completely destitute of certain faculties which are possessed by the European populace. There are, for instance, at times a hundredfold more gleams of taste and poetical genius in the brain of the most **beggarly lazzarone** of Naples than in that of the republican mechanic or farmer of the New World. The houseless young vagabonds of Paris have transient flashes of chivalric feeling and greatness of soul which the American worker never equals. This is because the national character of the Italians is impregnated with a love of art and because generous sentiments are one of the distinguished traits of the French character. The very lowest classes of each nation have some portion of the national spirit. But it does not belong to the multitude to be poets and artists in Italy, or models of chivalry in France. Their perfection, above all and in every country, consists in knowing and fulfilling their duties to God, to their country, to their families, to themselves, in assiduous and honest industry, in being good citizens, good husbands, and good fathers; in providing for the welfare and guarding the virtue of those dependent upon them. In order to make a fair comparison between the multitude in Europe and the multitude in America, we should consider them in reference to these qualities; for these belong to all varieties of the human race and all forms of civilization, and upon their development and stability among the mass depends the strength of empires. . . .

American democracy certainly has its faults, and I do not think that I can be accused of having extenuated them. I have not concealed its rude demands upon the higher classes, nor its haughty airs of superiority to other nations. I will even admit that, in many respects, it is rather as a class and in the lump that it recommends itself to favor. The individuals that compose it are destitute of those hearty and affectionate qualities by which our French peasantry would be distinguished if it were once delivered from the wretchedness which now brutalizes it. But it is in the mass and as a whole that I now judge the American multitude. . . .

Far be it from me to apologize for the **brutal and savage and sometimes bloody excesses** which have lately been so often repeated in most of the large towns in the United States. Should they continue, the American democracy will be degraded and will lose forever the high position it now occupies. But criminal as these acts are, it would be unjust to impute them to the American people and to condemn to ignominy the whole body of these incomparable laborers. Popular excesses in all countries are the work of an imperceptible minority, which the existing system in the United States is powerless to restrain. That system needs, then, some amendment which shall enable it to preserve the good qualities of the nation in their purity and which, indeed, seems already on the point of being introduced, for theories of absolute liberty are evidently losing favor in the United States.

It would be a mistake to infer from what has been said that American civilization is superior to our own. The multitude in the United States is superior to the multitude in Europe; but the higher classes in the New World are inferior to those of the Old, although the merits of the latter are more virtual than real and belong rather to the past or the future than to the present; for the higher classes in Europe, both aristocracy and bourgeoisie, turn their good qualities to little account either on behalf of themselves or the people. The higher classes in the United States, taken as a whole and with only some exceptions, have the air and attitude of the vanquished; they bear the mark of defeat on their front. As they have been always and in almost all circumstances much mingled with the crowd, both parties have naturally borrowed many habits and feelings from each other. This exchange has been advantageous to the multitude but less so to the higher classes. Each of the two is, therefore, superior in one of the two great elements of society and inferior in the other. This is the system of compensation.

TERMS AND DEFINITIONS

Ark of the Lord: Ark of the Covenant, the fundamental symbol of Judaism.

Bacon: Francis Bacon (1561–1626), English writer and politician who helped popularize the experimental, inductive method of research.

Beggarly lazzarone: homeless street people who beg for a living.

Brutal and savage and sometimes bloody excesses: reference to the rash of racist and anti-immigrant riots that plagued U.S. cities in the antebellum period.

Descartes: René Descartes (1596–1650), French mathematician and philosopher who discovered analytical geometry and is remembered for positing "I think, therefore I am".

Fetish: an object believed to have supernatural power for healing, etc.

Institute: the most prestigious association of intellectuals and scientists in France.

Lyons: city in France famous for silk production.

Manitou: Algonquian term for the spirit or life force believed to animate the entire world and everything in it.

Profanum vulgus: Latin idiom meaning uneducated masses of people.

Peccadilloes: minor fault or sin.

Rheims: city in France where kings were crowned and noted for the production of lace.

Soapstone: a soft talc in rock form often mistaken for soap.

Voltaic pile: an early form of electrical battery.

FRANCIS GRUND

PATRIOTISM, AMERICAN STYLE

Having spent nearly a decade in the United States before he wrote The Americans in Their Moral, Social, and Political Relations *in 1837, Austrian immigrant Francis Grund (1798–1863) had ample opportunity to compare the brand of patriotism that was developing in his new home with that which had long prevailed in Europe. Grund immigrated to the United States at the age of twenty-nine and spent much of his time writing school textbooks; he later wrote campaign biographies of several presidential candidates aimed at galvanizing support among German-speaking voters. He also published a Philadelphia-based journal,* Age, *until his death during the Civil War. While European patriotism was grounded in ties of "blood, land, and belief," Grund argues, the American brand rested almost entirely upon shared belief in the political principles expressed in the Declaration of Independence and the Constitution. In addition, he sees a powerful and necessary connection between that political philosophy and "the hope of acquiring property and consideration, which their institutions hold out to all persons, without distinction of birth or parentage."*

Though the Americans, in general, have fewer prejudices than any nation in Europe, and possess, therefore, less of a national character, though they have no community of religious feeling, yet there exists amongst them an uniformity of thought and sentiment, which is sufficient to mark them as a distinct people. These sentiments are principally political, or have reference to their habits of industry. The Americans present the singular spectacle of a people united together

by no other ties than those of excellent laws and equal justice, for the maintenance of which their lives, their fortunes, and their sacred honors stand mutually pledged. The American commonwealth consists of a community of reason
and good sense; its empire, therefore, is the largest, and its basis the most unal-
terable on which the prosperity of a people was ever established. They revere
the theory and foundation of their government, to which they transfer most of
their local attachments, their love of country, and those generous sentiments,
which the contemplation of the gigantic scenery which surrounds them is calculated to inspire. There is, at present, no room for **idyllic poesy** and romance, but
the energetic development of the nation may soon furnish matter for an epic.

An American does not love his country as a Frenchman loves France, or an
Englishman England: America is to him but the physical means of establishing
a moral power—the medium through which his mind operates—"the local
habitation" of his political doctrines. His country is in his understanding; he
carries it with him wherever he goes, whether he emigrates to the shores of the
Pacific or the Gulf of Mexico; his home is wherever he finds minds congenial
with his own. Americans have been reproached with want of love for their native country but, with such an enlightened attachment to their moral and political institutions, it is difficult to fix upon the limits of the empire which must
eventually be theirs, or upon the boundary line which they shall not overleap
in their progress. The patriotism of the Americans is not confined either to a
love of their country, or to those who are of the same origin with them. It relates to the mind, and to the habits of thinking and reasoning. Whoever thinks
as they do is, morally speaking, a citizen of their community, and whoever en-
tertains opinions in opposition to their established theory of government, must
be considered a natural enemy to their country.

The moral influence of this process of reasoning on the prospects and future power of the United States is incalculable. It has made America the representative of a doctrine which is fast gaining ground throughout the civilized
world; it has extended her physical and moral dominion, and created for her
friends and allies in every nation and in every clime. It has made her cause the
cause of humanity, and her success the triumph of reason over ignorance and
prejudice. What people could now make war on America, without retarding
the progress of their own freedom? What arm would not drop palsied in aim-
ing a blow at American liberty? What mariner would wish to extinguish the
beacon-light which directs the course of his navigation? It has made the Americans strong within themselves, and invulnerable from without. Their political
doctrines have become the religion and confession of the people of all countries. Like the truths of Christianity, they have had their apostles and their
martyrs and, like those truths, they are destined to become the universal faith
of mankind.

Neither can the patriotism of the Americans be called a vague and indis-
tinct feeling; on the contrary, it is clear and defined, and has a definite aim. It
is not an instinctive attachment to scenes with which they are acquainted from
childhood, or to men to whose familiar converse they are accustomed. It consists in the love of principles, for which they are ready to make every sacrifice,

and which, in the outset, they preferred to their homes. The American pilgrims carried their country in their hearts, and their government in their minds. Their character was formed before they touched the soil which was to nourish them, and has ever since remained superior to local circumstances. The Americans entered the wilderness as masters, determined to subdue it; and not as children of nature, nursed and brought up in its bosom. They could not at first love what was not their own; and when it became theirs, they had already changed its face. The succession of changes was so rapid that scarcely one could leave a permanent impression on their minds. They treated nature as a conquered subject; not as a mother who gave them birth. They were the children of another world, who came thither to burn, ransack, and destroy, and not to preserve what they had found. They burned the forests, dug up the bowels of the earth, diverted rivers from their course, or united them at their pleasure; and annihilated the distances which separated the North from the South, and the East from the West.

I have said that the patriotism of Americans is not a vague and indefinite feeling, but that it is consisted in a strong attachment to principles. I say so still. The principles which they cherish are those of liberty, and they are sufficient to raise them to a proud eminence amongst the nations of the earth. They establish a moral empire more durable than human feelings, and less susceptible of changes. I will now add that the Americans love their country, not, indeed, as it is, but as it will be. They do not love the land of their fathers, but they are sincerely attached to that which their children are destined to inherit. They live in the future, and make their country as they go on.

It often appeared to me as if the whole property of the United States was only held by the Americans in trust for their children, and that they were prepared to render a religious account of their stewardship. See with what willingness they labor to secure an independence to their children! with what readiness they take a part in the national improvements of their country! with what cheerfulness they quit an already fertilized soil, and emigrate to the "far west," to make more room for their offspring! how ready they are to invest their fortunes in undertakings which can only benefit their progeny! Are these not proofs of a genuine patriotism? Is this not the most exalted love of country of which history furnishes us with a record? A mere local attachment to the soil, however it may influence the domestic happiness of a people, is, of itself, hardly capable of imparting that national impulse which directs the feelings and actions of individuals to a common center, and makes them sacrifice their own private interests to the general good of the whole. It must be a spiritual essence, a community of the highest faculties of the mind, which shall make men look on one another as brethren, and unite them as members of one and the same family. It was the spirit of the Romans which created and preserved Rome, as it was the highest principles of religion which united the Israelites into a nation, and led them out of the land of bondage. It was religious liberty which led to the settlement of the British American colonies; and the same feeling is yet sending thousands to the shores of the New World. It is the cement of the American confederacy, and the very essence of their commonwealth.

I am aware it will be urged that it is not so much the liberal institutions of America as the immense resources of the country, the fertility of the soil, and the vast extent of commerce, which are the causes of the constant emigrations to the United States. This, however, is but begging the question; for, without those institutions, the resources of the country would not yet be developed, the soil would not yield its produce, and the commerce of the country would still linger under onerous laws. It is the love of freedom, the note of being exempted from **burthensome taxes,** and the expectation of being able to call their own what they shall earn by their honest toils, which causes most Europeans, and especially the Germans, to emigrate to the United States, in preference to the equally fertile but ill-governed states of South America. The security and good faith of the American government act at least as much as an enticing cause as the hope of realizing a competence. The early settlements of the British North American colonies, their political progress, and the present prosperous condition of the United States, may be alike traced to the love of liberty, which, from the commencement, distinguished the Americans; and the history of the individual states sufficiently proves their inhabitants set a higher value on political and religious freedom than on the physical advantages of the soil, and the means of acquiring riches. . . .

Property, in some of the Latin American republics, is acquired with as much, or more, facility than in the United States, but there is no security for its preservation, while the latter offer, in this respect, greater guarantees than any other country, England and France not excepted. There are no conflicting elements which threaten an immediate change or overthrow of her established institutions. The opposition in America is powerless, and never refers to the principles of government, but only to particular measures. No class of society in the United States is opposed to republican institutions, as there is no political party whose permanent interests are opposed to the majority of the people. Neither is it the policy of the United States likely to involve the country in a foreign war and, if in a national broil the republic should become a belligerent party, her political and geographical position is such that she has little to fear from an enemy.

The Americans have kept good faith with all nations and, by the most unexampled economy, discharged their national debt. Their credit is unrivalled, their honor unquestioned, and the most implicit confidence placed in their ability to fulfill their engagements. They have, thus far, received strangers with hospitality, and put no obstacles in the way of their progress. They have not monopolized a single branch of industry, but let foreigners and native citizens compete fairly for an equal chance of success. They have established liberty of conscience, and compelled no person to pay taxes for the support of ministers of a different persuasion from his own. They have abolished all hereditary privileges; but let all men start free and equal with no other claims to preferment than that which is founded on superiority of intellect. In short, they have made their country the market for talent, ingenuity, industry, every honest kind of exertion. It has become the home of all who are willing to rise by their own efforts, and contains within itself nearly half the enterprise of the world.

These are the true causes of the rapid growth of America which, joined to her immense natural resources, must make her eventually the most powerful country on the globe. It is the principle of liberty, carried out in all its ramifications and details, which has produced these mighty results. The states of **Buenos Aires** and Brazil contain immense fertile plains, blessed with a climate vastly superior to that of the United States, watered by streams which may vie with the Mississippi; but no earnest attempt seems, as yet, to have been made to settle them; and of the thousands of emigrants from Europe, scarcely a handful have seen the **La Plata**, or ventured themselves on the **Amazon.** The physical advantages are on the side of South America; but every moral and political superiority is permanently established in the United States. . . .

But the strongest tie which unites the Americans into a powerful nation is, nevertheless, the hope of acquiring property and consideration, which their institutions hold out to all persons, without distinction of birth or parentage. The idea may be **prosaic,** but it is, nevertheless, a correct one. What unites the citizens of a country more effectually than their common stakes of rights and property? The more they have to defend, the better will they defend it. Must not the stoutest patriotism relax in a country, in which a man is born only to be the footstool of those above him; in which the most persevering exertion can hardly protect him against want, and in which he must leave his children without inheritance, to lead the same weary life as their father. How must it affect his pride and honest ambition to be marked from his birth as an inferior being, though the faculties of his mind ought to make him the peer of the favored! What stimulus to industry is there in the thought that labor is incompatible with respectability, and that the highest title to respect is the having inherited a fortune? The Americans alone, of all nations, have completely overcome these prejudices. In their country the same rights, the same privileges are offered to all; industry is an honor, and idleness a disgrace; all a man earns is his own, or goes unimpaired to his children; no beginning is so humble but what it may lead to honor; and every honest exertion is sure of its adequate reward. As long as the institutions of America are productive of such happy results, it is but natural that the people should cling to them as the principal cause of their boundless national prosperity.

TERMS AND DEFINITIONS

Buenos Aires: Argentina.
Burthensome taxes: taxes that place a heavy financial burden.
Idyllic poesy: poem or prose describing a pleasant scene out of memory or imagination.

La Plata and **Amazon:** major rivers in South America.
Prosaic: dull, uninteresting, or ordinary.

DOMINGO FAUSTINO SARMIENTO

THE MORAL DEFECTS OF LIBERTY
AND EQUALITY

To the Argentine-born Domingo Faustino Sarmiento (1811–1888), North Americans were a strange mixture of religious piety, aggressive materialism, and sporadic outbursts of violence. Educator, journalist, author, and statesman, Sarmiento was exiled from his native land to Chile between 1840 and 1852. Returning to Argentina, he served successively as minister of public instruction and interior, governor of San Juan, minister to the United States, and president of the Argentine Republic from 1868 to 1874. It was during the period of his Chilean exile that he wrote Travels in the United States in 1847. *In it, he disagrees with Chevalier and Grund by insisting that widespread liberty and equality in the United States gives free rein to the "moral defects" that afflict the masses of people, and justifies their subjugation of nature and people. However, he also puts considerable faith in what he calls "the forces of unification, purification, and improvement."*

Previously I have said something of the physical geography of the United States, which, if it is not the basis of that country's prosperity, is its principal servant, in the same way that a man's fingers are the faithful executors of his thoughts. There is also a moral geography in that country, whose key features I should point out. Already knowledgeable about the land, you will now come to know something of the civilizing currents which carry to the far corners of the Union improvement, light, and moral progress.

You are familiar with the history and geography of the first thirteen states in the American Union. During two centuries the great political and religious ideas which England successively brought forth from its bosom were deposited there. Bancroft has made an inventory of those ideas, placing each of them in the locale where it was first introduced by, for example, the Pilgrims in New England, the Quakers in Pennsylvania, and the Catholics in Maryland. This colonization was less a matter of men who moved from one country to another than of political and religious ideas which required air and space in which to breathe and expand. Their fruit has been the American Republic, which came along very much before the French Revolution. The **Declaration of the Rights of Man** made by the Congress of the United States in 1776 is the first page in the history of the modern world, and all political revolutions which follow it on this earth will be a commentary on those simple, common-sense statements.

The Declaration of Independence was like the command to "Be fruitful and multiply" that God gave to the Hebrews. From that moment, ideas and men began moving into the interior of the country. The Republic began giving birth to territories that were later converted into states, like a polyp putting out new tentacles from its body. Study the history of the South American republics from their independence on, and you will see what a difference there is. Chile subdivides its old provinces, but without increasing either the amount of populated territory or the number of cities. The old **United Provinces of the River Plate** are seen to dismember their territory and form with the fragments rickety and absurd states, while the provinces which still carry the Argentine name are depopulating themselves day after day, their old infant cities being extinguished like lights being turned off. In 1790, Maine, for example had 96,000 inhabitants; in 1800. 151,000; in 1810, 228,705; in 1830, 400,000; and in 1840, 501,793. In 1790, New York had 340,120 inhabitants; in 1800, 586,766; in 1810, 959,949; in 1820, 1,372,812; in 1830, 1,918,608; and in 1840, 2,428,921.

But, in addition to concentration, there is also expansion. Mississippi appeared on the scene in 1800 with 8,850 inhabitants, and by 1840 it had already counted 375,651 souls. Arkansas was not heard from until 1820, when it presented a population of 14,273, but by 1840 it had nearly 100,000. Indiana had 4,762 in 1810, but thirty years later it had 685,866. Finally, Ohio, which in 1800 had a registered population of 40,365 had by 1840 grown by a million and a half. You would be astonished by this flood of men which the first settlers in a wilderness watch arriving and establishing themselves around them. The man who pointed this out to me was not old, and yet he had seen the birth, development, and growth of one of the great states. Where do these men come from, since today there are no **Deucalions** throwing rocks over their shoulders to produce them? European immigration is only the second most important source of these waves of people, even though its sum may be considerable. It is the older or adult states which beget these men who keep appearing. The INDIAN HATER goes first, scattering the members of that extraordinary, instinctive race; persecuting the savage is his only creed, exterminating the indigenous peoples is his only desire. No one has commanded it. He goes to the forest with only his rifle and his dogs to hunt the savages, putting them to flight and making them abandon the hunting grounds of their fathers. Afterwards come the SQUATTERS, who are misanthropes looking for solitude in which to dwell, danger for excitement, and the work of felling trees for relaxation. The PIONEERS follow at a distance, opening the forests, sowing the earth, and spreading themselves over a great area. Immediately the **CAPITALIST IMPRESARIOS** are there, with immigrants as their laborers, founding cities and towns as the terrain counsels. At once the proprietary class, machinery, and industry arrive from the old states, and youth immigrates to make its fortune.

In this expansion of the American population civilization has well-marked levels, almost disappearing at the extremes of the Union—in the West because of the distance between inhabitants and the primitiveness of rural life, and in the South because of the presence of slaves and of Spanish and French traditions. Half a century would be enough for the incurable barbarism of the Argentine plains to establish itself in the far points of the Union were it not for the ebb and flow of vital elements of regeneration which dominate the country, keeping everything moving and insuring that the most distant and most isolated places are kept from stagnating and degenerating. In the United States, European immigration is a barbaric element. Who would have believed it! Except for natural exceptions, the European—Irishman or German, Frenchman or Spaniard—comes from the neediest classes, is usually ignorant, and is not accustomed to the republican practices of the land. How can it be assured that the immigrant will at once understand that complicated mechanism of municipal, state, and national institutions, and, more important, that he will become like the Yankee in his love for every one of these, linking his existence and his very being to them in such a way that he would fear for his life or conscience if he neglected these institutions and what they represent? How can he become accustomed to the meeting, in which at every moment he is urged to express his sentiments? And once these are expressed, once he has voted a series of "**and to be further resolveds,**" how can he experience that relief of a great weight having been lifted which the American feels when he has terminated an argument or demolished the opposition's point of view? And so it is that foreigners in the United States are the burden of scandal and the leaven of corruption annually introduced into the bloodstream of that nation which for so long has been educated in the practices of liberty. The Whigs, who are the more nationalistic party, have tried many times to put restrictions on immigration, and also to prolong by many years the study an immigrant must engage in before obtaining his political rights. The **Nativist Party,** which today is extinct, tried to create a kind of fanatical nationalism very much like—although with different aims—our own **Americanismo.** But this dissipated in the new states when the first dark clouds of prejudice began to appear. The older states can disregard the foreigners because they are already densely populated and offer little incentive to the newcomer. But this, through necessity, is not the case in the Western states, where citizenship is practically bought at public auction and where the years necessary for establishing residence have been energetically lowered and requisites excused.

Society in the United States is very well organized to counter this relaxation of rules in order to disseminate population over the country, and splendid results would long ago have been produced if it were not an interminable task while **i barbari** keep coming from Europe by the hundreds of thousands, and while there are lands by the thousands of millions of acres to be cleared. The forces of unification, purification, and improvement are so important that, if you will permit me, I will go on describing them.

The daily mail service works remarkably well. The post comes to the front doors of every far-off town and leaves there in some public document a topic of conversation and some news of what is happening in the nation. You know that it is impossible to barbarize wherever the post, like a daily rainfall, dissolves all indifference born of isolation. Do not forget that the postal system in the United States covers 134,000 miles, in some places assisted by the telegraph. I am omitting the civilizing and **catalytic influence** of the periodical press.

Trial by jury calls men from the fields at any time to come together and decide criminal cases and this judge, the common man, listens to the prosecution and the defense, weighs the arguments, considers the laws, gains experience in this role, and judges with total security of conscience. The tradition of the jury has created the horrible civil crime known as **Lynch Law,** which is unpunishable. Just as Jesus said,"wheresoever three shall be gathered in my name, I will be with you," LYNCH'S LAW says to the Yankee of the forests,

"Wherever seven men meet in the name of the people, justice will be in your hands." Be careful in the FAR WEST, or in the slave states, of angering men when there are seven of them together, or you may be strung up by those judges, who are more terrible and arbitrary than the **invisible judges of the secret courts of ancient Germany.** The law permits it, and those grim consciences will remain free of any remorse, feeling no more and no less than the member of the **Spanish Inquisition** who, having used all his tricks to get his victim to the blaze, watches him burn. Religion and democracy fall into crimes when their principles and objects are exaggerated.

The election of the President exerts no small civilizing influence. The American engages in fifty elections a year. Defeated in the election for the Council on Public Education, he throws himself into the campaign for sexton of his church. If he loses there, he waits with doubled passion the election for ATTORNEY, the election for mayor, the election for state representative, or that for governor. For a whole year he is filled with bad feelings about one and love for another candidate for the presidency, and he gets just as worked up over the congressional elections. At the time of a presidential election the Union is shaken to its very foundations. The SQUATTERS come out of their forests like shades evoked by a conjurer. The fate of every last tortoise of them is involved in the outcome. There is the danger of not surviving the triumph of the Whig candidate, who is regarded as the reactionary one. If the election returns banish his hopes, the American clenches his fists and retreats to his dwelling, swearing to make up his losses in the election for pastor of his faith.

The election of the President is the only bond which unites all the far corners of the Union, the sole national concern that moves all of the people and all of the states at the sacred contest is, therefore, an awakener, a school, and a stimulant which revives a life otherwise made drowsy by isolation and hard work.

But what really stirs up Americans are their religious sentiments. A lukewarm Catholic from one of our countries would, without doubt, be astounded to see the grand and elevated scale on which religion is carried on in the midst of extreme liberty. Of course the Bible is all over the Union, from the LOG-HOUSE in the forest up to and including the hotels of the big cities, the effects of its daily reading working for good and for ill. I say "for ill," too, because an attachment to the letter of its text produces disastrous consequences in narrow minds.

TERMS AND DEFINITIONS

Americanismo: superpatriotism in Latin American countries.
"And to be further resolveds": sarcastic reference to the ordinary business of political bodies.

Bancroft: Hubert Howe Bancroft (1832–1918), American historian and publisher.
Capitalist impresarios: wealthy entrepreneurs who dominate the economy of a region.

Catalytic influence: the factor most responsible for setting events in motion.

Declaration of the Rights of Man: the author confuses the French Declaration of 1791 with the Declaration of Independence.

Deucalions: Son of Prometheus who created men out of stones after the Great Flood by throwing them over his shoulder.

I barbari: foreigners regarded as barbarians.

Invisible judges of the secret courts of ancient Germany: mythical courts where the accused had no rights.

Lynch Law: extralegal execution of suspected criminals.

Nativist Party: minor political party opposed to immigration and easy naturalization.

Physiognomy: outward physical appearance.

Roto: lowest social class in Argentina.

Spanish Inquisition: a religious court during the fifteenth and sixteenth centuries used to punish "heretics" and political dissenters where the accused had few, if any rights.

United Provinces of the River Plate: the forerunner of Argentina.

JULIUS HERMANN MORITZ BUSCH

"THE SUBORDINATE CHARACTERISTICS OF THE YOUTHFUL NATION"

Visiting the United States in 1851, the German journalist and publicist Julius Hermann Moritz Busch (1821–1899) wrote Travels Between the Hudson and the Mississippi, 1851–1852. *In it, he presents an unusually astute and well-balanced assessment of the current state and future directions of American society and culture. Although Busch insists that "love for individual liberty" is the primary trait of the American character, despite its treatment of racial minorities, he also forthrightly examines four secondary or subordinate characteristics that exert contrary pressures. As a result, he concludes that the nation must resolve some of its inner contradictions to realize its great potential. After his return to Germany, Busch served in the department of state of the government headed by Prince Otto von Bismarck.*

America, now, is a young country populated by diverse elements; in addition these elements have different interests in the West than in the East, different interests in the North than in the South. With the irresolution resulting from this, it is not easy to say what is the chief aspiration of the nation. However, if we look at its annals, we recognize at once that its basic impulse is the love of individual freedom. It is pushing its way—in part consciously, in part merely instinctively—toward democracy, the government of all, by all, for all. Nevertheless, there are for individuals as for nations also temporary secondary goals, and these are pursued so actively at times that the observer can be deceived about the constant basic impulse. Wealth is such a secondary goal in America at present. Currently the dollar is the dominant goal in the consciousness of the people. The passion for it has increased astoundingly since the beginning of the century, and the two roads that lead to it—business and politics—are almost the only ones upon which the so-called better class is to be encountered. To the goals correspond certain traits in the life of the individuals as well as of the nations. Just as every nation has its destiny, so every nation has its character. If we look over the history of every single nation, we encounter a pattern that advances toward us continually—sometimes clear, sometimes more blurred—from the language, the laws, the religion, the customs, the art, and the literature. . . .

It is not to be denied that when this yardstick is applied, much in the life of the Americans appears to be an exception. It is true that they sell the freedom of three million humans—who, without a doubt, are inferior to them mentally as well as physically, but who nevertheless are humans—for an annual income of less than three million bales of cotton. And it is likewise true that they have knowingly trodden under foot sacred rights in other connections. Nonetheless, however, and despite all exceptions, in the history as well as in the present of the nation, nothing appears with such clearness as that love for individual liberty and that striving to realize it.

I have attempted to substantiate this in preceding chapters. Here we are more concerned with those subordinate characteristics of the youthful nation that, branching off from its character or having come to it from the outside, modify that basic pattern and in part impair that basic impulse. They are signs of the times, and it is important to examine carefully the most prominent of them if one wishes to get a correct picture of the nation. The first of these characteristics is hostility toward all authority. Every single thing must state its reason and say why it exists and what justifies it to be so and not otherwise. From this results an absolute lack of respect, which not infrequently becomes **impiety.** Nowhere does the past count as little as here. "Our fathers did it this way," someone says. "Well, what does that mean?" answers the American. "Well, now, our fathers were giants compared to us," replies the friend of the past. "Oh, not in the least," responds the other. "They were nothing but big boys, and we are not only a great deal taller, but, standing upon their shoulders, we can see a great deal farther. We are the old ones, not they, and so we very gladly accept their wisdom and thank God for it, but keep off our necks with their authority." Furthermore, the example of ancient nations neither frightens the American nor does it teach him. Slavery was a curse for Athens and Rome. "It makes no difference to us," says **Jonathan.** "We aren't Greeks or Romans, but republicans and good Christians of the New World. We live in the nineteenth century, and although slavery may have caused all sorts of trouble there and at that time, it is an advantage for us—for we make money with it." Contemporary nations are just as little an example. No ordinary American wants to listen when the institutions of other nations, for example, in school or military matters, are praised. He understands all that much better, and even if he didn't understand it better, it would still be unpatriotic to admit a superiority of foreign states. To him the Mexican War is a miracle of modern military leadership that has covered him with eternal fame.

But while he stubbornly refuses to admit and emulate the good points of other nations, he imitates their follies and weaknesses without hesitation—especially in the higher classes of society. Like all upstarts, he makes a point of aristocratic customs, hoping that strangers will admire him if he adopts a coat of arms with lions and leopards instead of with the hand tools that enabled him to earn the money to have it painted.

From this hatred of all authority—which, however, does not prevent him from urgently inquiring what they think of him in Europe—comes an aversion toward everything old. This is one of the explanations for the continual change in all affairs of the American. His house, his books, even his churches must always be new. The frame house that the eye encounters so frequently here, freshly painted every year if possible, is a suitable emblem for this incessant striving for renewal. But this love of change is also expressed in more important matters. It is asked: What right to existence does this or that law have? Upon what is the existence of the government based? Who gives the majority the right to dictate its will to the minority, to limit commerce, levy taxes, and the like? If the entire nation forms a committee to make decisions about an important matter, then certainly a shoemaker or a brushmaker will form a committee all by himself and take the opposite position. The state of South Carolina is a nice little sample of this kind of self-reliance and this disregard of all authority. This tiny little speck of land, with scarcely half as many free white inhabitants as the city of New York, believes, nonetheless, that it represents the best part of the patriotism and the political wisdom of the nation. This "chivalrous" little state crows with swollen comb: If the Union does not pass such laws as suit us, if it doesn't permit us the expansion of our institutions and doesn't grant us the tariff that we desire, then we'll say "No," we'll secede from the federation, and we'll leave the other twenty-nine states to their fate. It's the same in church matters. America is the land of heresies and sects, partly because it is hostile to any authority. To be sure, there are also people in America who are interested in antiquity, but they appear in the crowd like individual stragglers of a bygone race. The present permits them a place and listens to them when they speak enthusiastically of old armor that has been discovered in an old ruin or hollow tree, of an **Indian Bible** dug up from the ground, or of fossilized mammoth bones. But they permit these and other remnants of the past to exert absolutely no influence upon the matters closest to their hearts, such as commerce, factories, and politics.

A second characteristic of the American is a certain philosophical trait, manifest in a questioning and searching after ultimate causes and general ideas. To be sure, one first looks for the facts, but then he looks immediately for the law of the fact and finally for the reason for the law. A sign of this is to be found in the titles of books and in the public lectures of traveling scholars. One is less concerned with treatises about the eye, the ear, and sleep; rather, one discusses the "philosophy" of seeing, hearing, and sleeping. Theological sects are not always the first to feel such a movement among the people. Still, almost all of them here, from the Episcopalians down to the Quakers, have a philosophical faction that has prospects of overcoming the conservative faction. This inclination has its representatives even in the pulpits, and it frequently happens that the "philosophy" of religion is preached to a devout circle. This holds true particularly in the East. There the young ladies have seriously taken up **Fourier's** ideas, the best and deepest thoughts of Germany are accepted and considered even more readily than in England, and shopkeepers and tailors lend an attentive ear when **Agassiz and Emerson,** men who certainly do not speak in a very popular vein, announce a series of lectures that, thereby, many an error slips in and that many a person participates simply for the sake of fashion; but even the circumstance that it has become the fashion indicates that such a philosophical trait runs through the nation. No doubt, too, that these opposing tendencies exist principally in the area of the church and that the old shouting about irreligion and freethinking often sounds louder than the word of the innovators. But, despite all this, it is evident that the future belongs to the latter, even though they will never be able to control the atheism that here and there makes a great show.

Despite this deep-running impulse, however, a closer examination shows a lamentable lack of principles. The validity of the traditional has been disavowed, but the authority of truth and justice has not yet been duly accepted. One does not want to be regarded as a boy, but is not yet old enough to step forth as a man who is aware of his intentions. So nothing is established as yet, and America presents the picture of a continual ebb and flow of opposing principles. In politics, no party has yet completely decided whether commerce should be restricted by laws, or whether it might not be better to leave it to the people to buy where they can get the goods most cheaply, and to sell where the most is paid. A similar indecision of opinion was revealed when the slavery question seemed to get into conflict with the stability of the Union, and it's no different with the internal improvements that the Democrats will finally have to leave to the central power to a certain degree. It's the same in matters of faith. Some declare that for them the Bible no longer is valid as the Supreme Court, but they dare not replace it with reason and conscience. Others act as though the Holy Scriptures were the highest authority for them, but if they should be asked their opinion about the miraculous birth and resurrection of Christ, they'd avoid answering with a "Yes" or "No."

A third characteristic of the American people is the unusual intensity of their living and striving, shown in their actions and talk, in their speculations, and in the **"revivals"** of the more serious sects. Everything that is done appears an exaggeration—and in most cases it is. Perhaps the Americans among all peoples have the most self-confidence, and so they behave like heaven-stormers—which often appears titanic, sometimes ridiculous. The soul of the Yankee leaves its work as soon as it's finished. His forefathers considered the Revolution a great deed. But he is already thinking about quite different revolutions. In his high spirits, which spring from his superabundance of vigor, he would like to join up with the entire world, with nature as well as with men. He considers a railroad from the Mississippi to the Pacific as a trifle. He talked about the incorporation of northern Mexico, and he effected it. He is now reaching for Cuba, for Central America, for the whole western continent—and he will take it. His deeds are not to be underestimated, but his hopes and desires go far beyond them.

If this intensity of living and hoping has its good side, it also has its bad. It produces haste, superficiality, and vanity. Seldom does it accomplish a completed work. English and German goods usually bear the mark of solidity, and French that of good taste—American goods usually lack both. One strives for the big, the many, and the spacious—not for strength and quality. One forgets that a thoughtful procedure is the shortest route to any goal and that a person who is certain about the end of his journey before he departs travels better than one who only thinks a little about it along the way. In America, speed is the chief requirement of all thoughts and desires. A Yankee vessel is recognized from a distance by the enormous number of sails that it carries. A Yankee state revises its constitution in such a rapid manner that a European would be almost frightened by it. In education, the goal is not to learn as much as possible but to snatch up rapidly as much as is absolutely necessary. From school, the boy plunges quickly into business life, and here his efforts are directed toward becoming rich rapidly—in this it frequently happens that he falls to the ground two or three times in the course of his life. His entire existence is a journey on a steamboat or railroad. He can't even remain quiet in sitting, so he puts his chairs upon rockers. Everything is activity, running and rushing. One is so bent upon creating and working that one has no time for enjoying and hence enjoys very little of the poetry of life. America has only two annual festivals and, even at these, there is more noise than pleasure. Everything is done "in less than no time," from the tanning of a cowhide to the training of a soul for the work and earning of life, and if flying is ever invented, it certainly will be done in the United States.

A fourth characteristic of the American way is its exaggerated love for material things. This is not limited to preferring the useful to the beautiful but consists in putting the external in place of the higher and more valuable internal and in putting money above the value of man. The American does not comprehend that a great man may be poor, and so the great man sells himself, and the crowd calls it a good piece of business. An otherwise quite intelligent and cultivated gentleman didn't know how to honor a painter except by pointing out that he had earned $20,000 with his paintings. It was typical that in Boston a man believed that he was praising a distinguished writer by remarking that his books had earned him more money than anyone else in the field.

One can object that other nations suffer from the same deficiency. True, but then one overlooks the difference. Elsewhere a man's possessions—his rank and wealth—are placed above the man himself, and this sort of materialism is not inconsistent with public opinion. In America it is an insult to the same and a challenge to the basic principle of the country. Moreover, in most civilized nations there is a hereditary propertied class who devote their lives to the sciences and arts and thus rise above the sphere of merely material elegance surrounding them. This class is rarely found in America. Young, rich people infrequently turn themselves to higher and nobler endeavors, but usually they strive either to transform their talents into gold or their gold into splendid houses, furnishings, coaches, and horses. If **Socrates** came to Boston, the **Athens** of the western continent, and set about to outwit the stockbrokers of the exchange (as he once did the **Sophists**), he would reap praise. On the other hand, if he followed his old method, the crowd would soon have forgotten him.

It is a feature of this disgusting materialism that one is proud of the wealth, which is but accumulated labor, and ashamed of the labor, which merely represents the striving for wealth. With all the talk about democracy, labor is honored less in the eyes of many Americans than in **Berlin or Leipzig**. Almost everyone whose exertions have been crowned by success is ashamed of the ladder by which he rose. The aristocrat who arrived in New York thirty years ago by the travel method of the apostles, carrying all his worldly goods wrapped up in a cotton kerchief, becomes red when he recalls that his father was a drayman or cobbler and that, out in the country, live a couple dozen cousins with his name who are distinguished only for their large hands and excellent memories. . . .

There are many contradictions in these secondary characteristics of the American way; they must be considered as signs of the times. Quality struggles with quantity; not a single one [of these characteristics] strives for harmonious relationships [with the others], and so they appear as national weaknesses. Whether these will improve, and soon, is a question that the future will answer. The present can only hope.

TERMS AND DEFINITIONS

Agassiz and Emerson: Louis Agassiz (1807–1873), American naturalist, and Ralph Waldo Emerson (1803–1882), American essayist, poet, and philosopher, both prominent Transcendentalists.

Athens: city that was the intellectual and cultural center of ancient Greece.

Berlin or Leipzig: large cities in eastern Germany.

Fourier: Charles Fourier (1772–1837), French utopian socialist whose followers founded model communities in the United States.

Impiety: antireligious attitude.

Indian Bible: Native American religious artifact.

Jonathan: fictional character used as the personification of the United States.

"Revivals": periodic religious rallies held to increase fervor or devotion.

Socrates: famous philosopher of ancient Greece (469–399 B.C.) who developed the question and answer method of reasoning and was the teacher of Plato, who, in turn, taught Aristotle.

Sophists: school of ancient Greek philosophers famous for their clever, and sometimes deliberately misleading, arguments.

MAJOR GEORGE WARBURTON

THREE NATIONS IN ONE

Of all the analyses of the current state and future of the ante-bellum United States, none was more blunt and skeptical than that given by Major George Warburton (1816–1857) in his essay entitled "Prospects For America." The essay was eventually published as chapter 10 of volume II of Hochelaga: Or England In The New World, *a book edited by his brother, world traveler and writer Eliot Bartholomew George Warburton, and first published in London in 1846. Critically acclaimed by the* London Quarterly Review *and* Blackwood's Magazine, Hochelaga, *the aboriginal name for Canada, enjoyed four printings. A British officer stationed in Canada, Warburton predicts a dire future for the survival of the United States as an entity, despite its obvious achievements. Unlike the other four observers, he finds almost no real sources of unity to counterbalance the tremendous internal diversity of the young nation. However, he takes great comfort from the fact that, together with Canada, the three separate sections will constitute an "Anglo-Saxon" coalition on the continent.*

There are at this present moment the germs of three distinct nations in the United States, differing more widely from each other in feelings and in interest than did England and the colonies at the time of the revolution. First there is the sober North—moral, enlightened, industrious, prudent, peaceful, and commercial, where society has taken an established form; the climate is severe, the niggard soil only rewards the careful husbandman, the industry of her people is the source of her wealth; the weaver's loom and the mechanics' skill are her mines of gold; her traders find their way over the desert, her ships over the ocean; wherever a mart is to be found, there will they be. Her sons are brave in war, adventurous in peace; in the revolution they bore the brunt of the fight; since then, the greatness of America in peace is due to them. They are at all times the bone sinew of the Union, but peace is their most congenial condition; in it, their great commerce is prosperous and safe; in war it is threatened, if not destroyed.

Next comes the turbulent West, with a fertility unexampled elsewhere, a climate which stimulates life and shortens its duration; all animal and vegetable productions shoot up, ripen, and wither in a breath, but still they spread over the land with wonderful rapidity. From the European kingdom and from the Atlantic cities of America, thousands of restless and adventurous men pour like a flood over these rich plains, and exuberant crops repay the clumsiest cultivation; when the productive earth grows dull under this wasteful husbandry, the tide rolls still further away, the Indian and the wild forest animals yielding to its strength; a few years changes the wilderness to a populous State, its centre to a city.

By far the greater part of the population of these countries are roving, energetic men, who merely till the land as a means of wealth, not as a settlement where their bones are to be laid and their children are to dwell after them. They have no stability or combination; they come from all parts of the compass, a great, strong, surging sea, each wave an isolated being. All the uneasy spirits who crowd thither from other lands, in a few years either sink under the noisome vapours from the rich alluvial soil, or enjoy plenty from its produce; each man acts for himself and wishes to govern for himself. The social conditions of all are nearly equal; there is but little chance of any of those dangerous organizations of society, which European states now, and the Atlantic states soon will, present, for a century to come. There will be ample room for all to grow rich on the spoils of the West. This western country, I consider, will be the last stronghold of democracy in America. By this I presuppose that everywhere this form of government must be ultimately abandoned, that it is merely tolerable now—a temporary expedient for an infant state, merely an affair of time. I shall state my grounds for this supposition presently. The conditions of the West are most fitted for these institutions, and these conditions are not likely to be altered for many years.

Population has increased so much of late years in that direction, that already the West holds the balance between the North and the South; in half a century it will overbalance both together. Far away, by the shores of Lake Superior—where, but a little time ago, none but the lonely trapper ever reached, are now cities; tens of thousands of men dig into rich mines or reap abundant crops, and in their steamers plough up the deep, pure waters, hitherto undisturbed by man's approach. On branches of the " **Father of Rivers**," which have yet scarcely a name, populous settlements are spreading over the banks. The rapidity of the growth of population and power in this region has no parallel in the world's history.

These people are confident in their strength; they live in a perpetual invasion; their great impulse is expansion. They are reckless of life, and but little accustomed to the restraints of law; skill and courage are their capital; their country is not a home, but a mere means of becoming affluent. The individual desires, from day to day, to pass on to other and richer lands, in hopes of a yet more abundant return for his labour; the aggregate of individuals desires the rich woods of Canada, the temperate shores of Oregon, and the fertile soil of California. They long to conquer them with the sword as they have conquered the Prairies with the plough; aggression is their instinct, invasion their natural state. This western division appears to me by far the most important of the three, the one in which the mysterious and peculiar destiny of the New World is to be in the fullest degree developed.

The South is the third of these divisions. It contains a population divided between the **Anglo-Saxon** and Negro races, the first rather the more numerous at present; but, taking a series of years, the latter has increased more rapidly than the former. It is well known that the whites hold the blacks in slavery, a bondage often gently enforced and willingly borne, but sometimes productive of the most diabolical cruelties that the mind of man has ever conceived. Altogether, the effect of these conditions is, that the ruling race despise and yet fear their servants, and use every ingenuity to deprive them of strength, as a class, by withholding education, and legislating to prevent the possibility of their combining together. The great mass of these slaves are dark and degraded beings, but in one respect they still keep up to the level of humanity—they long to be free. It is known that, by their own arms, the attempt would be hopeless, for they are far inferior to the whites in mind and body. Some people think that nature has condemned them to this inferiority; others, that it is only a transient condition, caused by this state of slavery. Some local outbreaks have indeed occurred, where the tyranny of the master was greater than the patience of the slaves; they were for the moment successful—long enough to shew how terrible is the vengeance for the pent-up wrongs of years; but they soon sank under the irresistible power which they provoked, and their awful fate holds out a warning to others.

Their liberation is not to be effected by any effort of their own. Their masters are united, bound together by this bond of iniquity; not only wealth is supposed to depend upon their upholding slavery, but their very lives. Were these degraded beings to be freed, and the sense of fear removed, no laws could restrain them; the wrongs of generations would be brought to an account; a "servile war" would ensue aggravated in horrors by the difference of race; no peace, or truce, or compromise, could end it; one or the other must perish or be subdued. The negro cannot subdue the white man, therefore he must be again a slave, or be freed by death from earthly bondage. So say those who defend the maintenance of this system in the South.

The ruling class in this part of America are proud and quick-tempered men: disdaining labour, free and generous in expense, slow to acknowledge authority, contemptuous of inferiors, jealous of the interference of others, they carry their despotic republicanism further than the other divisions. They are in themselves essentially an aristocracy, a privileged class. On several occasions, these fiery spirits have objected to the influence of other States of the Union. For instance, South Carolina almost went to war with the Federal Government rather than submit to an **obnoxious commercial regulation.** A member in this same state said, in the House of Representatives at Washington, "If we catch an abolitionist in South Carolina we'll hang him without judge or jury." But, indeed, even their laws enable them to inflict a very severe punishment on such an offender.

To retain the institution of slavery in the laws of the country is the great object of this division; for this object it is necessary they should hold the preponderating influence in the government of the country. This they have generally accomplished, having supplied by far the greater number of Presidents of the Union; they have carried their point of annexing Texas as a slave-holding State. By forming an alliance with the West, they have succeeded in electing a president favourable to the free trade so necessary to their interests; forgetting that by his views on other subjects they run the risk of provoking war, so fatal to their commerce and so dangerous to the existence of their cherished institution. This alliance is, however, but temporary; it has no solid foundation; the West loves not slavery, neither does the North. . . .

In the North, the conditions of the people are approaching to those of Europe. The mere productions of the earth have ceased to be their dependence; their trading or manufacturing towns have grown into cities, their population is becoming divided into the rich and the poor; the upper classes are becoming more enlightened and prosperous, the poor more ignorant and discontented. Increased civilization brings on its **weal and woe,** its powers and its necessities; as these proceed, it will be soon evident that the present **State-of-nature**

Government is no longer suitable; the masses will become turbulent, property will be assailed by those who want; and the wealthy and their dependents will be ranged in its defence. Perhaps foreign wars may add to these difficulties, and to the temptations to "hero worship," always so strong in the human mind, but especially so in America. The result will probably be a monarchy, supported by a wealthy powerful commercial and military aristocracy—and a certain separation from the West.

As these three divisions increase in population and in wealth, the diverging lines of their interests will become more widely separated, doubtless so widely separated that the time is not far when they will even incur the monstrous evil of breaking up the Union, and providing each as much against the other as against foreign nations. The general political tendency of the present time is to increase the powers and isolation of the different States; even the smallest grant of public money for works of defence or improvement is watched with jealous care by the districts not benefiting by it; the balance of power is also a constant subject of anxiety; the admission of Texas was, on this principle, energetically opposed by many in the North.

It is very plain that, in half a century, these divisions will each be strong enough to stand alone. The north, by that time will have a larger population and commerce than England has now, and it is more than probable that it will also be willing to stand alone. There are two ties which at present act in keeping up the Union—the necessity of mutual support, and patriotism. The first will cease with their increasing strength; in the second I have no great confidence: even at this present moment it is but an interested patriotism, and will cease with the interests, which cause it. They have no inheritance of glory handed down to them through centuries; with them is wanting the tie of affection which binds the heart to the land where lie the ashes of the honoured ancestral dead—their mutual relations are those of **foundlings** to one another; their love of country that of the **Nabob for the pagoda tree.**

The want of pride in the Americans is made up for by the most astounding conceit; they perpetually declare to each other their wisdom, virtue—in short, perfection; and will not allow even a share of this merit to other nations. They persuade themselves that they are, as I have frequently heard them say "a chosen people." But this shallow conceit is very easily wounded, and will probably be a great cause of ultimate dissension, for if one portion—still of course thinking themselves perfection—disagree permanently on any great principle with another portion, who equally think themselves perfection, the chances are that they will find very great difficulty in convincing each other, or in compromising the matter under discussion. Neither the fiery and intelligent Southern, nor the sedate and sensible Northern, is likely to give way.

I consider that the separation of this great country will inevitably take place, and that it is absolutely necessary for the peace and freedom of the world that it should. In half a century, if they remain united, they will be beyond doubt the most powerful nation of the earth. In the aggressive policy, certain in a great republic, will lie the danger of their strength. The extraordinary rapidity of events in America startles the observer; ten years here corresponds to a hundred in older countries, with respect to the changes that will take place. . . .

The probable separation of the great republic into distinct governments will not, I am convinced, interfere with her mission. Let the states assume what combinations they may, their prosperity and civilization is certain. The whole of the North American continent, and not improbably the Southern also, will one day belong to the Anglo-Saxon race. The progress of Canada, under a totally different system of government, has been quite as rapid as that of the States, and the progress of the States when separated will no doubt continue the same. It will, however, be a happy thing for the world when their vast power ceases to be concentrated.

TERMS AND DEFINITIONS

Anglo-Saxon: supposed ancestral heritage of modern-day English people.
"Father of Rivers": Mississippi River.
Foundlings: babies deserted by their parents and found by others.
Nabob for the pagoda tree: a person who worships material prosperity over all else.
Obnoxious commercial regulation: South Carolina's opinion of the Tariff of 1829.

"Servile war": wars fought by slaves or lower classes for freedom and rights.
State-of-nature Government: government with minimal powers and authority.
Weal and woe: mixture of good and bad occurrences.

THINKING THINGS THROUGH

1. On the whole, do these five observers agree or disagree more on the components of the American character?

2. If someone had read only these five commentaries would their overall impression of the American character be favorable or unfavorable?

3. On what aspects of the American character do the five seem to have a general consensus?

4. How do you think that the other four might react to Sarmiento's discussion of the forces that divide and unite Americans?

5. How do you think that the others might react to Busch's discussion of the four subordinate qualities of the American character?

8

Manifest Destiny

A. The International Context

At the dawn of the nineteenth century, the United States population scarcely exceeded five million people. The nation had but sixteen states, the furthest west of which was Tennessee. In 1850, with the admission of California, the United States extended from the Atlantic to the Pacific. From "sea to shining sea," a nation of 23 million people spread across thirty-one states. The great "continental republic," a dream since the early days of the nation, had become a reality. Contemporary Americans typically do not find anything remarkable in their nation's great territorial extent. Nor do they give much thought as to the means by which the new nation gained so much territory in so relatively brief a period of time.

The North American continent of 1800 remained a theater of rivalry and scheming among several European powers, most prominently Spain, England, and France. Spain still held its vast American colonial empire. Its viceroyalty of New Spain, stretched from the Isthmus of Panama to the northern boundary of California, and also included the Floridas. Above that line, it claimed rights to some of the Oregon territory, an area claimed as well by England, France, and the United States. France, its power in North America broken by defeat in the Great War for Empire, gained in 1800 what would become known as the Louisiana Territory through a secret treaty with Spain (the Treaty of San Ildefonso). At the same time, various Native American nations controlled vast stretches of territory. Competition between settlers and Native Americans was becoming increasingly intense in the trans-Appalachian West (the area between the Appalachian Mountains and the Mississippi River), where over a sixth of the nation's population now lived.

The expansion of the United States, therefore, played out against a background of international competition and

intrigue. It involved both diplomatic maneuvering and sub-
stantial warfare. Expansionism unfolded in two stages. The
first, from the 1800s to the 1830s, witnessed the acquisition
of the Louisiana Territory, the War of 1812, and relentless
pressure on Native American lands and societies. The second
stage, from the 1840s to the 1850s, featuring a still more ag-
gressive and powerful nation, comprises the era of "manifest
destiny." It saw the Mexican War, the United States' first for-
eign war with a nation other than England. Mexico lost a
major portion of its national territory, and the vast South-
west and California became part of the American nation.
Manifest destiny also meant further expulsion of Native
American peoples from their lands.

Shortly after signing the Treaty of San Ildefonso, Spain
(which had not yet formally transferred power to France) re-
voked the right of American citizens to deposit trade goods
in New Orleans. Mindful of the vital commercial importance
of the Mississippi River to the trans-Appalachian west,
Thomas Jefferson dispatched a mission to France, then under
the rule of Napoleon Bonaparte, with the intent of purchas-
ing New Orleans.

The resulting Louisiana Purchase nearly doubled the na-
tion's size, but it also helped propel the United States into the
War of 1812. In 1803, England and France once again were
engaged in war, one that would last until 1814. This latest
contest between the Western world's greatest powers affected
the United States because its national prosperity depended on
trade across the Atlantic. Several young members of Con-
gress, collectively known as War Hawks, called enthusiasti-
cally for war. Mostly westerners, they claimed that British
Canada had been furnishing armaments to the Indians, espe-
cially to the new confederation established by the great
Shawnee leader Tecumseh. The fact that Spain was allied with
England gave southerners—who were anxious to obtain the
Floridas—a reason to support the call for war.

With its best troops and officers engaged in the conflict
with France, England devoted relatively little attention to the
conflict with the United States. In fact, Russia, allied with
England, offered to mediate between England and America,
so that the British forces could concentrate fully on the war
with France.

England rejected that offer, and the War of 1812 dragged
on until 1814. Its end brought the United States no new terri-
tory. However, in the course of the conflict, Tecumseh, fighting
on the side of the British, had been killed. The collapse of his

confederacy made the northwest far more accessible for American settlers, and spurred further westward movement. Also, during the war Andrew Jackson had defeated the Creeks and secured title to much of their Mississippi territory; he then had moved on into Spanish Florida and taken the city of Pensacola.

An 1818 treaty between England and the United States set the fortieth parallel as the northern boundary of the Louisiana territory. It also provided for a joint Anglo-American occupation of Oregon. The following year, now heavily engaged in trying to suppress independence movements flaring throughout its American colonies, Spain signed the Adams-Onís treaty with the United States which established the boundary between the Spanish southwest and the Louisiana Territory. In effect, this ended all Spanish claims to the Pacific Northwest above California. In return, the United States abandoned its shaky claim that the Louisiana Purchase had included much of Texas.

In the 1840s, "Oregon fever" spread in response to reports that exceedingly fertile land was to be had in the Willamette Valley. American migration to the region gave name to a well-worn path carved out by wagon trains—the Oregon Trail. Soon American settlers in the region, scornful of other national claims, urged the United States to take over the territory. About the same time, many settlers began veering south from the Oregon Trail and moving into California. By then California formed part of the nation of Mexico, which had gained its independence from Spain in 1824. As in Oregon, American settlers had little patience for the formal claims of other nations.

This restless expansionist fever, gained a name—"manifest destiny"—in 1845, when New York newspaper editor John L. O'Sullivan suggested that in spreading its people and system of government across the continent the nation was in fact fulfilling its divinely ordained destiny. It is worth noting that expansionist nations often have couched their acquisition of territory or rule over other peoples in such terms. The Roman Empire, for example, spoke of its great civilizing mission and the positive impact of the "Roman Peace," imposed on previously warring and restive peoples. And when Great Britain carved out a formidable new colonial empire in the later nineteenth and early twentieth centuries, it would speak of a "pax Britannica" or British peace.

While Oregon and California danced in American consciousness, it was "the Texas question" that catalyzed the last *great continental territorial acquisitions of the United States. Like California, Texas formed part of Mexico. That nation's independence had been followed by a period of turmoil marked by a contest between centralists and federalists. While differing on that issue, Mexican leaders substantially agreed as to the dangers posed by the ongoing expansion of their northern neighbor.*

Mexico's population and power concentrated mainly in the central valley around the capital, Mexico City. The vast northern frontier, including Texas, the Colorado river valley, and California, largely remained unsettled. Only a string of missions and forts testified to the Mexican presence. Spain, which had held the area prior to Mexico's independence, feared that its lightly held territories might fall prey to a land-hungry United States. To forestall this possibility, in 1821 Spain had actually invited American settlers into Texas, hoping their presence would deter any aggressive moves. A newly independent Mexico continued that policy.

As it turned out, American settlement had the opposite effect. The "Texans" never made much effort to acculturate to Mexican norms. Furthermore, they resented being subject to the jurisdiction of both the state of Coahuila (of which Texas formed part) and the national government in Mexico. Matters came to a head in the 1830s, when a centralist faction in Mexico gained control of the national government. They crafted a new constitution that greatly limited the autonomy previously enjoyed by the state governments. The government also outlawed slavery throughout Mexico. This measure directly threatened the livelihood and way of life of the American in Texas.

Disgruntled Americans in Texas, joined by a significant number of Mexicans who also opposed the new centralizing policies, rose in revolt, demanding a return to the federal system. This movement soon resulted in an outright declaration of independence. In 1836, General Sam Houston, in command of the independence forces, gained a decisive victory over the Mexican army led by Antonio López de Santa Anna. Bargaining for his own freedom, Santa Anna signed a treaty recognizing Texas's independence. Since he really had no authority to sign any such treaty, Mexico never recognized his action, nor the independent nation of Texas, as legitimate. However, continuing political problems virtually paralyzed the Mexican government, and it was unable to mount any forces to regain control of Texas.

The idea of becoming a state of the United States had al-ways enjoyed support among the American settlers in Texas. The rising ferment over slavery, however, made the Texas question politically divisive. England was happy to see an independent nation arise in the Southwest, seeing it as a bar-rier to further United States expansion. At that time England still claimed the Oregon territory, and always remained con-cerned about potential United States thrusts into Canada; it also welcomed the prospect of gaining another secure source of cotton for its textile mills. England quickly recognized Texas as an independent nation and signed a commercial treaty. So did France.

As the campaign for the presidential election of 1844 in the United States heated up, questions of territorial expan-sion gained importance. James K. Polk won the Democratic party's nomination in large measure because he supported the annexation of both Texas and Oregon. A popular slogan dur-ing the presidential campaign, "fifty-four forty or fight!" called for U.S. control of the Oregon territory up to that lati-tude. For a while it seemed possible that America and En-gland might again find themselves at war. However, an 1846 treaty between the two nations settled the matter peacefully.

The Texas question, however, had no such resolution. In fact, it was the prospect of war with Mexico that had caused the United States to resolve its differences with England. When the national election saw Polk victorious, outgoing president John Tyler, himself an expansionist and plantation owner, asked Congress to approve the annexation of Texas. It became a state in December 1845.

Having previously informed the United States that it would regard annexation of Texas as an "unfriendly act," Mexico now responded by breaking diplomatic relations. Ten-sions further escalated because of conflicting U.S.–Mexican claims regarding the southern boundary of Texas. Even though they represented different views on internal affairs, two successive Mexican governments angrily rebuffed a U.S. diplomatic mission that had sought to resolve this issue. The fact that the mission offered to buy New Mexico and much of California confirmed Mexican fears that the United States had its mind set on taking Mexican territory.

When U.S. and Mexican forces clashed in the disputed territory, President Polk, asserting that American blood had been shed on American territory asked for, and received, a Congressional declaration of war on Mexico. Declared on

May 13, 1846, the war officially ended with the Treaty of Guadalupe Hidalgo of February 2, 1848, in which Mexico acknowledged the more southern boundary line and, coincidentally, that Texas now belonged to the United States. During the war the United States annexed both New Mexico and California. Mexico's final territorial loss occurred with the Gadsden Purchase of 1853 which saw the transfer of a strip of land from present-day El Paso west towards Lower California as a potential southern route for a transcontinental railroad. That purchase ended the United States' territorial expansion in North America, save for the later purchase of Alaska from Russia in 1867. While the United States had grown enormously, Mexico had lost about half of its national territory, most of it through a conflict it recalls as the "War of the North American Invasion."

The expansionist fever of those days also led to pressures on other parts of Latin America. In 1848, for example, the United States failed in an attempt to buy Cuba from Spain. Over the next few years, the United States turned a blind eye to several private expeditions—organized and equipped on American soil, and including mostly American citizens as troops—that attempted to take Cuba by force. The possibilities of official U.S. action to take Cuba surfaced during the Pierce administration in the 1854 Ostend Manifesto. The 1856 Democratic Party Platform specifically endorsed the annexation of Cuba. Other informal expeditions, known at the time as filibusters, included those by the American William Walker, who actually for a time in the 1850s gained control of Nicaragua.

B. International Views

The great westward surge of the United States prompted a great deal of foreign commentary, some of which was very positive. In the 1830s to 1850s, liberalism gained strength in Europe. In some cases, reform movements arose; in others, revolutions. Liberals of that era admired the United States, seeing it in many respects as a model for their own societies. They tended to see America's growing continental empire as reflecting the dynamic energy of its people. America was a land of growth and progress. Those who wrote from this perspective held very little sympathy for either the Native Americans or the Mexicans. "Backward" peoples were doomed to disappear because they could not compete with more energetic civilizations. The Native Americans, then, were the inevitable victims

*of progress. As for Mexicans, their own unenlightened and cor-
rupt government had doomed them to stagnation.*

*This liberal European view of manifest destiny as a
grand, admirable process often disappeared when expansionism involved specific national interests. The British, for example, frequently pointed to the overly aggressive nature of
America when discussing such subjects as the boundaries between British North America and the United States. Similarly,
locked in its own controversy with America regarding Oregon, England tended to portray the United States as the insti-
gator of the war with Mexico. For example, the* London
Times *in 1846 observed: "The annexation of Texas must be
taken as one entire transaction, originating with General
Jackson nearly twenty years ago, and ending with Mr. Polk's
declaration of war; but twenty years of fraud and hypocrisy
have not lessened the enormity or mitigated the violence of
this depredation."*

*Of course, those most directly affected by American ex-
pansionism voiced the most thorough condemnations. Mexican commentary on relations with the United States during
the heyday of manifest destiny, whether at the time or subsequently, may acknowledge the degree to which the failures of
their own government played some role in the debacle. However, overwhelmingly they portray the United States as behav-
ing in a predatory fashion. People in other Latin American
nations also grew concerned that Mexico's fate might become
their own. The various filibustering expeditions added to their
anxiety about U.S. expansionism.*

*The selections which follow exemplify these varying
views of manifest destiny while touching on many of the
major events of the era. The view of European liberals is reflected in the first two readings. A Hungarian couple, Ferencz
and Theresa Pulszky discuss the plight of the Native Americans, or as they put it the "red man," focusing especially on
Tecumseh. Adam De Gurowski, a Pole, discusses manifest
destiny as a fulfillment of American republican principles.
The next selection, signed only as being from "the British
public," focuses on the Oregon dispute, and appeals for its
peaceful resolution. The anger of Mexicans over the annexation of Texas marks the work of José María Tornel y
Mendível, who served as Mexico's secretary of war during
the Texas revolt. A Chilean, Francisco Bilbao, writing in
1856 concludes this chapter with a critique of U.S. attitudes
and behaviors toward Latin America.*

FERENCZ AND THERESA PULSZKY

TECUMSEH

Ferencz (1814–1897) and Theresa (1815–?) Pulszky accompanied the Hungarian liberal revolutionary leader Lajos Kossuth on a journey through the United States in 1851-52. They penned a three volume account of their travels, White Red Black, Sketches of Society in the United States During the Visit of their Guest, *which appeared in 1853. In this selection on "The Red Race," they clearly express prevailing Western-world sentiment regarding race, progress, and civilization. So, for example, while noting the admirable qualities they recognize in Tecumseh, observe also their easy condemnation of the "savages," and their assumptions regarding the superiority of the Anglo-Saxon.*

Who could speak about Indians without mentioning their greatest man, Tecumseh? Tecumseh himself had, in early youth, distinguished himself among his tribe, in their encounters with the hunters of Kentucky, during and after the revolutionary war, and acquired an influence over his nation by his bravery, his sense of justice, and his eloquence. He was not acknowledged as chief of his own tribe, either in peace or war; he was but a brave, though he soon wielded greater power and influence than any chief. Not entirely unacquainted with the arts and sciences of the whites—in fact he could read and write—pervaded by the loftiest patriotism, and fully aware of the ultimate fate of his race, unless the tribes were to attain the consistency of a nation, he not only took up the plans of Pontiac, but carried them further.

Pontiac's aim was merely the destruction of the English forts in the west, by a sudden and simultaneous attack, but, beyond the defeat of his enemies, he did not form, or at least not actively prepare, any scheme of future organisation. But Tecumseh's aim was nobler,—it was not the destruction of the enemy, but the reformation of his own race, and the ultimate amalgamation of the tribes into one nation. He traced the rapid decline of the red man principally to the intemperate use of spirits, and to the hostility of the tribes amongst themselves. Hence while the English, and later the Americans, were always able to war or to negociate with only one section of the Indians at a time, they were subdued and bought up piecemeal. His efforts were therefore directed to two principal points: the reformation of the savages, whose habits made them unfit for continuous exertion,—and the rousing of the feeling, that the interests of the Indians were identical, that therefore no treaty or sales of land to the United States, should be admitted without the united consent of all the tribes.

Tecumseh, well aware that no reformation of nations ever has been carried without religious enthusiasm, now imparted his plan to his brother Elshwatawa [Tenskwatawa], who was not less distinguished for his eloquence than the courageous chief himself. Elshwatawa accordingly began to dream dreams, and to see visions, of which the reports spread in the wilderness with the swiftness of the electric spark. The public mind was aroused, credulity and superstition began to extend its circles, until the fame of the prophet, and the divine character of his mission, pervaded all the Indian country. His precepts were purely moral; he preached humanity, peace, and good-will among the tribes, and especially temperance and union. In a short time, pilgrims from remote tribes sought, with fear and awe, the head-quarters of the prophet; proselytes were multiplied, and Tecumseh, the principal of the believers, mingled with the pilgrims.

Having thus prepared his way, and created a centre for his agitation, Tecumseh set out, in 1809, to perambulate the country of the different tribes, on the Lakes across the Mississippi, and in the South. He visited sometimes on his way General Harrison, at Vincennes, who was always busy in buying Indian lands for the government, and watching suspiciously the movements of the Shawanese [Shawnee] brothers, though he could not find any fault with them. They did not deny that they had occasionally seen English officers and traders, who, perhaps in anticipation of the war in 1812, were encouraging the Indians to contend for their rights; but they disclaimed any part in the combination to attack the American settlements, which was discovered amongst the tribes on the Mississippi and Illinois. Nor is there reason to believe, that they were insincere in this respect. Their scheme was yet far from being ripe, and Tecumseh had no intention to fight the battle of the English, and to endanger his plans of reform and union by an untimely outbreak in favour of white foreigners. On the other side, he solemnly protested, in 1810, against General Harrison's treating with several tribes, contending that the treaties were illegal and unjust, as the territory ceded by them was not the property of any single tribe, but of the red men at large.

The American government, of course, repudiated the new principle of the Shawanese brothers, that the purchases should be thenceforward made from a council, representing all the tribes united as one nation, and the officials of the government began to see in Tecumseh "the successor of Pontiac." So strong was this impression, that in a council, held in 1811, in a grove of trees close to General Harrison's house, when Tecumseh began to speak with some vehemence on the wrongs inflicted upon the Indians by the whites, who had driven them from the seacoast, and would soon push them into the lakes, and declared that it was his intention to take a stand, resolutely opposing any further intrusion upon the Indian lands, the general assumed a threatening attitude, guns were levelled on the Indians, and Tecumseh severely reprimanded, though his party had no guns under their blankets, and no treacherous disposition whatever. The council terminated by leaving on both parties the conviction that an ultimate conflict could not be avoided; but Tecumseh did not think it yet immediate, and went down to the South to seek allies amongst the Creeks and Cherokees.

The conflict being inevitable, it was desirable to have it ended before Tecumseh's plans had been matured, and the absence of the warrior favoured the enterprise. Though the general sent a message of peace to the prophet, he knew too well that the Indian fanaticism, raised by the appearance of a strong camp in the immediate vicinity of their sacred settlement would induce them to accept a battle, so much the more, as the general's little army, scarcely 900 men, was not superior to the Indian forces.

Harrison was not deceived by his estimate of the red man's character. In the morning of the 7th of November, he was furiously attacked. The prophet had given assurances to his followers, that the Great Spirit would render the arms of the Americans unavailing; that their bullets would fall harmless at the feet of the Indians, who would fight in full light, whilst their enemies would be involved in darkness. He continued his incantations and mystic rites during the battle, but, after a sharp action, his followers were routed. The prestige of the prophet was destroyed, the settlement of Tecumseh broken up, his village burnt, his camp trampled down, the tribes which had already joined in the confederacy were dismayed, and all further progress stopped.

In the next year the war with England broke out, and Tecumseh, with his friends followed the fortunes of the English. By his bravery and humanity—a rare virtue with an Indian—he got the appointment of brigadier-general in the English service; but he had the strong conviction that his star had set. He sought and found his death in the battle of the Thames. He deemed flight disgraceful, and stood his ground when the English were already defeated—in life and in death the bravest of the Indian " Braves."

It is easier to pity the red race, and to mourn over its fate, than to devise a plan for saving them from destruction, unless they give up their hunting propensities, and turn either shepherds or agriculturists. The co-existence of the hunter and of the ploughman in the same country is utterly impossible. It is not only the constant encroachment of the agriculturist on the hunting-ground, by the extension of the tilled soil, but even the noise of the village, the clearing of the woods, the roads which connect the distant settlement, and the regular intercourse on them, frighten the deer, drive away the wild buffalo, and deprive the Indian of his means of subsistence. Pressed back by progressive civilisation, seeing his supply of game constantly diminishing, in the presentiment of his ultimate fate, he rushes upon the settlements of the white, and destroys them: a war ensues; the bravest of his race fall in the strife, victims of the superior skill, and often of the treachery of their white enemies, whilst the remnant of the tribe, decimated by imported vices and diseases, lingers for a time, mixes with the oppressors, and is absorbed by them through a generation of half-breeds. The red race in North America is doomed to extinction. The activity of the Anglo-Saxons is fatal to every idle race; they are the great colonisers of the modern age, but not the civilisers of savage nations. Wherever they settle, the inferior race is swept away from the country. And this process of extermination is nowhere more rapid than in North America.

The United States, which had successively bought up the lands of the Indians from the Alleghanies to the Ohio, from the Ohio to the Mississippi, and from the Mississippi to the Missouri, felt their duty of providing them with an ultimate home, from whence they should not again be disturbed, and where, under the guidance of government officials, they might accustom themselves to agricultural and industrial pursuits. An immense tract, occupying all the country from the boundary of the state Missouri to the frontiers of Texas, and from the Red river to the Kansas, was purchased of the wild tribes for a permanent abiding place for those Indians, who were removed from the settled part of the Union. This tract is called "the Indian Territory." The soil is fertile here, with excellent water; it is rich in minerals, and studded with fine timber. The whites are not allowed to settle in the Indian Territory. Traders may visit it; blacksmiths and gunsmiths, teachers and missionaries reside there with the permission of the chiefs and of the Indian agent, but no encroachment on the territory is permitted to the pioneer who covets its beautiful climate. The government has, besides, paid the costs of the transportation of the tribes, erected a portion of their dwellings, fenced and ploughed a part of their fields, furnished them horses and cattle, erected school-houses, supported the teachers, and made provision for the subsistence of the new emigrants. It forbids hostilities amongst them, but does not meddle further with their internal administration, though it recommends them to abolish the hereditary chieftainships to make all the rulers elective, and to unite the tribes—constituted in a certain similarity to the States—under a general government like that at Washington.

Civilisation is thus put within the reach of the Indians. The plans of Tecumseh can here be carried on in peace, as the red men are protected during the epoch of transition against any attack or competition of their enterprising neighbours. They have, at last, got a fair trial for their energies and they can now show whether they are able to endure the state of an agricultural society, or whether they are to be swept away by the tide of colonisation, with the elk, and deer, and buffalo; "improved off" from the face of the earth.

Terms and Definitions

Pontiac: an Ottawa chief who was one of the leaders of a 1763 "rebellion" on the Appalachian frontier.

ADAM DE GUROWSKI

Manifest Destiny: A Positive View

A German-educated Polish nobleman, Adam G. De Gurowski (1805–1866) was involved in anti-monarchical insurrections in Poland in the 1840s, and subsequently moved to the United States. He greatly admired America, seeing in it the fulfillment of the ideas of nineteenth-century European Liberalism. The following selection comes from his 1857 book, America and Europe. *De Gurowski's various references to the "Yankee," relate to his disdain for the slave-holding southerner, who he did not regard as being true to American principles. Note as well his reference to the American continent as being "unpeopled," a comment which implies that the displacement of Native Americans did not count as an act of aggression.*

It was not . . . to conquests of a filibustering character, that the American republic owes its rapid, and almost miraculous extension. Its ways and means are original, and, up to this time, unused in history. They differ from all the modes of extension used in all other epochs, and by all other nations or sovereigns; they are truly American, and constitute a cardinal difference between the history of the States of the Old World, and that of the United Republic.

It is a common-place saying, thrown out by the partisans of absolute and monarchical governments in the face of republics and democracies, that these are always aggressive and greedy of conquest. With the exception of Rome, history does not justify this saying. All the monarchies, of whatever age, nature, and form, have been always warlike, conquering, and aggressive. All of them extended their possessions by invasions and conquests, and uninterruptedly imbrued the annals of the human race in blood. Republics have been few, democracies still fewer; and any one, even superficially familiar with history, ought conscientiously to acknowledge, that they have been less aggressive than monarchies.

Still less are justified the modern European assertions, made by governments and political writers, concerning the insatiable desire to extend the American nation. In face of their past history, as well as of their present uninterrupted proceedings, it does not behoove any of the European states to upbraid America. While America purchased and extended itself over the wilderness and unpeopled solitudes, England almost daily overthrows and absorbs organized, populous, and rich empires in India, extending over thousands of square miles, and with millions and millions of population. English conquests are destructive; American purchases and annexations are organic and creative. France and Russia extend their dominion, the one in Africa, the other in Asia; and their conquests, in their civilizing purpose and character, as well as in that of the regions over which they are extended, have a certain similitude to the American annexation.

The consciousness of carving out the manifest destiny of this continent, inaugurates a new distinct policy for America, in her relations with others, above all with European governments. The technical name of this policy, called the Monroe doctrine, is only its partial enunciation. In its full comprehension, this policy is the utterance of maturity and manhood, the fulfilment of the historical mission.

This continent ought to be independent and sheltered from any direct, that is, governmental, or indirect, political and diplomatic influence, to be exercised in any way by European powers. It is natural to the free Union, to look for an end of the colonial dependency of any region on this continent upon what is called the mother countries; it is natural to see the Americans extend their flag, to shield other States here from the baneful breezes of European policy. The European monarchies, based all of them without exception on prerogatives and privileges, surrounded by various kinds of aristocracies, are conjured not to allow a republic to start among them, to preserve the royal and aristocratical brotherhood untouched. It is natural and logical that this commonwealth wishes and tends to be surrounded by a cluster of sister democracies. It is logical and natural that it tends to see the whole continent fully emancipated. No dependency ought to exist.

The natural bonds between Europe and America are only those of commercial intercourse and exchange, and of ideas and notions; all on the footing of absolute political equality. It is natural and logical for the United States, that, embodying a new and higher social principle in its vigorous growth and expansion, they should assert their rights, and speak to the old world peremptorily in the name of the new one. The American Republic does not interfere with the annexations and extensions carried out by various European powers on the other parts of the world;—but it is her most sacred duty to repel any encroachments of Europe on the soil of America, as well as to repel the intervention of European policy in any relations, domestic or external, of the North or South-American States. It is duty and right to put a term in the name of this new world, to the arrogant and unjustifiable assumption of European monarchical governments, to regulate in any way the affairs of this hemisphere. The real supremacy of Europe in the arts, in several branches of manufactures, industry, science, and literature, will by itself preserve its influence. This supremacy, of which the European people are the creators, is independent of the action on it of the governments. These civilizing and pacific channels alone can unite the two worlds. Europe might still serve in many mental and intellectual respects, as a master to America; nevertheless the action of the currents is reciprocal. But the governments of Europe are not so constituted as to exercise any beneficial influence on this continent. Against them alone is to be directed, in its fullest meaning and extent, the Monroe doctrine. The European governments, on the contrary, in questions of general policy, must yield to the principles asserted by the American Republic.

From whatever point of view we regard the question, Europe has not a right to interfere on this continent. Only, if America should tread down the sacred principles wherein she originated; if America should swerve and abandon the luminous orbit of freedom and civilization, pervert her character, and use her power for extending and implanting slavery in regions where it does not exist or where it has been already abolished; in one word, if extension of the Union should become synonymous with bondage and chattelhood, with the slave-trade; then only as the positions would thus become reversed, and Europe defend a holier principle, her intervention and her defense of sacred human rights would be justified before the tribunal of justice,—morality, civilization, and history.

Europe ought not to have any footing on the American continent. Justly, likewise the European powers will never allow to the American Republic to acquire any foothold in Europe. In this respect, both the continents ought to be absolutely independent and free of each other. Under no pretense, American interference with European internal affairs, with wars or revolutions, would be justified. Principles and example are the only agencies—moral ones—of the action of America on the old world.

There is no danger that the preservation of the martial spirit, in the free and civilized States of the Union will degenerate, and become tantamount to a savage, reckless spirit of assault, invasion, and piracy. The population of those

States value the worth of civilization, of peace and its blessings; they prefer the quiet pursuits of agriculture and industry, the family hearth, to the roving idleness of military bands and expeditions.

America as a nation is so situated that her extension, even if aimed at indefinitely, can be accomplished more easily by peace than by aggression. The band of the federation is limitlessly elastic. To it gravitates—at present it may be imperceptibly—the North and the South—Canada as well as the republics of Central America. That the result of such union will be the successive disappearance and dissolution of the **creole race** in its own shiftlessness, is almost indubitable. In Louisiana, Florida, the original native elements, living on equal rights with the new comers, preserving their respective idioms in all the everyday and domestic relations, vanish or are absorbed, dissolved, by the preponderating influence of the language used by the law, in politics and in business, used for general and public education, as they are absorbed by the influx of new occupants. The same will occur with the Spanish inhabitants of the central states or of Cuba, if they shall enter the Union. They will yield the path to the northern man, (not however to the slavery extenders and pirates,) to his superior activity, industry, culture, robustness of mind and of body. And those among the natives who may be able to keep step with the men of the North, will merge in the new culture and language, and only the family names will tell of the original difference. It is this certainty of absorbing by the superiority of intellectual muscle, other populations coming in contact with him, that increases in the American of the North his faith in the manifest destiny. By this superiority, and by peaceful arts, industry, commerce, he attracts; by them he increases the national wealth in colossal proportions; and can buy lands, paying for them millions, as he did to the Indians, and annex. (Canada, united already by identity of birth, of language, and of interests, must finally by her own free choice throw away her royalist livery, and become an independent and self-acting member of the federation.)

The preservation of the martial spirit is not therefore an agency or a lever for the fulfillment of manifest destinies—as those destinies are not pregnant with the curse and calamities of war. War is inborn among the nations of past and of modern Europe, it exhausts their material resources, demoralizes their respective populations, disabling them for freedom and for its acting soul—self-government. War in the life and development of America is an excrescence on the social body, an excrescence produced by an irritating action from without, or by the fermentation of the impure elements created inwardly in the body by the deviation of a part of the nation from the fundamental principles of reason and justice, from which America draws her life.

European powers, as well as European nations, daily and daily more clearly understand, that the prosperity of that hemisphere increases with the preponderating influence of North America. England gets more than the lion's share of the gold from California, transformed as by a spell from an unknown solitude into a flourishing community, by the expansive energy, the activity, the constructiveness of the freemen from the free States. The creative and untiring activity of these genuine Yankees covers the pestilential marshes with railroads, clears the forests, subdues wild nature, and aids the surplus of European populations to take possession of those primitive, or badly cultivated regions. The free North Americans are alone born to start, to create, to organize, and direct new communities, and thus to facilitate the efforts of Europeans. They alone possess the required self-consciousness and energy, and above all the inborn faculty of social organization. By the extension of American freedom Europe becomes benefited, and new and prosperous marts are opened as outlets for her industry. War will not therefore prevent the progress of America, and is not necessary to forward the fulfillment of her manifest destiny.

TERMS AND DEFINITIONS

Creole race: as used here, a reference
to the mixed-race inhabitants of
Spanish America.

"THE BRITISH PUBLIC"

OREGON IS NOT WORTH A WAR

Relations between England and the United States had improved somewhat in the decades after the War of 1812. Nonetheless, "Twisting John Bull's tail," that is, making derisive comments about England, remained popular in the United States, particularly among politicians, who wanted to whip up a crowd. The bellicose posturing on both sides of the Atlantic with regard to the Oregon territory suggests the still-delicate nature of the relations between the two English-speaking nations. The following selection, an anonymous antiwar appeal to people in the United States from "The British Public," written in 1846, stresses the positive ties of language and culture that unite the two countries. It also criticizes politicians for inflaming public passions.

We address ourselves at once to the great question, on which have long enough been balanced the peace and prosperity of two of the greatest nations in the world. A declaration of war is the death-warrant of thousands. This terrible truth, engraven in indelible characters on the records of the past, calls aloud upon every successive generation to inquire by whose authority and on what ground such sentence is pronounced.

On the point now at issue between you and us, we have not to plead either ambiguity or mystery; and we are not yet plunged head-long into the midst of a quarrel, in which there can be no pause, and from which there can be no retreat. The nature of our difference is at least clearly avowed, and easily understood; and on the strength and sincerity of that avowal, we appeal to your candour, your intelligence, and your sober judgment. The conviction is perhaps gaining ground, that a rupture is not now to be feared. It is not an unreasonable hope, that war will now be averted. But the evil next in magnitude, to open violence, is a state of irritability and anxiety, such as we have long enough endured; and such as leaves an ever-open door for a sudden and terrible collision. We have long enough stood on the brink of the precipice. The public mind has long enough been tortured by suspense. We ask you to join us in a decisive effort, *to terminate, once for all,* this senseless agitation; and to substitute, for an unworthy jealousy, those feelings of good will which alone are compatible with our highest and noblest destinies.

We would bring the entire question to the test of those simple and intelligible principles by which we regulate our ordinary pursuits;—in a word, to the test of common sense. We address you as brethren, not merely on the broad principle of universal kindredship. We claim a closer, a nearer relation. We acknowledge the same progenitors; we speak the same language; and we have to a great extent a community of laws. Thousands who have found in your land a home, claim among us their nearest earthly connexions; vast and increasing intercourse cements our innumerable and varied interests. We are bound together by all that can influence the noblest feelings of our nature, by all that can address the understanding, or appeal to the heart. If there are any two nations in the world that have the strongest reasons for desiring the continuance of peace, and friendly intercommunication they are the people of England and yourselves.

We turn then to the potent cause which has been declared sufficient to awaken the slumbering spirit of national animosity, to call forth mighty fleets and slaughtering armies trained to the trade of Destruction, and equipped with all the horrid paraphernalia of devastation and Death. What do we propose to purchase or what do we hope to acquire at so tremendous a cost? What is it that we thus coolly put in competition with so terrible an amount of human life? Is it the salvation of an empire? Is it the existence of a kingdom? Is it the safety of ourselves and our families, or the Preservation of our homes? No; but to settle a question about a title, or a boundary; to decide the proprietorship of territory. And is it possible that this is the real ground on which we propose to imbrue our hands in each other's blood? Is this the policy which represents the honest feeling of enlightened communities in this age of knowledge and civilization? It is impossible. The insinuation is disgraceful. Such a proposition is compatible with the ferocity of a savage, or the wild dreams of a maniac, but it is abhorrent to all that is worth the name of sense and good feeling, both in England and America. What then is the prospect before us, should we arrive at the preposterous conclusion to fight about the Oregon boundary? Among the multitude of chances and dubious results what can we discover of certainty? The most perspicacious eye cannot foresee on which side victory would declare itself. After a protracted and bloody struggle, it might even be on neither. It has been said, and no doubt truly that "all the strength and prejudices of both nations would be brought into play." You then at least are capable of inflicting upon *us* inconceivable mischiefs and calamities. We have at least the power of a somewhat proportionate retaliation.

We turn, then, to "the real value of the point at issue." Let any man of common intelligence declare, if he can, what the people of England really know or care about Oregon. We are as much interested in the question of its proprietorship as we are in that of the Great Desert of Africa; and we do not doubt, that apart from the excitement of the moment every intelligent man among yourselves has a precisely similar feeling.

As dogs are incited, first to snarl, and then to fight, by idle boys who stand by and enjoy the sport, exactly so it is with nations. Some simple incident gives rise to the first growl. Some journalist or scribbler is immediately wroth, magnifies the occasion, and makes some insulting comment. A rejoinder is soon at hand, more haughty and more provoking. Thus the quarrel proceeds. Does some leading journal or some public man discover an insult offered to our "national honour?" No time is to be lost in arousing our indignation. Our "dignity" must be maintained. Let us call to mind the glory of our ancestors. Let us boldly assert our rights. Let concessions be speedily demanded. Let America beware how she rouses the "British Lion."

Suppose on the other hand, some American statesman, or suppose a score of them, heated by enthusiasm, or urged by ambition, should inflate themselves with an idea of their growing importance, claim the empire of the world, and defy the interference of Great Britain. Very flattering is this no doubt to pride, very exciting at the moment, very much to the point as an appeal to human passions. But who among thinking men does not perceive its genuine character, and deplore the infatuation in which it originates? Without some such incitement as this, and without any factitious agency, are these the sentiments which in the midst of your industry, your vast commerce, your intelligence and your enlightened policy, you deliberately entertain, or fondly cherish? Would you willingly be judged by the character and movements of a knot of vain and violent politicians? You would not; and the injustice is only equaled by the folly that would charge the imprudence and the recklessness of such men upon a whole nation.

We call upon you to join us in putting an end to this mischievous and senseless system. We invite you to join us in adopting a course more accordant with the possession of rational faculties, more worthy of our intelligence, and more in character with the majesty of a great and powerful people. A doubt respecting the rational mode of settling the Oregon dispute, is only worthy of a darker age. We ask, *what conceivable obstacles stand in the way of a just and enlightened arbitration?* This is our real inquiry, and one which it is impossible to evade. The welfare of the world is involved in its issue. The destiny of millions may be contingent on its solution. It is an animating reflection that the door is still open for honourable negociation: it is impossible therefore to abandon the hope of an honourable arrangement. The appointment of a competent commission is within our reach: nothing but a mutual good-will to the undertaking is wanting for its realization. Is it objected that the decision might be unjust?

It is no part of our object here to investigate the actual merits of the question. We appeal to you on the simplicity of its character, and its unquestionable susceptibility of adjustment; and if nothing short of *mutual concession* be compatible with our mutual interest, it were the height of injustice to assume that you would be more reluctant than ourselves, to yield to the dictates of reason and humanity. It is at least as noble to abate our claims for the sake of peace and friendship, as it is to urge and enforce them till the ties of brotherhood are severed. There is every thing in favour of a peaceful decision; there is everything against an appeal to arms. The total loss of Oregon would be as nothing compared with the mischiefs and horrors of a war. We look at the subject as affecting the welfare of millions.

Far be it from us to affix the stigma of injustice or violence on any man, or set of men, among you. There is such a thing as misguided or mistaken patriotism. There is such a thing as an elevated, though it be a ruinous and mischievous sense of honor; and while an unprincipled selfishness is not to be mistaken, it must not be forgotten that integrity and misdirected zeal are not incompatible. We cannot however shut our eyes to the fact, that the unequivocal desire for peace evinced by the British government, has been but imperfectly reciprocated. Every attempt to effect a compromise has by some parties been resisted. We do not inquire who these parties are; but we ask, Are they *the millions* among you? We do not believe it. We find no evidence of such a fact. By misrepresentation of British feeling by distorted and exaggerated statements, by the excitement and indignation of men, whom you would fain believe to be your friends and protectors, you may possibly be brought to acquiesce in the necessity, if not to join in the spirit, of a bloody contest. We therefore appeal to your own independent judgment against a wild fanaticism; to the best and noblest feelings of your nature, against wicked attempts to excite a blood-thirsty desire for conquest. We urge you fearlessly to scrutinize the motives and the principles of men who would reject every proposition for a peaceable adjustment. It must be an unprecedented combination of circumstances which excludes all possibility of amicable arrangement.

The course you adopt is most momentous; for it stands associated with the great fact, that both in England and America, public opinion is irresistible. Its unequivocal expression carries every thing before it. It remains with the millions to decide if they will, the great and vital question, of war or peace. It argues nothing against the growing conviction in this country in favour of the latter, that England has still a large military and naval force, that she has even now scarcely retired from a blood-stained field. A long and complicated train of events cannot always be broken at a given point. The dispute about Oregon is scarcely begun; the sword is not yet unsheathed; now is the golden moment for the adoption of a humane and enlightened policy, in opposition to the maxims of by-gone ignorance, or a blind and savage ferocity. We appeal to you on the circumstances of the present juncture. We ask, can war be avoided now? We say that it can.

JOSÉ MARÍA TORNEL Y MENDÍVEL

A MEXICAN VIEWS
MANIFEST DESTINY

Like the Native Americans, Mexico stood in the way of U.S. expansion. The independence of Texas, popularly cast in our country in terms of the villainous general Antonio López de Santa Anna and the heroic Texans who died in the cause of freedom at the Alamo, never was recognized officially by the Mexican government. Writing just after Sam Houston took office as first president of the independent nation of Texas, José María Tornel y Mendível, Mexico's secretary of war during the Texas uprising, scathingly criticized the United States for its aggressive expansionism. He also disputed the grounds put forth by the Texans to justify their revolt, and, accurately as it turned out, warned his own countrymen of the looming menace of the United States. His critique later appeared in a 1837 book, Texas and the United States of America in their Relations with the Mexican Republic.*

For over fifty years—that is to say since its origins as a nation—the dominant thought of the United States of America has been to take over a great portion of the lands formerly owned by Spain and which now are part of the nation of Mexico. Democrats and Federalists, all their parties, whatever their names, have been in agreement with regard to expanding the boundaries of the republic in all directions, using every means in their power and guided by shrewdness, fraud and deceit.

Jefferson, that hero of the most exalted democratic principles, the philosopher who had the greatest influence on the law and policies of his country, the statesman who imbued it with its specific national character—which became evidenced in the actions of swarms of frontiersmen and settlers—delighted his compatriots with the prospect of expanding to the Isthmus of Panama while promising as well that the colossus [the U.S.] would also one day extend to the banks of the Saint Lawrence. The atheist of Monticello well understood the propensities of his countrymen, and to gain widespread popularity, he fomented their dreams of domination, even though they were based on no right other than that of force. Therefore, one rarely encounters an American who does not celebrate Jefferson as some sort of demigod, because they see him as the person who has revealed their destiny as a people. . . .

Unfortunately . . . we always have acted with the openness, weakness, and inexperience that characterizes new nations. Our restless, tumultuous neighbor presented himself to us as our teacher and encouraged us to copy his institutions. All too late we now understand that once established in our land, these inevitably would produce naught but constant anarchy, the destruction of our resources, the weakening of our national character, and, hence, render us incapable of resisting the inroads and attacks of the modern Rome.

To covet, wait, and then act characterize the distinctive nature of the American people and its government; none in the civilized world can match their limitless claims. Once they have decided upon an objective they covet, they lie in ambush awaiting the appropriate moment, all the while feigning disinterest. And then, when circumstances seem to be favorable, they stop at nothing to achieve their objective. This is an historical truth, a truth obvious to everyone, a truth as bright as the noonday light.

When Spain still retained some power, and was strengthened by its alliance with France, America respected its rights. . . . When the Spanish people rose in revolt against Napoleon, it threw the affairs of the Peninsula into chaos, and the weak revolutionary governments could scarcely maintain their existence. This combination of factors proved propitious for the schemes of the United States, which, scarcely able to conceal its pleasure, now began to act without the hypocritical mask which previously had disguised its designs.

The thinking men of the United States understood that their own successful independence movement was the prelude to the political emancipation of the entire New World, and that sooner or later, Spain's colonies would realize that resistance to a distant, tyrannical power could be successful. These men realized as well that the United States' longer existence as an independent nation, its material achievements, and the experience of its own fighting forces would afford it a preeminent position to guide the fortunes of the new nations: assisting Spain's colonies in their independence struggles would unfailingly strengthen the United States.

Despite its advantageous position, its nascent naval power, the warlike nature of its inhabitants, the strength displayed in its own struggles, its abundant natural resources and the prospects of its industries, the United States could not hope to achieve a higher rank among the world's nations so long as its standing was compared to the great powers of Europe. The appearance of other new independent peoples in the Americas would change this situation. Aiding the independence movements in Spanish America—whether by example, advice, or material assistance was therefore in the self-interest of the United States. It would enable the U.S. to achieve its coveted objectives. . . . Egoism is an inherent aspect of the nature of the Anglo-American peoples. If they proclaim or uphold the august rights of nations to liberty and independence, this does not proceed from the desire to aid a just or holy cause. It is their own interests, that they seek, their own advancement that they tirelessly pursue. Who today does not recognize the real and only reason for the United States' early support for the independence of the Spanish colonies?

In issues relating to the acquisition of the Floridas, in the never-ending attempts to bring the American zodiac to the banks of the **Rio Bravo,** the United States has followed the same path, shamelessly marked by the same tricks and pretensions, violent attacks and bad faith. Do not all the ancient republics—even the ever-ambitious Rome—pale in comparison to this tempestuous democracy that extends its arms from the Atlantic to the Pacific, and which plans to absorb an entire continent? At times she advances through the power of illusionary claims which pave the way for her diplomatic intrigues; however, she does not shy away from the use of force and war.

The colonization of Texas by adventurers from the United States was an assured way to despoil Mexico of its territory *without impairing or violating existing treaties.* Is there anyone who fails to see the manifestly deceptive nature of a policy that seized upon this recourse to mock the most solemn and sacred pledges that are entered into by nations?

The treaty by which Spain ceded Louisiana to France included the stipulation that its inhabitants could settle freely in any portion of the territory. The Anglo-Americans cleverly used this as a pretext for going to Texas—alleging that as members of some Louisiana families, they felt loyalty for the Spanish government. This occurred towards the end of 1820, and by the beginning of the following year, the Americans already had obtained permission to bring 300 families into Texas, with the proviso that they be of the Catholic faith and swear obedience and loyalty to Spain.

Moses Austin headed the expedition. By happenstance, his name foreshadowed the invasion which ultimately would occur, traversing the desert and arriving in the promised land. One marvels at such adroitness on the part of the leader of *the new chosen people of God,* and at the ignorance and lack of forethought on the part of the Spanish authorities. They ought have reflected on the fact that the United States begins and carries out its conquests through silent paths, without imperiling peaceful relations with the nation whose territory it plans to despoil; that instead of openly hostile measures, it uses artfully disguised means and expedients, ones seemingly slow and ineffectual, but which unfailingly succeed.

Opening the door for the Americans was a big mistake. Not very long ago, so as to have grounds to justify their rebellion, the American colonists alleged that they had joined Mexican society with the proviso that Mexico would remain a federal republic. Since this had not proved the case, they argued, the pact with the government no longer held any force, and they thus had the right to govern themselves as they wished.

The great majority of the inhabitants of Texas are from the United States, particularly its western frontier; the percentage of land speculators among them is considerable. Among those speculators are some who . . . exercise great influence on United States policy. This has contributed to the formation of a population in Texas that is Anglo-American rather than Mexican. Neither their predilections, manners, language, nor policy distance them from their country of origin, nor inspires within them any sense of feeling for the country which adopted them. What ought have been anticipated as the outcome of this: only that the colony would organize and consolidate itself in order to marshal its forces against the very mother country which had provided the opportunity for them to grow and develop. Who does not in this see the mark of the longstanding desire to take our land? What could deter the covetous Anglo-Americans? Nothing. They had the power.

In April 1833, a convention was held in San Felipe de Austin, and approved a constitution separating Texas from the state of Coahuila and giving it its own independent, sovereign government. Stephen F. Austin. . .was sent to Mexico City to argue that, in accordance with the law, it fulfilled all the conditions to be a separate state. Rebuffed for impudent behavior, he tried to excuse himself on the grounds that he was not all that conversant with the Spanish language.

Nonetheless, such was his perfidious nature that on his return to Texas on 2 October, defying the wishes of the national government of Mexico he instructed the Texas authorities to establish an independent government.

Finally, the day came when, enticed by the advantages produced by multiple unforseen circumstances, they entirely ripped off the veil of deceit and openly declared their independence from Mexico. On 2 March 1836 a convention of Texas delegates issued a formal declaration of independence. But this amounted to nothing more than the expression of long-standing actions and desires. Nonetheless, the justice of this action is supposedly supported by an astonishing set of fictitious charges. They assert that the Texans were invited and admitted to the country in accord with a contract under a written constitution, and that from the moment that constitution was annulled, their own obligations ended as well. Mexico, imprudently generous to the colonists, consented to their supplications, admitting them into our nation, because they wanted and requested that association. We have noted that at the time the first concessions of land were made to them, the national government was a monarchy, and that multiple other changes subsequently have occurred, none of which gave them any right to deny their allegiance since there never was any condition stipulating a particular governmental form.

The principal complaint alleged by the rebels is that they were not allowed to establish an independent state governed by their own constitution. Even had the federal system remained, it is not at all certain that Texas truly has the elements and resources requisite for an independent existence. As for the subsequent change in government that occurred, one would have expected the colonists to defer any action until the results of the changes became clear. And, we have seen that the congress raised Texas to the level of a department [state] separating it in that fashion from Coahuila.

The Texans accuse us of having neglected elementary education, a charge which clearly highlights their bad faith. As is known, under our system, education falls under the respective city councils. The city council of Texas had that right, and even assumed other prerogatives denied such bodies. Why, then, did they not take care of this issue if it indeed was of such interest to them? In addition, in Texas the city council levied taxes and spent revenues without any interference by Mexican officials. If they did not provide funds for their children's education, the responsibility rests with them. The Texans have representation in the state congress. They ought have promoted there the things they saw as important, as they did with regard to land issues, the primary object of their desires, the principal object of their insatiable greed.

Finally, before God and man, the rebels attempt to justify their criminal uprising by claiming it is a response to repressive measures to which they have been subjected by what we know is an all-too-indulgent Mexican government. An inherent attribute of sovereignty is the right to use force to reign in rowdy elements, punish those who rebel, and maintain order. Can the United States claim any other basis in law for sending troops to Florida to punish the Seminoles and Creeks? That which is a right for one nation ought be a right for all. The civilized world already has judged the Texans' actions; it rejects the reasons proffered for their declaration of independence.

Whenever possible, the Anglo-Americans have worked against our country's interests and inflicted harm upon us. Their navy provided assistance for an uprising of American citizens in Upper California. No such revolt ever would have occurred had its leaders not counted on receiving such support. Doubtlessly as well, the bloody revolt in New Mexico resulted from the actions of U.S. agents, a supposition confirmed by the fact that the insurrection's leaders sought refuge in United States territory.

This rapidly traced picture of the horrid policy of the United States ought sufficiently alert Mexicans as to the dangers they face, and, naturally, it will inspire a desire to exact revenge for so many acts of violence and oppression. Vanity inspires the imagination of the Anglo-Americans, and in their self-flattering dreams, they see us as pygmies, objects of scorn, just as our lands are objects of their covetousness. "All other nations," says a celebrated writer, "seem to have reached their natural limits, while the United States continues easily and with alacrity along a path whose ultimate end the human eye cannot foresee."

The loss of Mexico will inevitably lead to the loss of New Mexico and of the Californias; and little by little our territory will shrink until we are reduced to an insignificant nation.

TERMS AND DEFINITIONS

Rio Bravo: this river is also known as the Rio Grande river. The Rio Bravo, in the southwest United States, forms part of the U.S.–Mexico boundary. The river flows from the San Juan mountains in southwestern Colorado to the Gulf of Mexico.

FRANCISCO BARQUÍN BILBAO

THE U.S. THREAT TO LATIN AMERICA

The new nations of Latin America often expressed admiration for the United States. They praised its emphasis on liberty, its form of government, and the great progress it had made in so short a period of time. Manifest destiny, however, alarmed many Latin Americans, and they began to see a different, a more threatening, United States. Francisco Barquín Bilbao (1823–1865), a radical political figure in Chile, traveled extensively in Europe during the 1840s. He wrote a book in 1856 with the title "America in Danger." The word "America" in that title refers not to the United Sates, but to Latin America. Although Chile itself had not suffered any intervention to that point, Bilbao wrote at a time of the several filibustering expeditions and in the aftermath of the Mexican War. Note the mixture of admiration for the many accomplishments of the United States, and anger over its arrogant behavior.

Today we behold empires reviving the ancient idea of world domination. The Russian Empire and the United States, two powers situated at the geographical as well as political extremes, aspire, the one to extend Russian slavery under the mask of **Pan-Slavism,** the other to secure the sway of Yankee individualism. Russia is very far away, the United States is near. Russia sheathes its claws, trusting in its crafty snares; but the United States daily extends *its* claws in the hunting expedition that it has begun against the South. Already we see fragments of America falling into the jaws of the Saxon boa that hypnotizes its foes as it unfolds its tortuous coils. First it was Texas, then it was Northern Mexico and the Pacific that hailed its new master.

Today the **skirmishers of the North** are awakening the Isthmus with their shots, and we see Panama, . . . suspended over the abyss and asking itself: Shall I belong to the South or to the North?

The **United States of South America** has sighted the smoke of the campfires of the United States. Already we hear the tread of the young colossus that with its diplomacy, with that swarm of adventurers that it casts about like seed, with its growing power and influence that hypnotize its neighbors, with its intrigues among our peoples, with its treaties, mediations, and protectorates, with its industry, its merchant marine, its enterprises—quick to note our weaknesses and our weariness, quick to take advantage of the divisions among our republics, ever more impetuous and audacious, having the same faith in its imperial destiny as did Rome, infatuated with its unbroken string of successes—that youthful colossus advances like a rising tide that rears up its waters to fall like a cataract upon the South.

The name of the United States—our contemporary, but one that has left us so far behind—already resounds throughout the world. The sons of Penn and Washington opened a new historical epoch when, assembled in Congress, they proclaimed the greatest and most beautiful of all existing Constitutions. . . .

That was the heroic moment of its annals. All grew: wealth, population, power, and liberty. They leveled the forests, peopled the deserts, sailed all the seas. Scorning traditional systems, and creating a spirit that devours space and time, they formed a nation, a particular genius. And turning upon themselves and beholding themselves so great, they fell into the temptation of the **Titans.** They believed they were the arbiters of the earth. . . .

Personality infatuated with itself degenerates into individualism; exaggeration of personality turns into egotism; and from there to injustice and callousness is but a step. They have not abolished slavery in their States; they have not preserved the heroic Indian races—nor have they made themselves champions of the universal cause, but only of the American interest, of Saxon individualism. They hurl themselves upon the South, and the nation that should have been our star, our model, our strength, daily becomes a greater threat to the independence of South America.

We know the glories and even the superiority of the North, but we too have something to place in the scales of justice.

We who are poor have abolished slavery in all the republics of the South, while you who are rich and fortunate have not done so; we have incorporated and are incorporating the primitive races, . . . because we regard them as our flesh and blood, while you hypocritically exterminate them.

In our lands there survives something of that ancient and divine hospitality; in our breasts there is room for the love of mankind. We believe and love all that unites; we prefer the social to the individual, beauty to wealth, justice to power, art to commerce, poetry to industry, philosophy to textbooks, pure spirit to calculation, duty to self-interest. We do not see the earth, or in the pleasures of the earth, the definitive end of man; the Negro, the Indian, the disinherited, the unhappy, the weak, find among us the respect that is due to the name and dignity of man!

That is what the republics of South America dare to place in the balance opposite the pride, the wealth, and the power of North America.

TERMS AND DEFINITIONS

Pan-Slavism: the idea of uniting all the Slavic-speaking peoples of eastern Europe.

Skirmishers of the North: a reference to the several filibustering expeditions to Central America and Cuba.

Titans: in Greek mythology, this family of giants tried to become rulers of the heavens.

United States of South America: No such union actually existed. However, from the days of their wars for independence, various Latin American leaders and intellectuals spoke of creating some type of grand confederation.

THINKING THINGS THROUGH

1. What similarities do you see in the attitudes toward the Native Americans expressed by the Pulszkys and de Gurowski?

2. To what extent does de Gurowski's assertion that America's expansionism differed from that of other countries seem accurate?

3. What similarities are there in the two Latin American authors' critique of the United States?

4. Compare the European liberals' assessment of manifest destiny with that of the Latin Americans. What accounts for the differences?

5. What does the selection on Oregon suggest about the nature of relations between the United States and England?

9

SLAVERY, ABOLITION,
AND THE IMPENDING CRISIS

A. The International Context

In December 1865, the Thirteenth Amendment to the Con-
stitution ended slavery in the United States. By that time,
slavery already had been eliminated in every independent na-
tion of the Americas except Brazil, and from all European
possessions in the hemisphere save Spain's colonies of Cuba
and Puerto Rico.

   The abolition of slavery in the United States, while
unique in some respects, formed part of a broader world
movement. Slavery was an ancient human institution (see
Chapter 3). Plantation slavery in the Americas, however, had
some distinctive characteristics. In the past, slavery had
tended to be a temporary, nonhereditary status. It was asso-
ciated more with the misfortunes of war than with any pre-
sumption of inherent inferiority. In the Americas, however,
slavery developed a specific racial dimension, and the status
of slave became permanent and inherited. In the United
States, at least in terms of law, slaves lost all humanity and
became simply property. The intertwining of the status of
slave with race imbued American slavery with social charac-
teristics that powerfully affected subsequent race relations
and social class systems.

   Although slavery existed throughout the Western Hemi-
sphere, it varied significantly from place to place. The eco-
nomic importance of slavery and, hence, the number of slaves
and prominence of the institution varied widely. For example,
in Canada, Argentina, and Chile, slavery had comparatively
minor importance. By contrast, it dominated the economic
and social landscape of Brazil, the West Indies sugar islands,
and the southern portion of the United States. In the 1770s,
slaves comprised approximately 90 percent of the population

of the British West Indies, but accounted for perhaps 1 percent of the population of Chile. Differences also occurred with
regard to the ease and frequency of manumission, the numbers of free persons of color, the ratio of the slave population
to that of the free, and the frequency and success of insurrections and other forms of slave resistance. Furthermore, the
very identification of race also varied. Throughout much of
Latin America, racial mixing resulted in the recognition of in-
termediate racial classifications. In the United States a "one
drop of blood" rule of descent maintained a rigid "black"-
versus-"white" dichotomy.

The process of abolition in the Americas also displayed
both general similarities and significant variations. In chrono-
logical terms, the first formal abolitions of slavery in the New
World occurred in the context of the wars of independence in
Latin America. The forerunner was Haiti where a revolt that
raged from 1789 to 1791 saw massive slave insurrections and
the end of both slavery and French colonial rule. In 1823 a
newly-independent Chile decreed the end of slavery, as did
the newly created Central American Confederation (which
included the present nations of Costa Rica, Guatemala, Honduras, Nicaragua, and El Salvador) the following year. Mexico followed suit in 1829. The next decades saw further
erosion of New World slavery. The chief remaining European
colonial powers acted to end the institution, beginning with
England in 1834, and then Denmark and France in the
1840s. In the 1840s and 1850s Uruguay, Colombia, Argentina, Venezuela, and Peru all abolished slavery.

Coincident with these movements in the Americas, serfdom, another system of servile labor, finally disappeared from
Europe. The years 1848–53 saw the emancipation of serfs
throughout the vast Hapsburg Empire. In the 1860s, both
Romania and Russia freed their serfs.

It seems clear, then, that abolition of slavery formed part
of a more general movement away from various traditional
forms of labor control and toward what would become
known as a system of free wage labor. Not surprisingly, one
explanation for slavery's end relates to the significant rise in
industrial production in the years from 1760 to 1840. This
industrial revolution particularly marked the experience of
England, and to a somewhat lesser extent France, Belgium,
Germany, and the United States.

Though confined to specific regions within those countries, industry's rise had broad impacts, including an accelerated rate of urbanization and the creation of a new industrial

working class. Although landed wealth retained its predominant economic and social position throughout the nineteenth century, industrial growth created new avenues for achieving money and status. Newly-rich industrialists altered the traditional upper class. The middle classes also expanded. A wage-based labor system, where workers independently contracted with employers, became common. These developments also contributed to a greater democratization of political systems and new possibilities for mass politics.

Great Britain, Europe's leader in industrialization, also led the Continent in a fight against the slave trade and slavery itself. Similarly, in the United States, the more industrialized and free-labor-based Northeast led the fight for abolition. In part, this reflected the obvious workings of self-interest. Neither Great Britain nor the northeastern United States saw their prosperity as linked to slavery.

At the same time, however, the abolitionist impulse also reflected new currents of thought regarding government and society that had been at the base of both the American and French revolutions, and had fed the rise of Liberalism in England. These related also to the idea of progress, which became a benchmark for much of the Western world. Measured in those terms, slavery along with serfdom increasingly seemed remnants of a backward age whose time had passed.

Religion provided the most direct and uncompromising attack on slavery. The Society of Friends, or Quakers, which had arisen in the 1640s in England, always had opposed slavery, but they represented only a small, lonely voice. In eighteenth-century England, however, a powerful new religious voice arose, one that uncompromisingly defined slavery as sin. The Wesley brothers, John and Charles, established so-called Wesleyan societies, reform evangelical Christian groups which by the 1790s became known as Methodists.

The Wesleys' critique of British society and policy included stinging indictments of slavery. They and their followers formed an important contingent in the coalition of reformers pressing England to take a stand against both the slave trade and slavery itself. That coalition also included new middle- and working-class groups who saw slavery not only as a moral issue but as a threat to free laborers.

The abolition movements in the Americas confronted many of the same issues. One involved the tension between a gradual rather than an immediate end to slavery. Those Latin American nations where slavery had great economic importance proceeded with great caution. Abolition unfolded in stages as a gradual process. One common approach first freed children born by slave mothers, and only later completely ended slavery itself. Gradualism also had its adherents in the United States.

The treatment of newly freed slaves was another question. While compensation to former slave owners commonly received discussion, and in some cases actually occurred, the freed men typically received no support to ease their transition. In the United States at the end of the Civil War, the Freedmen's Bureau represented a positive exception to this practice, but it soon fell by the wayside. Instead of assistance, throughout the Americas freed slaves often encountered schemes which sought to bind them in some fashion as laborers. In Cuba, for example, the government imposed an eight-year "apprenticeship" to keep newly-liberated slaves under the control of their former masters. Denmark used that same expedient in its colonies in the West Indies. Having freed its slaves in 1848, the following year, the government imposed a Labor Act, which forced them to sign yearly labor contracts. That law remained in force until a massive protest forced its repeal in 1879.

Violence of various kinds, both episodic and organized, marked the process of abolition in the Americas. Only in the United States, however, did it take the form of a civil war. Even Brazil, where slave-owning planters represented the wealthiest and most politically powerful families, managed to abolish slavery without that type of upheaval. The peculiar spatial distribution of U.S. slavery, replete with differing economic and social visions, clearly complicated the issue of abolition and contributed to creating the irrepressible conflict.

B. International Views

Two factors dominate international views of slavery in the United States: religious reformism and the rise of political liberalism. British abolitionism had strong ties to New England, the center of the U.S. movement against slavery. Antislavery societies in England regularly corresponded and cooperated with their counterparts in America. The Second Great Awakening, which exploded over the first several decades of the nineteenth century, reflected religious currents emanating from England. This new current of religious reform, swelled the ranks of those opposing slavery. Seeing slavery as sin, they had little patience with gradualism or compromise.

European liberals uniformly denounced slavery. For many of them, the American Revolution and the subsequent great democratic experiment in America had provided both inspiration and a model of enlightened liberal principles in practice. The existence of slavery in the United States therefore pained them greatly. A comment in an 1855 letter by Alexis de Tocqueville, renowned then and now for his insightful comments on the nature of democratic culture and society in the book Democracy in America, *accurately captures this feeling: "As the persevering enemy of despotism everywhere and under all its forms, I am pained and astonished that the freest people in the world is, at the present time, almost the only one among civilized and Christian nations which yet maintains personal servitude." Those working for the abolition of serfdom also saw an obvious connection between their efforts and the fight against slavery in the United States. The fact that the United States represented one of the last bastions of slavery also prompted broad international commentary.*

The following selections reflect the prominent role of religion, liberalism, and the British. They begin, however, with an eighteenth-century French liberal, J. P. Brissot de Warville, an admirer of U.S. political principles, which he sees as incompatible with slavery. Writing in the 1830s, a British woman, Fanny Kemble, draws a dismal picture of slavery's multiple cruelties to women. Hiram Wilson, an American delegate to the General Anti-Slavery Convention, sponsored by a British antislavery organization, discusses runaway slave communities in Canada. Frederick Milnes Edge, an English journalist writing in the years immediately prior to the Civil War roundly denounces the U.S. South, portraying it as opposed to freedom. In the concluding selection, the famous French liberal and author Victor Hugo writes in defense of John Brown.

J. P. BRISSOT DE WARVILLE

THE STATE OF AFRICAN AMERICANS AND THE FINAL DESTRUCTION OF SLAVERY

J. P. Brissot de Warville (1754–1793) had a distinguished career as an author and essayist over the latter portion of the eighteenth century. An ardent liberal, he became intrigued with the American experience, seeing in it a potential model for the people of a still-monarchical France. The following selection comes from his book New Travels in the United States of America Performed in MCCCLXXXVIII. *Published in 1793, the same year de Warville was guillotined in Paris for*

*his participation in the French Revolution, the book reflects his admiration for liberty and repub-
lican forms of government. Like other European liberals of his day, he saw an incongruity in the
existence of slavery in a democratic country. Note that he does foresee a path toward abolition in
the United States, and that he draws a sharp distinction in this regard between the northern and
southern portions of the new nation.*

Scarcely was independence declared, when a general cry arose against this commerce. It appeared absurd for men defending their own liberty to deny liberty
to others. The Congress, in 1776, declared the slavery of the Blacks to be incompatible with the basis of Republican governments. Different legislatures
hastened to confederate this principle of Congress. Three distinct epochs mark
the conduct of the Americans in this business—the prohibition of the importation of slaves—their manumission—and the provision made for their instruction. All the different States are not equally advanced in these three objects.

A numerous party still argue the impossibility of cultivating their soil
without the hands of slaves, and the impossibility of augmenting their number
without recruiting them in Africa. It is to the influence of this party, in the late
general convention, that is to be attributed the only article which tarnishes
that glorious monument of human reform, the new federal system of the
United States. It was this party that proposed to bind the hands of the new
Congress, and to put it out of their power for twenty years to prohibit the importation of slaves. It was said to this August assembly, *Sign this article, or we
will withdraw from the union.* To avoid the evils which, without meliorating
the fate of the Blacks, would attend a political schism, the convention was
forced to wander from the grand principle of universal liberty.

But, though this article has surprised the friends of liberty in Europe,
where the secret causes of it were not known; though it has grieved society in
England, who are ready to accuse the legislators of a cowardly defection from
their own principles; yet we may regard the general and irrevocable proscrip-
tion of the slave trade in the United States as very near at hand.

This conclusion results from the nature of things, and even from the article itself of the new constitution now cited. Indeed nine States have already
done it; the Blacks which there abound are considered as free. There are then
nine asylums for those to escape to from Georgia; not to speak of the neighbourhood of the Floridas, where the slaves from Georgia take refuge, in hopes
to find better treatment from the Spaniards.

When you run over Maryland and Virginia, you conceive yourself in a different world; and you are convinced of it when you converse with the inhabitants. They speak not here of projects for freeing the negroes; they praise not
the [abolition] societies of London and America. No, the indolent masters behold with uneasiness the efforts that are making to render freedom universal.
The Virginians are persuaded of the impossibility of cultivating tobacco without slavery; they fear that if the Blacks become free they will cause trouble; on
rendering them free, they know not what rank to assign them in society;
whether they shall establish them in a separate district, or send them out of the
country. These are the objections which you will hear repeated every where

against the idea of freeing them. The strongest objection lies in the character, the manners, and habits, of the Virginians. They seem to enjoy the sweat of slaves. They are fond of hunting, they love the display of luxury, and disdain the idea of labour.

The free Blacks in the Eastern states are either hired servants, or they keep little shops, or they cultivate the land. They do not venture themselves on long voyages, for fear of being transported and sold in the [West Indies] islands. Those who keep shops live moderately, and never augment their affairs beyond a certain point.

The reason is obvious: the Whites, though they treat them with humanity, like not to give them credit to enable to undertake any extensive commerce, nor even to give them the means of a common education, by receiving them into their counting-houses. If, then, the Blacks are confined to the retails of trade, let us not accuse their capacity, but the prejudices of the Whites, which lay obstacles in their way.

The same causes hinder the Blacks who live in the country from having large plantations. Their little fields are generally well cultivated; their log-houses full of children decently clad, attract the eye of the philosopher, who rejoices to see, that, in these habitations, no tears attest the rod of tyranny.

There exists still too great an interval between them [free Blacks] and the Whites, especially in public opinion. This humiliating difference prevents those efforts which they might make to raise themselves. Black children are admitted to the public schools; but you never see them within the walls of a college. Though free, they are always accustomed to consider themselves as beneath the Whites.

We may conclude from this, that it is unfair to measure the extent of their capacity by the examples already given by the free Blacks of the North.

But when we compare them to the slaves of the South, what a difference we find!—In the South, the blacks are in a state of abjection difficult to describe; many of them are naked, ill fed, lodged in miserable huts on straw. They receive no education, no instruction in any kind of religion; they are not married but coupled. Thus they are brutalized, lazy, without ideas and without energy.

The Americans of the Southern States treat their slaves with mildness; it is one of the effects of the general extension of the ideas of liberty. The slave labours less; but this is all the alteration made in his circumstances, and he is not the better for it, either in his nourishment, his clothing, his morals, or his ideas.

The lands inhabited by the whites and free blacks, are better cultivated, produce more abundantly, and offer everywhere the images of ease and happiness. Such, for example, is the aspect of Connecticut, and of Pennsylvania.

Pass into Maryland and Virginia, and as I said before, you are in another world;—you find not there those cultivated plains, those neat country-houses, barns well-distributed, and numerous head of cattle, fat and vigorous. No: every thing in Maryland and Virginia wears the print of slavery; a starved soil, bad cultivation, houses falling to ruin, cattle small and few, and black walking skeletons; in a word, you see real misery and apparent luxury, insulting each other.

They begin to perceive, even in the Southern States, that, to nourish a slave ill, is a mistaken economy; and that money employed in their purchase does not render its interest. It is perhaps more owing to this consideration than to humanity, that you see free labour introduced in a part of Virginia, in that part bordered by the beautiful river Shenadore [Shenandoah]. In traveling here, you will think yourself in Pennsylvania. Such will be the face of all Virginia when slavery shall be at an end.

FANNY KEMBLE

THE CRUEL LIFE OF WOMEN IN SLAVERY

An actress of considerable reputation in London who also wrote poetry, Frances Ann ("Fanny") Kemble (c. 1809–1893) traveled to the United States in 1833. The following year she married a Georgia planter named Pierre Butler. While residing on Butler's plantation, she wrote numerous letters to relatives in England. Some of these, which included detailed discussions of slavery, appeared in a book, Journal of a Residence on a Georgian Plantation in 1838–1839. *As is evident from the following account, she found slavery morally offensive, particularly with regard to its treatment of women. Known as an outspoken person, Fanny Kemble ultimately divorced Butler and returned to England. After a time, she came back to the United States, lived in Massachusetts and Pennsylvania, and then in her late sixties, returned once more to her native England.*

It has occurred to me that whereas the increase of this ill-fated race is frequently adduced as a proof of their good treatment and well-being, it really and truly is no such thing, and springs from quite other causes than the peace and plenty which a rapidly increasing population are supposed to indicate. In the first place, every woman who is pregnant, as soon as she chooses to make the fact known to the overseer, is relieved of a certain portion of her work in the field, which lightening of labor continues, of course, as long as she is so burdened. On the birth of a child, certain additions of clothing and an additional weekly ration are bestowed on the family; and these matters, small as they may seem, act as powerful inducements to creatures who have none of the restraining influences actuating them which belong to the parental relation among all other people whether civilized or savage. Moreover, they have all of them a most distinct and perfect knowledge of their value to their owners as property; and a woman thinks, and not much amiss, that the more frequently she adds to the number of her master's livestock by bringing new slaves into the world, the more claims she will have upon his consideration and good will. This was perfectly evident to me from the meritorious air with which women always made haste to inform me of the number of children they had borne.

The women who visited me yesterday evening were all in the family way, and came to entreat me to have the sentence (what else can I call it) modified which condemns them to resume their labor of hoeing in the fields three weeks after their confinement. . . . their sole entreaty was that I would use my influence to obtain for them a month's respite from labor in the field after childbearing. Their principal spokeswoman, a woman with a bright sweet face, called Mary, and a very sweet voice, which is by no means an uncommon excellence among them, appealed to my own experience; and while she spoke of my babies, and my carefully tended, delicately nursed, and tenderly watched confinement and convalescence, implored me to have a kind of labor given to them less exhausting during the month after their confinement. All these women had large families, and *all* of them had lost half their children, and several of them had lost more.

The settlement at St. Annie's is the remotest on the whole plantation, and I found the squalidest, wretchedest huts, and most miserably, filthy, and forlorn creatures I had yet seen here. . . . There was an old crone called Hannah, a sister, as well as I could understand what she said, of old House Milly, whose face and figure, seamed with wrinkles, and bowed and twisted with age and infirmity, hardly retained the semblance of those of a human creature, and as she crawled to me almost half her naked body was exposed through the miserable tatters that she held on with one hand, while the other eagerly clutched my hand. One or two forlorn creatures like herself, too old or too infirm to be compelled to work, and the half-starved and more than half-naked children apparently left here under their charge, were the only inmates I found in these wretched hovels.

Before closing this letter, I have a mind to transcribe to you the entries for today recorded in a sort of daybook, where I put down very succinctly the number of people who visit me, their petitions and ailments, and also such special particulars concerning them as seem to me worthy of recording. You will see how miserable the physical condition of many of these poor creatures is; and their physical condition, it is insisted by those who uphold this evil system, is the only part of it which is prosperous, happy, and compares well with that of Northern laborers. Judge from the details I now send you; and never forget, while reading them, that the people on this plantation are well off, and consider themselves well off, in comparison with the slaves on some of the neighboring estates.

Fanny has had six children; all dead but one. She came to beg to have her work in the field lightened.

Nanny has had three children; two of them are dead. She came to implore that the rule of sending them into the field three weeks after their confinement might be altered.

Leah, Caesar's wife, has had six children; three are dead.

Sophy, Lewis's wife, came to beg for some old linen. She is suffering fearfully; has had ten children; five of them are dead. The principal favor she asked was a piece of meat, which I gave her.

Sally, Scipio's wife, has had two miscarriages and three children born, one of whom is dead. She came complaining of incessant pain and weakness in her back. The woman was a mulatto daughter of a slave called Sophy, by a white man of the name of Walker who visited the plantation.

Charlotte, Renty's wife, had had two miscarriages, and was with child again. She was almost crippled with rheumatism, and showed me a pair of poor, swollen knees that made my heart ache. I have promised her a pair of flannel trousers, which I must forthwith set about making.

Sarah, Stephen's wife; this woman's case and history were alike deplorable. She had had four miscarriages, had brought seven children into the world, five of whom were dead, and was again with child. She complained of dreadful pains in the back, and an internal tumor which swells with the exertion of working in the fields; probably, I think, she is ruptured. She told me she had once been mad and had run into the woods, where she contrived to elude discovery for some time, but was at last tracked and brought back, when she was tied up by the arms, and heavy logs fastened to her feet, and was severely flogged. After this she contrived to escape again, and lived for some time skulking in the woods, and she supposes mad, for when she was taken again she was entirely naked. She subsequently recovered from this derangement, and seems now just like all the other poor creatures who come to me for help and pity. I suppose her constant childbearing and hard labor in the fields at the same time may have produced the temporary insanity.

Sukey, Bush's wife, only came to pay her respects. She had had four miscarriages; had brought eleven children into the world, five of whom are dead.

Molly, Quambo's wife, also only came to see me. Hers was the best account I have yet received; she had had nine children, and six of them were still alive.

This is only the entry for today, in my diary, of the people's complaints and visits. Can you conceive a more wretched picture than that which it exhibits of the conditions under which these women live? Their cases are in no respect singular, and though they come with pitiful entreaties that I will help them with some alleviations of their pressing, physical distresses, it seems to me marvelous with what desperate patience (I write it advisedly, patience of utter despair) they endure their sorrow-laden existence. Even the poor wretch who told that miserable story of insanity, and lonely hiding in the swamps, and scourging when she was found, and of her renewed madness and flight, did so in a sort of low, plaintive, monotonous murmur of misery, as if such sufferings were "all in a day's work."

I ask these questions about their children because I think the number they bear as compared with the number they rear a fair gauge of the effect of the system on their own health and that of their offspring. There was hardly any one of these women, as you will see by the details I have noted of their ailments, who might not have been a candidate for a bed in a hospital, and they had come to me after working all day in the fields.

I have had an uninterrupted stream of women and children flowing in the whole morning to say "Ha de, missis?" Among others, a poor woman called Mile, who could hardly stand for pain and swelling in her limbs; she had fifteen children and two miscarriages; nine of her children had died; for the last three years she had become almost a cripple with chronic rheumatism, yet she is driven every day to work in the field.

Another of my visitors had a still more dismal story to tell; her name was Die; she had had sixteen children, fourteen of whom were dead; she had had four miscarriages: one had been caused with falling down with a very heavy burden on her head, and one from having her arms strained up to be lashed. I asked her what she meant by having her arms tied up. She said their hands were first tied together, sometimes by the wrists, and sometimes, which was worse, by the thumbs, and they were then drawn up to a tree or post, so as almost to swing them off the ground, and then their clothes rolled round their waist, and a man with a cowhide [whip] stands and stripes them. I give you the woman's words. She did not speak of this as anything strange, unusual, or especially horrid and abominable; and when I said: "Did they do that to you when you were with child?" she simply replied: "Yes, missis." And to all this I listen—I, an Englishwoman, the wife of the man who owns these wretches, and I cannot say: "That thing shall not be done again; that cruel shame and villainy shall never be known here again." I gave the woman meat and flannel, which were what she came to ask for, and remained choking with indignation and grief long after they had all left me to my most bitter thoughts.

HIRAM WILSON

CONDITION OF THE COLOURED PEOPLE IN CANADA

England remained at the forefront of the nineteenth-century movement to abolish slavery. One important institution in this struggle was the British and Foreign Anti-Slavery Society. In 1843, it held its second General Anti-Slavery Convention, which, true to its name, considered questions pertaining to the fight against slavery in Europe, Africa, the East Indies, and the Americas. Large-scale slave insurrections in the United States proved relatively rare. As the existence of the "underground railroad" suggests, runaways—that is, slaves fleeing from the south—were a more common form of resistance. The Reverend Hiram Wilson, an American subscriber to the conference, working in concert with an escaped slave, had established the British American Institute to help resettle fugitive slaves in Canada. In the following selection, he discusses the flight of slaves from the United States to Canada, and the conditions they encountered there. Note the various references to cooperation between British, Canadian, and American abolitionists.

I have no doubt that a very deep sympathy is felt in the bosom of every delegate on behalf of the refugees from American slavery in the province of Canada. The circumstances of our meeting, and the pressures of business crowding upon us, require me to be very brief, and merely to give you a synopsis of the immense amount of matter that might be adduced in respect to them. I stand here as the representative and advocate . . . on behalf of the most interesting fragment of the human family to be found on the face of the earth.

You have been much interested with the statements from the Vigilance Committee of New York, with regard to the numerous cases of flight from bondage: I represent not far from 12,000 of my native countrymen, who have emerged from the prison of slavery, and made their way to Canada. They are a marvellous people. There is something marvellous in the ideal of liberty producing such a transforming influence; they are emphatically men of one idea, that seems to get into the top end of the chattels,converts them into self-propelling locomotives, and moves them in a Northerly direction till they cross the line to Canada. There are not far from a thousand births occur annually along the national line that separates the United States and British America They are a people remarkable in regard to their birth. They are of noble birth, more distinguished even than the birth of princes and princesses in this country. The latter are born into infancy but the refugees are born at once into British manhood. The number of males to females is perhaps as two to one; and the entire coloured population in Canada would number not far from 16,000; indeed some have estimated them at 20,000. They are located in different districts—in Gore-in-the-Home in Niagara, in London and in the Western districts. It was my privilege, about seven years since, to commence my labour as an itinerant ant among them, with a view to promote their improvement, and to elicit their testimony concerning slavery as it was thought that this might be of great service to the Anti-slavery enterprise. For eighteen months I was under the patronage of the American Anti-Slavery Society, and procured from the refugees their testimony as to the horrors of the prison house, from which they had fled. They represent every slave state in the American Union and at the same time every variety of complexion between those of the fairer hue and the jet black. The great majority of the coloured refugees in Canada are from the more Northern slave states; they are continually arriving from what are called the slave-breeding states—Delaware, Maryland, Virginia, and Kentucky. I remember hearing it stated by Joshua Coffin, who is interested in the Vigilance Committee, and who is familiar with the condition of Delaware and Maryland, that such is the tendency to fly Northward, that 20 years would abolish slavery in those states merely by flight. It is not to be supposed that very many of them can come from the more Southern states; I have seen them, however, from New Orleans and Mobile—from the cotton plantations of the South, as well as the sugar-growing regions.

The climate of Canada, especially the more South-Western districts, is mild and salubrious, and the transition to them from the more Northern slave states is but very slight. They are generally, a healthy, athletic, and vigorous-minded people. I am bound in duty to state, that there exists amongst the White inhabitants of Canada a vast amount of prejudice against colour. In certain places—as, for instance, Kingston and Toronto, and a few others, where the preponderating influence is English and Scotch—there is but very little ground of complaint; prejudice obtains only to a faint degree; whilst in other parts, especially along the frontiers and the West, the prejudice is intolerable. The coloured youth generally are shut out from the white schools; they are not suffered to be educated in common with the white people. We have founded an institution of learning on the manual labour system. I would here remark, for the satisfaction of those who intrusted [their] money . . . that we have made a purchase of 200 acres of land of first rate quality, erected a public building, and three small dwelling-houses. During the last year we have made improvements, and brought twenty-five acres under cultivation, and in the course of the winter we received and instructed sixteen young men of colour, every one of whom, I believe, without exception, was a fugitive from slavery.

I have here a testimonial signed by one hundred and fifteen coloured men in the vicinity of our new institution about seventy of whom have been in the military barracks at Chatham as soldiers; but at the time I left they were expecting their discharge. The testimonial is as follows.

"To the British Philanthropists, the undersigned coloured citizens and soldiers of Chatham, Canada West, do hereby express our sincere thanks to our friends in England for the interest they have manifested in our welfare as a people, and for the means they have already furnished in aid of the education of ourselves and our children."

I have . . . a letter from a coloured youth who is now a student at Oberlin, but who has been engaged for some time in teaching his brethren in Canada.

"Tell the dear people in England that our united cry and petition is, that they will remember our bonds, and to give us what help they can to get an education, which is the key, and the only key to unlock the handcuffs of the American slave-drivers. Tell the friends, of our bonds, tell of our ignorance tell of our stripes, tell of our sorrows, and tell them we don't know where to look for help. If our friends in England will not hear our complaints, if they turn away from us, we are certainly done, and there is no hope for us, but we must die in American slavery."

The slaves who possess the strongest minds are those who escape to Canada and hence the great encouragement to educate them. There are now two or three very efficient agents traversing the Northern states, who were fugitives to Canada. They are now lecturing in the Eastern states. I allude to the Clarkes whose father was an Englishman. It is of great moment to train up for the anti-slavery conflict, those who have themselves suffered in the wretched state of slavery. In the temperance reform the tee-totallers who have come out of the ditch can best tell the miseries of drunkenness; and it is of importance that we should have those to advocate emancipation who can reveal the invisible horrors of the prison-house. I have, since I left the Lane seminary, been the servant of servants and am willing to be the servant of British philanthropists to do your bidding to act in accordance with your wishes by operating in the most efficient and powerful manner within the limits of my feeble capacity, against slavery and against that terrible prejudice to colour which prevails to so great an extent in Canada. I wish you to feel that the responsibility of carrying on this work devolves on this Convention, and on those in this kingdom who sympathise with us. We do not ask American abolitionists to withhold their hands, or to excuse themselves from doing this work; but we especially call on the friends of humanity throughout Great Britain to enlist in this enterprise, according to their means, and to render that amount of aid which their wisdom may dictate.

FREDERICK MILNES EDGE

Slavery Is Doomed

Frederick Milnes Edge, an Englishman, resided in the United States for five years as the agitation over the expansion of slavery into the territories heated up. Working as a journalist, he covered the 1856 presidential election, which saw the Democrat James Buchanan triumph over the first presidential candidate fielded by the Republican Party, John C. Frémont. Edge's sympathies clearly rested with the antislavery position. The following selection comes from his 1860 book, Slavery Doomed, or the Contest Between Free and Slave Labor in the United States. *In it, he comments broadly on the American scene, paying particular attention to enlighten Europeans as to the peculiar governmental system of the United States, where states shared sovereignty with the national government. He also comments at length on the expansionist aims of southerners, and links them to the Ostend Manifesto.*

If a question arise in any part of Europe or Asia, involving the conquest or annexation of some petty principality, Great Britain immediately becomes vitally interested. Territories far distant, barren, and thinly peopled are invested with ridiculous importance, whereas that immense Republic beyond the Atlantic is a sealed book to us, although the source, mainstay, and support of England's prosperity. . . . we know nothing of the impending crisis in that country, and ignore the storm which is ready to burst.

This year, the United States elect a President in the place of Mr. Buchanan. For the first time in the history of the Republic, the two principles of Free and Slave labour stand face to face.

It is necessary that Europeans should understand that the issue pending between the Free and the Slave States is not one of the abolition, but of the extension or non-extension of Slavery. The thirteen States which originally formed the Union, agreed to a constitution which prevented negro vassalage being interfered with in those portions of the Confederation where it then existed; and every succeeding State on entering the Union bound itself not to meddle with the internal affairs of any other State. To all intents and purposes, except that of mutual defence against foreign aggression, the various States of the North American Confederation are as separate and distinct sovereignties as Austria and Prussia. Thus, for example, a murderer in the State of New York cannot be seized in New Jersey, or any other State, except upon requisition of the governor of the former to that of the latter, who causes the offender to be arrested by his own officers, and delivers him across the frontier to the authorities of the State where the crime was committed. Slavery is a *State*, not a *Federal* institution, and it must therefore be understood that *Slavery can only be abolished by the legislature of the State where it exists*. What the Free North is labouring to effect is, to prevent the legalization, and, consequently, the existence of Slavery in the wide-spreading territories of the Republic not yet sufficiently peopled to form into States. In effecting this—in declaring that henceforth and for evermore Slavery shall no further extend within the Republic—the accursed system of African serfdom will eventually die out—become, in fact, stifled by the freedom surrounding it. Only so far is the Republican, or Free State party, Abolitionist.

It is necessary that this position be clearly understood, for there are certain individuals in the United States whose views and aims are of the most ultra abolitionist character, and whose writings are well and favourably known in Europe. The Republican party, whilst endorsing all their remarks upon the moral aspect of the question—what, in America, is called "the higher law"—declares that the abolition of Slavery in any State or States by federal authority is not their object, because *not within their province or power*.

A work has lately appeared in America entitled, *The Impending Crisis of the South, and how to meet it*. The author, Hinton Rowan Helper, is a citizen of the Slave State, North Carolina, and he proves conclusively that the "peculiar institution" is ruining the southern portion of the Confederation. Such works as this *Impending Crisis of the South* and *Uncle Tom's Cabin* are read and generally approved in the northern portion of the Union, but have little or no effect upon the political action of that section.

Careful not to offend the north too rapidly, the Slave oligarchy . . . turned its attention outside the Union and commenced **filibustering attempts** southward. Central America, Cuba, and Mexico, suffered continual raids from armed bands, composed almost exclusively of Southern men and officered and equipped by them. The Government at Washington *publicly* disowned these attempts, knowing at the same time that the Legislatures of various Southern States were finding equipments for the robbers from their arsenals, and funds from their treasuries. The object of the South—for most of the leaders of that section of the country were interested in the plot—was preponderance at Washington. If they could annex any one of the above-mentioned countries, they would immediately add three or four additional States to the Confederation, representing twice the number of United States Senators, and a proportionate number of Representatives in the Lower House. But the North saw through their object, and if Cuba, Costa Rica, or Mexico do not now belong to the Union, *it is only because the Free States would not consent to the annexation. At any time during these ten years, one or all of those countries could have been Americanized, in defiance of any Government in Europe.* The people of the United States number upwards of 30,000,000; the whole population is accustomed to the use of arms from their youth up; their resources are infinite; their public debt next to nothing; and they are within a stone's throw of their object. Nothing else prevented the consummation but the determination of the Northern States to oppose the policy of the South; and we shall find, on examination, that the leaders of public opinion in the Free States have always been the firmest opponents of filibusterism and annexation. That the extension of Slavery is the sole cause of this brigand policy was pointedly asserted by Senator Seward no later than March last.

It is but right that Englishmen should know who are the causes of these vile attempts periodically made upon the independence of neighbouring States. They all proceed from that party whose one great aim is the perpetuation and extension of Slavery. It was the advocacy, the championship of this policy which caused Mr. Buchanan to be the nominee of the dominant party in the Union at the Presidential election, and he has directed the concerns of his country during the past four years, because he stood pledged to the Slave oligarchy to do his utmost to annex Cuba to the Confederation.

During the administration of General Pierce, the pro-Slavery democracy determined upon making a violent effort to obtain the island of Cuba, and Mr. Soulé, United States plenipotentiary to the Court of Madrid, was charged with the mission of effecting a purchase. Mr. Soulé, an emigrant Frenchman, naturalized in the State of Louisiana, had obtained this advancement to the dignity of ambassador on account of his ultra pro-Slavery and democratic [party] principles. Since his relinquishment of diplomatic functions he has devoted himself to the development of filibusterism, being the recognized agent and factotum of the celebrated **William Walker,** of Nicaragua infamy. No more suitable envoy could be selected for forcing a sale of Cuba at the buyer's own price; but the democratic party in the Southern States well knew that the mission would be one of difficulty, and orders were, therefore, sent out by the President to the American Ministers at the Courts of St. James (Mr. Buchanan) and the Tuileries (Mr. Mason) to meet Mr. Soulé and confer with him as to the speediest mode of obtaining the desired result. The Ministers to England and France were selected, not merely on account of their offices being the most important in the American diplomatic corps, but because the governments of those two countries were understood to be the protectors of Spain and the guaranteers of her possessions in the Antilles.

The three plenipotentiaries met, first at Ostend, and subsequently at Aix-la-Chapelle. The result of their deliberations was the paper known in the United States as the "Ostend Manifesto." (The Ostend Manifesto is not merely important as the expression of opinion of three prominent statesmen, but it is also "the destiny," the rule of action of the pro-Slavery American Democracy. This extraordinary diplomatic paper having offered a price for the island, and informed the Spanish people that they must have it by fair means, if possible, fixes its own value on the proposed purchase, tells Spain she is in want of the money, and coolly suggests how she should use that money when she has got it.)

Is there in the whole range of diplomacy so vile a document as this? The only excuse which any of the pro-Slavery band can give for it is the specious one that the Manifesto was not intended for aught else than the guidance of the President of the United States. But it is precisely because the principles it advocates, and the line of action it suggests, were intended for home consumption, that it is so monstrous. . . . because Messrs. Buchanan, Mason, Soulé, and Pierce, acting *for* the Democratic party, desired to show to England, France, and Spain, that sooner or later, Cuba must, *should*, belong to the United States; and in order that they might hereafter be able to say to Spain, in justification of their seizing it,—*"Why didn't you take our dollars when we offered them? We told you how it would be."*

It is now well known throughout the Confederation, that a regularly organized body exists in the Southern States, which is gradually "Americanizing" the island, enlisting the disaffected Cubans in a secret society, and preparing them for a signal to rise—a signal which will come from the American Slaveholders when they know the forces of the Confederation are ready to back them. This band of conspirators, whose rallying point is New Orleans, has existed for several years, their proceedings being winked at by successive Administrations, until the Ostend Manifesto gave them a *quasi* endorsement, and Buchanan and Co. told them,—*"Get the crop ready and we'll help you to cut it."*

The Methodist Church in the United States is directed and governed by a "General Conference," but the Southern portion of the sect has long been restless and defiant of their Northern brethren. The Conference never meets but the question of Slavery brings discord into their councils; and it could scarcely be otherwise, where one portion of the body believes "the peculiar institution" to be a duty, and the other a crime.

The Episcopalians, Presbyterians, and Catholics in the South bear but a small proportion to the above-mentioned sects, whilst Congregationalism may scarcely be said to exist. These churches do honour to their principles by the little connection they have with Slavery, and it is from their pulpits that are heard the fiercest denunciations of the system.

All that could be done by most of the **parent societies** in Great Britain to induce their brethren in the Southern States of the American Union to put away this reproach from their Church, has been nobly and conscientiously performed. **Mr. Spurgeon** has lately poured forth his eloquence against the iniquity, and has had the honour, like a second Luther, of having a volume of his sermons publicly burnt in one of the Slave States. But we have yet to learn that the Methodist Conference in this country has taken any action on the question, except to give Slaveholding Methodism a species of approval. The reverend gentlemen who visit the United States as deputations from the Parent Society have never taken that stand which was expected of them by the Northern members, but have held out the hand of fellowship to ministers and members from the Slave States, and endeavoured to steer a middle course betwixt right and wrong.

We are well aware of the difficulty attending the discussion of such a question in a foreign country, but we are at a loss to understand how English ministers of the Gospel can reconcile it to their consciences, to give the tacit consent to Slaveholding which their unmanly silence warrants. No other body of Christians possesses an organization so capable of concentration. The Methodist Sanhedrin or Conference, wields a power only equalled by that of the Pope and a General Council. Its ramifications extend, and its decrees are implicitly followed, throughout the civilized world and a declaration on its part that it will no longer recognize any body excusing or defending Slavery will do more towards limiting and eventually destroying that cursed system than the action of any other Church whatever. Will the Methodists of Great Britain take that stand against the iniquity which their brethren in the Northern States of the American Union have so long expected of them, and assist in removing from their sect the reproach of being "the great Slaveholding Church?" We hope so, but we fear. The Methodist Conference and Connection are so intensely conservative that, no matter what the law may be, *provided it is law,* they will render to it implicit obedience. It is precisely because the question of American slavery has become a political one that they do not interfere with or oppose it. Not so acted and taught their founder.

The Southern States of the American Union are following the example of the infatuated Louis the Fourteenth of France. As he drove into exile thousands of his subjects engaged in manufactures and trade, who sought refuge in England and laid the foundation of our manufacturing supremacy, so are the Slave States now driving from their confines thousands of freed coloured men. Where are the exiles to go? The Free States are too crowded and Canada too cold for them. Can we not offer them an asylum in Jamaica and other colonies? They are the cream, the best of their race; for it is by long-continued industry and economy that they have been enabled to purchase their freedom and joyfully will they seize the hand of deliverance which Great Britain holds out to them. We only want additional labour; give us that and we shall very soon cultivate our own cotton.

Another consequence of the triumph of the Free State party in November will be hailed with satisfaction by every tax-paying Englishman. We shall no longer be compelled to keep up expensive fleets on the coast of Africa [see Chapter 3] and in the Mexican Gulf, for the new Government at Washington will reverse the foreign policy of the Slave power, and render the Slave-trade impossible.

TERMS AND DEFINITIONS

Filibustering attempts: Paramilitary expeditions by private American citizens to Cuba and Central America in the 1840s and 1850s, they often had tacit assistance from the U.S. government.

Parent societies: a reference to the English-based Wesleyan societies.

Mr. Spurgeon: Charles Haddon Spurgeon (1834–1892), a well-known evangelical minister in England.

William Walker: Born in 1824, Walker led an 1855 filibustering expedition to Nicaragua, and briefly ruled that nation as president. He was killed in 1860 during an abortive attempt to take Honduras.

VICTOR HUGO

Thoughts on John Brown

The existence of slavery in the United States caused great discomfort for European Liberals, who long had admired the nation's democratic character and institutions, seeing in them a model for the Western world. Typically, then, they viewed the South as having become corrupted through slavery. As a result, it had lost the virtuous character exemplified by George Washington and Thomas Jefferson. In the following section, the great French author Victor Hugo (1802–1885), whose Les Misérables *remains one of the classic works in Western literature, comments on the actions of John Brown. Hugo sympathizes totally with the radical abolitionist view that portrayed Brown as a martyr to liberty.*

To the Editor of the London News, Dec. 2, 1859:

When our thoughts dwell upon the United States of America, a majestic form rises before the eye of imagination. It is a Washington!

Look, then, to what is taking place in that country of Washington at the present moment. In the Southern States of the Union there are slaves; and this circumstance is regarded with indignation, as the most monstrous of inconsistences, by the pure and logical conscience of the Northern States. A white man, a free man, John Brown sought to deliver these negro slaves from bondage. Assuredly, if insurrection is ever a sacred duty, it must be when it is directed against Slavery. John Brown endeavored to commence the work of emancipation by the liberation of slaves in Virginia. Pious, austere, animated with the old Puritan spirit, inspired by the spirit of the Gospel, he sounded to these men, these oppressed brothers, the rallying cry of Freedom. The slaves, enervated by servitude, made no response to the appeal. Slavery affects the soul with weakness. Brown, though deserted, still fought at the head of a handful of heroic men; he was riddled with balls; his two young sons, sacred martyrs, fell dead at his side, and he himself was taken. This is what they call the affair at Harper's Ferry.

John Brown has been tried with four of his comrades. What has been the character of his trial? Let us sum it up in a few words:—

John Brown upon a wretched pallet, with six half gaping wounds, a gunshot wound in his arm, another in his loins, and two in his head, scarcely conscious of surrounding sounds, bathing his mattress in blood, and with the ghostly presence of his two dead sons ever beside him; his four fellow-sufferers wounded, dragging themselves along by his side; justice in a hurry and over-leaping all obstacles; an attorney, Hunter, who wishes to proceed hastily, and a judge, Parker, who suffers him to have his way; the hearing cut short, almost every application for delay refused, forged and mutilated documents produced, the witnesses for the defense kidnapped, every obstacle thrown in the way of the prisoner's counsel; two cannon loaded with canister stationed in the Court, orders given to the jailers to shoot the prisoners if they sought to escape, forty minutes of deliberation, and three men sentenced to die! I declare on my honor that all this took place, aye, not in Turkey, but in America!

Such things cannot be done with impunity in the face of the civilised world. The universal conscience of humanity is an ever-watchful eye. Let the judges of Charlestown, and Hunter and Parker, and the slaveholding jurors, and the whole population of Virginia, ponder it well: they are watched! They are not alone in the world. At this moment, America attracts the eyes of the whole of Europe.

John Brown, condemned to die, was to have been hanged on the 2d of December—this very day.

But news has just reached us. A respite has been granted to him. It is not until the 16th that he is to die. The interval is a brief one. Before it has ended, will a cry of mercy have had time to make itself effectually heard?

No matter! It is our duty to speak out.

Perhaps a second respite may be granted. America is a noble nation. The impulse of humanity springs quickly into life among a free people. We may yet hope that Brown will be saved.

If it were otherwise, if Brown should die on the scaffold on the 16th of December, what a terrible calamity! The executioner of Brown—let us avow it openly—would be neither the attorney Hunter, nor the judge Parker, nor the Governor Wise, nor the State of Virginia; it would be, though we can scarce think or speak of it without a shudder, the whole American Republic.

The more one loves, the more one admires, the more one venerates that Republic, the more heart-sick one feels at the contemplation of such a catastrophe. A single State ought not to have the power to dishonor all the rest, and in this case there is an obvious justification for a federal intervention. Otherwise, by hesitating to interfere when it might prevent a crime, the Union becomes a participator in its guilt. No matter how intense may be the indignation of the generous Northern States, the Southern states force them to share the opprobrium of this murder. All of us, no matter who we may be, who are bound together as compatriots by the common tie of a democratic creed, feel ourselves in some measure compromised. If the scaffold should be erected on the 16th of December, the incorruptible voice of history would thenceforward testify that the August Confederation of the New World, had added to all its rites of holy brotherhood a brotherhood of blood, and the *fasces* of that splendid Republic would be bound together with the running noose that hung from the gibbet of Brown!

This is a bond that kills.

When we reflect on what Brown, the liberator, the champion of Christ, has striven to effect, and when we remember that he is about to die, slaughtered by the American Republic, the crime assumes an importance co-extensive with that of the nation which commits it—and when we say to ourselves that this nation is one of the glories of the human race; that like France, like England, like Germany, she is one of the great agents of civilization; that she sometimes even leaves Europe in the rear by the sublime audacity of some of her progressive movements; that she is the Queen of an entire world, and that her brow is irradiated with a glorious halo of freedom, we declare our conviction that John

Brown will not die; for we recoil horror-struck from the idea of so great a crime committed by so great a people.

Viewed in a political light, the murder of Brown would be an irreparable fault. It would penetrate the Union with a gaping fissure which would lead in the end to its entire disruption. It is possible that the execution of Brown might establish slavery on a firm basis in Virginia, but it is certain that it would shake to its centre the entire fabric of American democracy. You preserve your infamy, but you sacrifice your glory. Viewed in this moral light, it seems to me that a portion of the enlightenment of humanity would be eclipsed, that even the ideas of justice and injustice would be obscured on the day which should witness the assassination of Emancipation by Liberty.

As for myself, though I am but a mere atom, yet being, as I am, in common with all other men, inspired with the conscience of humanity, I fall on my knees weeping before the great starry banner of the New World; and with clasped hands, and with profound and filial respect, I implore the illustrious American Republic, sister of the French Republic, to see to the safety of the universal moral law, to save John Brown, to demolish the threatening scaffold of the 16th of December, and not to suffer that beneath its eyes, and I add, with a shudder, almost by its fault, a crime should be perpetrated surpassing the first fratricide in iniquity.

For—yes, let America know it, and ponder on it well—there is something more terrible than Cain slaying Abel: It is Washington slaying **Spartacus!**

TERMS AND DEFINITIONS

Spartacus: a slave and gladiator who led a major revolt against Rome; the revolt failed, and Spartacus was executed in 71 B.C.

THINKING THINGS THROUGH

1. Identify the common elements in the arguments of de Warville and Hugo. What does this commonality indicate regarding the liberal critique of slavery?

2. What images of the U.S. South appear in the various selections?

3. If you were a foreign delegate to the World Anti-Slavery Convention, how might you have reacted to Hiram Wilson's report? What opinion would you have of the United States?

4. Identify some of the human costs of slavery as related by Venture Smith, in Chapter 3, and Fanny Kemble.

10

INTERPRETATIONS OF THE CIVIL WAR

A. The International Context

No event in the history of the United States was more intensely "American" than the Civil War. Virtually all of the three million men who fought and the 618,000 who died were Americans, either by birth or recent immigration. The number of Americans killed in the Civil War was only 20,000 less than the 638,000 who have died in all of the country's other wars combined, and over 200,000 more than the number of Americans who died in World War II. Nearly 2,000 out of every 100,000 people in the country's population died during the Civil War, compared to just over 300 per 1,000,000 in World War II, the nation's second most costly conflict. For four long, bloody years, and for decades after its official conclusion, the struggle permeated every aspect of the nation's society, economy, polity, and culture. It touched the lives of every single American in some significant way. Even the war's most widely recognized causes—disputes over the nature of the federal union and over the spread of slavery into the western territories—were quintessentially American, having risen directly out of the young republic's unique attempt to apportion power between the several states and its national government, and out of its unprecedented attempt to continue "half-slave and half-free." Well before April 1861 —and well after April 1865—the attention of most Americans was turned resolutely inward, focusing on the nation's life-and-death struggle as if the rest of the world had disappeared.

At the same time, however, the eyes of much of the rest of the world were just as resolutely fixed upon the United States. Many hoped or feared that this aggressive young nation that had made such a remarkable impact upon international affairs in such an incredibly short time was about to self-destruct. For some, the American Civil War was a trial

*by fire to determine whether "a government conceived in lib-
erty and dedicated to the propositon that all men are created
equal" and "a government of the people, for the people, and
by the people" could really endure. For others, it was an or-
deal by combat between those committed to the perpetuation
of human slavery out of self-interest and racial hatred and
those dedicated to achieving the ideal of universal human
freedom and brotherhood. Liberals in Europe, Latin America, and elsewhere generally saw the Union as the champion
of all that they held most sacred. Many conservatives viewed
the Confederacy as the bastion of those ideals and institutions that were being brutally destroyed by the onward march
of modernization, industrialization, and urbanization. Most
governments, however, watched with a far more pragmatic
eye, attempting to calculate what impact a victory by either
side would have on their country's relative position within
the international balance of power and wealth. Meanwhile,
the virtual destruction of the cotton trade resulting from the
Union blockade of southern ports devastated the textile industry in Great Britain, France, and the Low Countries. A
large portion of the industrial working class was unemployed
and faced economic disaster. Many of their leaders, as well as
those sympathetic to their plight, urged European involvement to break the blockade and end the conflict.*

*This was a question so crucial to some European govern-
ments that they were forced to ponder the wisdom of intervention on one side or the other, whether diplomatic,
economic, or even military. Other rulers, especially Napoleon
III of France, saw the total immersion of the United States in
Civil War, and its consequent inability to enforce the Monroe
Doctrine, as a golden opportunity to regain a significant portion of their lost wealth and power in the Western Hemisphere. Still others recognized the conflict as an unparalleled
opportunity to assess the actual operation, under battlefield
conditions, of the advances in military science, tactics, and
weaponry in the half century since the end of the Napoleonic
Wars. For all of these observers, calculators, commentators,
and potential participants, the American Civil War was an
event of enormous international interest and consequence,
one whose course and eventual outcome would have a significant impact in several corners of the world for decades.*

*Nor were the leaders of the Union and the Confederacy
ignorant of the international implications, and possibilities,
that the Civil War presented. Seeing their position as somewhat analogous to that of the thirteen American colonies on*

the eve of the Revolutionary War, many Confederate leaders were well aware that it had taken significant economic and military intervention by France and other European countries to guarantee the eventual triumph of the United States in 1783. Some openly predicated their approval of secession, with its almost certain consequence of war, on the assumption that Great Britain's putative dependence on "King Cotton" to feed its insatiable textile mills would eventually force it to provide the Confederacy with substantial aid. Perhaps it might even dictate direct military intervention. At the very least, Confederates hoped that Britain and France would recognize the belligerency and independence of the Confederacy, thereby entitling it to various rights under international law. Perhaps Britain and France would challenge the Union's maritime practices, and offer to mediate on the premise of southern independence. The United States was confident of its ability to prevail without outside intervention, and determined to prevent the Great Powers from using the war as an opportunity to reassert their power in the Western Hemisphere. It bent nearly all of its diplomatic efforts in the direction of neutralizing the powers and of establishing cordial relations with the rest of the world. Much of that effort involved publicizing its war aims in the most favorable light possible, and in interpreting the rules of belligerence and neutrality to their greatest possible advantage. Ironically, the latter meant an almost complete reversal of roles from those that the United States, Great Britain, and France had played between 1775 and 1815, with the United States as assertive belligerent, Britain a scrupulous neutral, and France and Britain vying with one another for the distinction of being the biggest thorn in the American side.

Somewhat surprisingly, the Union cause found its most sympathetic audience among the leaders of the most despotic of all the European Great Powers. Russia was ruled by a divine-right monarch, dominated by a feudal aristocracy, and peopled largely by peasants not yet freed from serfdom. The unlikely cordial relationship between Russia and the United States dated back to the American Revolutionary War, when Czarina Catherine the Great had pragmatically organized the League of Armed Neutrality. That coalition boldly proclaimed its adherence to a set of neutral maritime rights that significantly hampered Britain's naval warfare tactics. Despite occasional crises, relations between the two disparate nations remained generally friendly over the years. They were actually enhanced during the Civil War, thanks largely to the mutual admiration between Secretary of State William Seward and Russian Ambassador Edouard de Stoeckl, an attachment that eventually resulted in the transfer of Alaska. Russian–American cordiality was further augmented by the "Russian Fleet Myth" in the autumn of 1863, when two Russian fleets almost simultaneously put in at San Francisco and New York, probably in search of repairs and provisions. Erroneously assuming that the two fleets had been dispatched to the United States as a sign of friendly solidarity, the Americans wined and dined the Russian crews lavishly. They proposed endless toasts to the Czar's health, and devoutly recited the prayer "God Bless Russia." In a more substantive gesture, the Czar rejected a French proposal for joint British-French-Russian mediation during an enforced six-month armistice.

Far more sinister and ominous were the intrigues of French Emperor Napoleon III. Jealous of the growing power of the United States, especially in the Western Hemisphere, Napoleon hoped to divide the nation in half, thereby rendering it vulnerable. Moreover, the ambitious emperor planned to gain control of Mexico by declaring it a puppet empire ostensibly ruled by an Austrian prince, Maximilian of Hapsburg. A Confederate victory would greatly enhance his success. Because their textile and other industries were heavily dependent upon cotton and other southern products, many Frenchmen were also sympathetic to the Confederate cause. They favored almost any measure short of military intervention. Early on, Secretary of State Seward warned the French foreign minister that recognition of the Confederacy would result in war with the United States. From October 1861 on, Napoleon periodically tried to engage Britain in a joint effort to break the Union blockade of southern ports. A year later, he unsuccessfully proposed the three-power intervention leading to a six-month armistice and mediation. Rebuffed by the other Great Powers, Napoleon approached Seward in January 1863 with an offer of direct personal mediation, which the American politely refused. Angered, Congress overwhelmingly passed a resolution declaring that future offers of mediation, or other attempts at meddling, would be considered an unfriendly act by the United States. Meanwhile, Napoleon continued his military support of Maximilian in Mexico, despite an anti-imperial revolution led by Benito Juárez, with whom Lincoln enjoyed a friendly correspondence. As the Civil War came to a conclusion, Congress and the U. S. military escalated the pressure upon

Napoleon to withdraw. The former passed a unanimous resolution to that effect, while General Ulysses S. Grant ordered
fifty thousand troops to the Mexican border. Faced with increasing threats of military intervention by the United States,
Napoleon finally withdrew his troops in 1867, leaving the
hapless Maximilian to his fate at the hands of a Mexican fir-
ing squad.

Napoleon notwithstanding, the biggest international
crises of the Civil War involved the United States and Great
Britain. Seward generally met these threats by alternately
threatening and flattering the world's greatest military power.
When Queen Victoria proclaimed British neutrality, thereby
tacitly recognizing the belligerency of the Confederacy, the
secretary of state responded with a message warning that "if
any European power provokes war, we shall not shrink from
it." He also firmly refused any suggestions of British mediation, and admonished them not to have any contact with the
"pseudo-commissioners" of the Confederacy. However, when
an American warship high-handedly removed two Confederate commissioners from the British mail steamer Trent, Seward smoothed over the situation. The British people
themselves were seriously divided over the war, especially before Lincoln issued the Emancipation Proclamation. Liberal
party leaders openly favored the Confederate cause, while
many working-class organizations supported the Union, despite the adverse impact of the blockade on the British textile
industry. In the long run, "King Corn," symbol of British dependence upon American foodstuffs, proved more powerful
than "King Cotton." The issuance of the Emancipation
Proclamation, which invested the Union cause with apparent
moral superiority, virtually ended any real chance of British
intervention. Above all, though, the British followed the
dictates of national interest, seriously contemplating involvement as long as there was the chance of an ultimate Confederate victory and abandoning the idea as soon as the tide of
battle turned to favor the Union forces. In a very real sense,
the Confederate defeats at Antietam, Vicksburg, and Gettys-
burg doomed any possibilities of meaningful foreign assistance. Even so, occasional crises continued to darken
U.S.–British relations, such as the discovery that Confederate
raider ships, such as the Alabama and the Florida, which
sunk over 250 Union ships, had been built in England. When
it was revealed that British shipbuilders also planned to sell
several Laird Rams (iron-clad steam-powered vessels
equipped with wrought iron "piercers" to penetrate wooden

hulls), American protests forced the government in London to prevent their delivery. When the final Union victory at Appomattox was followed quickly by the assassination of President Lincoln, even the pro-southern English press celebrated the victory and mourned the tragedy, hailing their former nemesis as "a true-born king of men," and as "a fellow Anglo-Saxon."

B. International Views

The Civil War also set off a furious debate among intellectuals and political activists in other parts of the world. That discussion was most intense and important in England and France because of the devastating impact that the conflict had on the economies of those nations, and because of the distinct possibility that one or the other of those two Great Powers might intervene in some fashion. One of the strongest arguments in favor of the legitimacy of the Confederate cause in England was made by a prominent law professor at Oxford University, Charles Lempriere. In it, he vociferously denied that slavery was the major issue in the war and strongly implied that his country might be forced to intervene because of belligerent actions by the U.S. federal government. One of the strongest contrasting cases was made by Edward Dicey, a highly respected English journalist and historian who spent much of the Civil War period in the United States. He insisted upon the centrality of slavery to the conflict and predicted ultimate victory for the Union forces, even though he praised the Southern people for their courage and determination. Across the English Channel, a distinguished French scholar, Édouard-René Laboulaye, penned a widely-read article against European mediation or intervention. Although painting a bleak picture of the economic impact of the war, especially on the working class in England and France, he contended flatly that a Confederate victory would bring even worse consequences. Staunchly advocating the Union cause throughout the war was Karl Marx, a German Jewish intellectual whose works would eventually be regarded by most Americans as completely hostile to the American way of life. Well over a century later, two of his disciples, Huo Guangshan and Guo Ningada, scholars of U.S. history in the People's Republic of China, reaffirmed those views. They portrayed Abraham Lincoln as a "capitalist revolutionary", whose triumph over slavery and "feudalism" was a milestone in the progress of human freedom.

CHARLES LEMPRIERE

AN OXFORD DON EMBRACES
THE CONFEDERATE CAUSE

One of the strongest voices advocating the Confederate cause in Europe was that of Charles Lempriere (1818–1901), member of The Inner Temple, a Law Fellow of St. John's College in the University of Oxford. Basing his opinion almost entirely on the constitutional issues involved, Lempriere staunchly defended the right of secession, while expressing highly skeptical attitudes toward the motivation and sincerity of the Union cause. His The American Crisis Considered *was published in London during the first year of the Civil War.*

Constitutionally speaking, according to the laws of the United States, the southern Confederation had an indefeasible right to withdraw from the Union, and had exercised that right legally. The position which the President assumed for the Northern section as constituting the State, and the Southern as in rebellion is not founded either in fact or in reason. In a plain truth, the exact expression is embodied in the witticism that the United States are become Untied. I now propose to test the proceedings of the Electoral Government in support of my proposition. Has there been any act of the legislature passed to define the relative position of the two contending sections? Not one. Has there been any declaration or State paper issued for the information of foreign Governments, or, in fact, any other than their own dependents, as to the rights claimed by the Government, the laws violated by the seceding States, or the legal powers by which the President and his Government are authorised in restraining by armed force a resistance against his rule? Not one. We are left to gather all these most vital points from speeches delivered irregularly, and often most obscurely worded, before tumultuous meetings. All the acts done are solely on the authority of the President of the United States, by the plenary power of himself alone, without any action of what in every people, government, or nation under the sun is supposed to represent the will of the body politic. Even the autocrats of Russia have never, in their proudest day of power, wielded so despotic a sway. What, then, is the secret of its easy adoption so far? It is the taking the lead in the onward rush of the passions which range in the minds of the masses, not the deliberate march of authority legally constituted and judicially exercised. It is, in fact, force and not reason—anarchy and not law.

No allowance is made for the difficulties in which the question of emancipation is involved. These people totally forget that they have no right to interfere with the question, unless they are prepared to pay for the negro's freedom, and his master is willing to sell him. They foolishly expect to coerce the Southern people to uproot their social fabric, and forever impoverish themselves and their posterity. . . .

The notion that was cherished for some time after the rupture that some means might be discovered of reconciling the contending sections has utterly and completely failed; and this from causes which were known and felt on the other side of the water, but have never yet found expression, partly from the hope, naturally felt, that the evil might not be irremediable, and partly from the dishonest way in which the writers in the press, and the press itself, at least for some time, have argued the views of the North, to the exclusion of the South, whose rights they have almost totally ignored. The question of abolition has been put forward invariably as the sole cause of disruption, in deference to the known feeling of England and Europe generally—whereas, there are far graver and deeper questions affecting the relations between the Northern and Southern States, which, for the last quarter of a century, have been antagonistic, and which have culminated to the present crisis. These we propose first to examine historically, and then to deduce reasons which preclude the hope of any fair or honourable settlement of the difference. In 1844, the Methodist Episcopal Church divided, the Northern section refusing to recognise the Southern on many grounds beside the question of slavery, and a feeling of bitterness arose which has never been appeased among the members of that community. I need not point out the refusal of admission to the State of Missouri, and the compromise which was ultimately effected—for its history is too familiar to require discussion—but only notice it in passing as one of the early causes of dissension. It has been uniformly felt by the South that in this, as in other cases, they had been unfairly dealt with by the legislature. In fact, since the compromise, the admission of every State south of the **Mason and Dixon's line** has been systematically resisted by the Northern statesmen, in open disregard of the plain bearing of the constitutional law on this head. This has been the cause of endless strife and bloodshed on all the border questions, when the votes of the settlers became of importance, and involves too deeply-rooted antipathies and prejudices ever to allow of reconciliation.

The systematic interference of the **Northern proselytisers** in the States south of the line was looked on, and most fairly so, as illegal and unjustifiable, while the manner in which it was conducted was as ruffianly as it was otherwise in defiance of all law and reason. The impression, founded on many years' experience, that so far from repressing or discountenancing such interference with the South, and forcing on them, as it were, a tyranny, the Northern statesmen took every opportunity of justifying what had been done, and sketching in no vague colours plans of subjugation, and further reducing into possession the Southern States, led all thinking men of the latter party to see that unless steps were taken at once to assert their independence their strength would be undermined. They found emissaries were sent with incendiary papers throughout the whole country—libels on the South were circulated throughout every town and hamlet, and especially in the schools. Not to go too far back, the first struggle for power, which illustrates the position of two sections, was the Fugitive Slave Law passed in 1850. This was, in fact, a compromise. The state of enmity between the North and South had become so virulent that such men as Clay, Webster, & Calhoun saw that a disruption was inevitable. They knew that, constitutionally, the South were right in resisting the open aggression of the North, and, morally, in defending their just title to the property which the law of the Union had guaranteed to them. On the other hand, the present secretary of President Lincoln, W. H. Seward, in the debate brought forward what has since been characterised as the **Higher Law Pressure,** stating as his principle of action the obligation on his conscience from a higher law than that of the law of the land, a mode of statesmanship more in accordance with the politics of **Cromwell's generals** that has happily occurred in the annals of history since that day—for no one can possibly prognosticate whither the force of conscience can compel a fanatic.

Although the slave right was the question on which the two parties came to an issue, on this as on other occasions when they met in open conflict, it cannot be denied that the graveness of the offence was the unwarrantable assumption of the part of the North to override the rights of the South by an unconstitutional exercise of power, and that it was so is proved not only by the arguments of Daniel Webster, the ablest, as the most temperate, of modern American statesmen, but, also, most palpably by the direction events took in the consequent settlement of this question, as well as the subsequent presidential contests. Previous to 1850, the separate States of the North had resisted the resumption of a slave who had escaped from his master—fourteen of them had passed laws in their State Legislatures to that effect. To meet the complaint urged by the owners of the slaves using the fair legal argument that the law of the land was bound to protect their property, Webster, Clay, and others brought in an Act to enable the slaveowner to pursue his slave into any State in the Union, and to call on the Federal authorities to assist him in recovering his property. Now, right or wrong, the law of the land did universally acknowledge the ownership of slaves, and the right accorded by this Act. "The Fugitive Slave Act" was affirmed by a majority in the Senate and in Congress after a long and bitter contest; and approved by Fillmore, the then President. From this date commenced the disruption of the Union. The Federal officers, acting under this law, have been systematically resisted in the execution of their duty, even after the affirmation of it by the solemn judgement of the Supreme Court of Judicature of the United States.

In almost every case, the expense and hinderance cost the owner more in recovering his slave than the property was worth, while, in many, he lost it altogether, and not seldom his life too, in the pursuit of it according to law. Now, however we may deplore and protest against the tenure of slaveholders, we cannot, by any principle known to civilised nations, ignore the fact, that the first duty a citizen owes the State is obedience to its laws, and resistance against their execution is an offence against the whole State. But, in the United States, not only was such resistance applauded by the Northern States, but it was made expressly the ground of asserting an unconstitutional supremacy over their equals in the Confederated Union. It was the injustice felt to be so done, and the right according to law which the South undoubtedly had, that swayed the nation in 1852, in their choice of Pierce—a New Hampshire candidate, who was in favour of carrying out the laws of the land—in preference to General Scott, the present commander of the Northern forces; and again, in 1856, in electing Buchanan, a Pennsylvanian, who avowed his intention of carrying out the law, by a large majority over Colonel Fremont. This proves incontestably that, up to that date, moderate and constitutional views prevailed in the body of the national electors; and the South, although they did not consider they had their full and fair share in the rights and privileges of the nation, yet acquiesced, in the hope that moderation and constitutional equity would guide the spirit of legislation.

The question of interest, which still more largely affects the motives which have induced both sides to hazard all their public and private ties, will be fully dealt with in a subsequent chapter. It is one which is totally ignored by every writer and speaker on the Federal side with a most patent unanimity—for they are aware how it tells against them. I shall, for the present, content myself with quoting a very late authority for my denial that the slavery question is the sole element of this fearful disruption, and asserting that it is very far in importance behind another, which has been studiously kept in the background by the North.

It is not slavery, but protection; it is not sentiment, but interest, which has destroyed the unity of the Great Transatlantic Republic. It is not any anxiety of New York to manumit the slaves, who raise the produce by which New York sends forth her volunteers, and makes her welcome them so warmly when they come back war-worn at the end of three months enlistment. The South, unless it were rich and productive as it lately was, would be of no use to New York. Nor is it the fear of danger to their "domestic institutions" which gathers the Southern host at Manassas Gap. It is, says Mr. Bernal Osborne, quoting **William Cobbett's** prophecy, not thirty years old, because the heavy import duties on British goods are neither more nor less than so many millions a year taken from the Southern States, and given to their Northern competitor.

Having thus endeavoured to show what appears to be the course of conduct which has caused the present disruption and future total disunion of the States of America, it only remains to consider what will be its effect upon England and the other powers of Europe. Commercially speaking, the opening of direct trade with the cotton, rice, and tobacco producing countries, unfettered by a prohibitory tariff, will of course be an advantage. Nor can the blockade which shuts out the world from this trade be long suffered to stand in the way. How it will be broken it is impossible to say; but if the experience of history is to guide us in appreciating the spirit with which the United States deals with foreign nations, there will not long lack an excuse. It would be well for England and France to seize the present opportunity for inculcating the Confederate States with a more liberal legal policy in dealing with slavery, and, without interference or dictation, advise as friends a modification of its disabilities. There is no indisposition on their part to ameliorate the condition of their slaves; and where a spirit of conciliation in lieu of coercion, of sympathy in difficulty in lieu of antagonism which threatens subjugation, suggests a course of policy which the sense of the civilised world approves, we have no doubt of a happy result to such intervention. We may add that the experience of the working of the law in Brazil, under similar circumstances, fully warrants such an anticipation.

Any other intervention is now happily out of the question; the Emperor Napoleon seems to be thoroughly in accord with the unanimous feeling of the people of this country, to keep out of this disastrous quarrel as long as it is possible to avoid it. But will it be always possible? Whatever ministry may hold the reins of office will know of a certainty at what price to value the abuse poured upon England by statesmen who require active co-operation from the subjects of a foreign government on a question of purely domestic interest. Our policy is quite assured, to remain perfectly neutral until some outrageous act against our national honour, or against the law or interest of nations in general, compels us to assert our influence in arms. Let the Federal Government look to it that they do not so force us. Already there are manifest signs that the old rule of uncontrolled democratic action is at work. Violent men are crying out that enough has not been done, and that the country requires more energetic men and measures. The voice of sensible expostulation has been long hushed. The world trembles at the mutterings of a thunder which, in so many instances in Europe, has ushered in amongst the convulsions of empires the utter extinction of law, of commerce, and even of security for life itself.

TERMS AND DEFINITIONS

William Cobbett: English writer and free trade reformer (1763–1835).
Cromwell's generals: reference to the fact that Oliver Cromwell's generals during the English revolution of the 1640s were considered fanatics in both religion and politics.
Higher Law Pressure: argument made by the abolitionists that the moral law condemning slavery took precedence over the Constitution's protection of it.
Mason and Dixon's line: boundary between Pennsylvania and Maryland surveyed by Charles Mason and Jeremiah Dixon in the 1760s and commonly regarded as the dividing line between the North and the South.
Northern proselytizers: northerners encouraging runaway slaves and abolition.

EDWARD DICEY

WHY THE UNION SHOULD AND WILL WIN

One of the most articulate voices raised in support of the Union cause in England was that of the prolific journalist and historian Edward Dicey (1832–1911). A future editor of the London Observer *and author of several books on nineteenth-century Europe, Dicey traveled around the United States as a reporter during the Civil War and developed a keen sense of American culture and its regional variations. Although he was remarkably balanced and objective in his 1863 book* Spectator Of America, *Dicey predicted that the Union's evolving anti-slavery position, epitomized in the Emancipation Proclamation, would eventually guarantee its victory.*

I hear constantly that the South only wants to establish its independence. If the European Powers could offer tomorrow to guarantee the independence of the Gulf States, the offer would be rejected without hesitation, unless the Confederacy could be secured also the possession of the vast regions that lie west of the Mississippi, whereon to ground new Slave States and Territories. The North is fighting against, the South is fighting for, the power of extending slavery across the American continent; and, if this was all that could be said, it is clear on which side must be the sympathies of anyone who really and honestly believes that slavery is an evil and a sin.

But this is not all that can be said. The present war is working directly for the overthrow of slavery where it exists already. If you look at facts, not at words, you will see that, since the outbreak of the war, the progress of the anti-slavery movement has been marvelously rapid. Slavery is abolished once for all in the District of Columbia, and no Senator can come henceforth to Washington, bringing his slaves with him. With a free territory lying in their midst, slavery becomes ultimately impossible in Maryland, as well as in Virginia. For the first time in American history, distinct national proposals have been made to emancipate the slaves. The proposals are impracticable and unsatisfactory enough, but still they form a solemn avowal of the fact that slavery is to be abolished. The slave trade has been finally suppressed, as far as the United States is concerned, and, after half a century of delay, Haiti has been recognized. These measures are no unimportant ones in the world's history; but what renders them more important is that they are due, not to popular enthusiasm, but to the inexorable logic of facts. Stern experience is teaching the North that slavery is fatal to their own freedom, and it is beneath the growth of this conviction that these blows have been dealt against the system. . . . At last, this growing conviction has terminated in its inevitable result, the Emancipation edict of President Lincoln. . . .

I, myself, plead guilty to a faith in the higher law, and hold that the Federal Government would have done more wisely and more justly if it had abolished slavery throughout the whole of the Union on grounds, not of temporary expediency, but of eternal justice. Still, I cannot condemn Mr. Lincoln, or his advisers, for their almost servile adherence to the letter of the law, as they construed it. By virtue of the war power, the Government has, or believes it has, authority to emancipate the slaves in the insurgent states, since it has power to perform any other act necessary for the preservation of the Union. But, by the Constitution, it has no more power to interfere with slavery in any loyal state than England has to interfere with serfdom in Russia. By the proclamation, the Federal Government has done everything that it could do legally with reference to slavery. That it has not done more is a complaint that cannot be brought justly.

It is no answer to statements such as these to vapor about the inhumanity of the North toward the free Negro. Anybody who knows England and Englishmen must be aware that if we had an immense foreign population among ourselves, belonging to an ignorant, half-savage, and inferior race, too numerous to be objects of sentimental curiosity, too marked in form and feature to be absorbed gradually, our feeling toward them would be very much that of the Northerner toward the Negro. The sentiment which dictates the advertisement, so common in our newspapers, of **"No Irish need apply,"** is in principle very much the same as that which in the North objects to the contact of the Negro. Moreover, in all the Northern States, after all is said and done, the Negro is treated like a man, not like a beast of burden. In half the New England States, the black man has exactly the same legal rights and privileges as the white, and throughout the whole of the older Free States the growth of public opinion is in favor of a more kindly treatment of the Negro. Somehow or other, the men of color in the Free States prefer their treatment, however inconsiderate, to the considerate care of slave-owners. There is nothing easier than for an emancipated or runaway slave, who has experienced the vanity of freedom, to recover the joys of slavery. He has only got to appear as a vagrant in a Slave State, and the state will take the trouble of providing him with a master free of expense; yet, strange to say, slaves are not found to avail themselves of the privilege. But, admitting the very worst that could be said of the condition of free Negroes in the North, a humane man must, I fear, conclude that, on the whole, it is better for the world that the American Negroes should die out like the Indians, than that they should go on increasing and multiplying under slavery, and thus perpetuating an accursed system to generations yet unborn.

Southern friends, whom I knew in the North, used to try hard to persuade me that the best chance for Abolition lay in the establishment of a Southern Confederacy. I do not doubt they were sincere in their convictions, but, like most Secession advocates, they proved too much. When you are told that the slaves are the happiest people in the world, and that slavery is the best institution ever devised for the benefit of the poor, you are surprised to learn, in one and the same breath, that the main object and chief desire of the Secessionists is to abolish slavery. Whatever may be asserted abroad, I have never seen any address or proclamation of the Southern leaders, in which the possibility of emancipation was even hinted at—in which, on the contrary, the indefinite extension of slavery was not rather held forward as the reward of success. That a social system, based on slavery, must fall to pieces ultimately, I have little doubt myself; but, "ultimately" is a long word. The immediate result of the establishment of the Southern Confederacy is obvious enough. A new lease of existence will be given to slavery; vast additional territories will be added to the dominions of slavery, and the cancer of slavery will spread its roots over the width and length of the New World. Those who wish the South to succeed, wish slavery to be extended and strengthened. There is no avoiding this conclusion; and, therefore, as I hold that the right of every man to be free is a principle even more important than the right of every nation to choose its own government, I am deaf to the appeal that the South deserves our sympathy because it is fighting to establish its independence. If the North had but dared to take for its battle cry the grand preamble of the Declaration of Independence:

"We hold these truths to be self-evident, that all men are created equal; that they are endowed by their Creator with certain inalienable rights; that amongst these are life, liberty, and the pursuit of happiness"; then it might have appealed to the world for sympathy in a manner it cannot now. That this cannot be, I regret bitterly. The North still ignores the principles contained in its great charter of freedom, but it does not repudiate them like the South. And, in the words of a homely proverb, "Half a loaf is better than no bread."

Facts, however, not words or sentiments, will decide the contest between North and South. The victorious cause may be better than the cause of victory, but after all the real question is which side will conquer, not which side ought to conquer. It would be absurd to enter in these pages on prognostications as to the military issue of the war, but there are certain broad features in the struggle which are too much lost sight of over here. Ever since the attack on Fort Sumter, the Northern frontier has advanced, and the Southern receded. The progress of the Federal armies has been slow enough, but all they have gained they have kept. No single town of any importance has been permanently recaptured by the Confederates; no single victory has ever been followed up, and no Southern army has ever succeeded in occupying any portion of Free State soil. Still Southern partisans would reply, with some show of reason, that these considerations, important as they are, do not affect the vital question of the possibility of the North ever subjugating the South. This is true; and, if the South was really fighting only to secure its independence, and to establish a Confederacy of the Gulf States, the answer would be conclusive. But, in reality, as I pointed out before, the struggle between North and South is, which party shall obtain possession of the Border States and the territories west of the lower Mississippi; which party, in fact, shall be the ruling power on the North American Continent? So far the successes of the North are fatal to the hopes of Southern Empire. The South would not value, the North would not fear, a Confederacy confined within the Gulf States; and yet the result of the campaign has been to render it most improbable that the Confederacy, even if successful, will extend beyond its present narrow limits. So far the North has gained and the South lost.

The war will be decided, not by any single defeat or victory, but by the relative power of the two combatants. Now, as far as wealth, numbers, and resources are concerned, it is not worth the trouble of proving that the North is superior to the South. As far as mere personal courage is concerned, one may fairly assume that both sides are equal. Anyone who has, like myself, been through the hospitals of the North, where Federal and Confederate wounded are nursed together, can entertain no doubt that the battles of the war have been fought on both sides only too gallantly. The one doubt is, whether the South may not be superior to the North in resolution, in readiness to make sacrifices, and in unity of action. If it is so, the chances are in favor of the South; but there is no proof as yet that it is the case. Much, and as I think undue, stress has been laid on the slow progress of enlistment in the North. It is very easy to talk glibly about what England would do in case she was at war, but if England did as much relatively as the Union States have done, it would be a grand and a terrible effort.

TERMS AND DEFINITIONS

"No Irish need apply": a common expression of blatant prejudice and discrimination against Irish Catholics in both England and the United States at that time.

ÉDOUARD RENÉ LABOULAYE

WHY THE UNION CANNOT CONSENT TO SECESSION

One of the most powerful European statements against Northern acquiescence in secession, no matter what it cost Europe in the short run, was that of Édouard-René Laboulaye (1811–1883), a member of the French Institute, professor in the College of France, a member of both the Chamber of Deputies and the Senate, and author of A Political History of the United States. *Writing in the* Revue Nationale de Paris *in 1863, Laboulaye details the severe impact that the war was having on the European economy, but nevertheless argues strongly that the long-term consequences of a Confederate victory would be far more disastrous. His essay was translated and reprinted in the* New York Tribune.

The civil war, which for two years past, has been dividing and ruining the United States, has its counter-blow in Europe. The cotton famine causes great suffering; the operatives of **Rouen and Mulhausen** are not less sorely tried than the spinners and weavers of **Lancashire**; entire populations are reduced to **mendicacy**; and to pass the winter they have no other resource, no other hope, than private charity and the succour of the State. Amid so cruel a crisis, among sufferings so little merited, it is quite natural that public opinion should grow restive in Europe, and bitterly reproach the ambition of those who thus prolong a fratricidal war. Peace in America, peace at any price, is the cry of thousands among us who are beset by hunger—innocent victims that they are of the passions and resentments that are steeping the United States in blood.

 These complaints are but too well founded. The world today is united in one compact, and peace is a condition of existence for modern nations that live by industrial pursuits. But, unfortunately, if it be easy to indicate the remedy, it is almost impossible to apply it. Up to the present moment, it is from the war itself only that we can expect the termination of the war. To throw herself into the contest and impose a truce by force of arms would be an enterprise in which Europe would exhaust her strength-and to what purpose? As **Mr. Cobden** has correctly said, it would cost less to feed with game and champagne the operatives who would have been ruined by the American crisis.

To offer our friendly mediation, at this time, is to expose ourselves to a refusal, if not even to exasperate one of the parties and to push it to extreme measures. In time, it is to diminish our chances of having our mediation accepted at a favourable moment. We are then reduced to the necessity of remaining spectators of a deplorable war that causes us infinite evils. We are reduced to the necessity of offering up our prayers that exhaustion and destitution may at length appease these infuriated antagonists, and compel them to accept reunion or separation. A sad position, undoubtedly, but one which has at all times been that of neutrals, and from which one cannot emerge without rushing into unknown dangers. If we have not the right to interfere, we have, at least, the right to complain, and to inquire for ourselves who are the really guilty parties in the war that strikes us too. The opinion of Europe amounts to something. It can, better than arms, precipitate events and lead us back to peace. Unfortunately, for two years past, public opinion, led astray, has been upon the wrong track, and in taking the bad side prolongs resistance, instead of causing it to cease.

In England and in France the South has found numerous able advocates; its cause has been put forward as the cause of justice and liberty. The right of separation has been proclaimed, and men have not recoiled from an apology for slavery. Today, these arguments are beginning to wear out. Thanks to certain publicists who care nothing for humanity; thanks especially to **M. de Gasparin,** light has dawned, and we now know what to think about the origin and character of the rebellion. To every candid observer, it is evident that all the wrong is on the Southern side. It is not necessary to be a **Montesquieu** in order to be able to comprehend that a party whom nothing threatens, and who, through ambition or pride, breaks the National Union and tears its country in two, has no right to the sympathy of Frenchmen. As for the canonization of slavery, that is a work that must be left to the spokesmen for the South. All the intellect and wit in the world cannot sustain that fallen cause. Had the Confederates a thousand reasons for complaint and revolt, there will ever remain upon their rebellion an indelible stain; no Christian, no Liberal, will ever interest himself for men who, in the broad light of the nineteenth century, boldly avow their desire to extend and perpetuate slavery. It may still be allowable to the planters to listen to theories that have intoxicated and destroyed them, but never can such sophisms cross the ocean.

The advocates of the South have rendered her a fatal service. They have made her believe that Europe, enlightened or seduced, would take her part, and would, one day, cast into the scales something more than sterile good wishes. This illusion has kept up, and still keeps up, resistance in the South: it prolongs the war and our own sufferings. If, from the very first day, as the North had a right to expect, the friends of liberty had pronounced boldly against the policy of slavery: if the partisans of peace upon the high seas, if the defenders of the rights of neutrals, had spoken in favour of the Union, and had repelled a separation that can profit England only, it is probable that the South would have rushed with less rashness into a course without visible issue.

Should the South, notwithstanding the courage and devotion of her soldiers, and the skill of her generals, fail in an enterprise which, in my opinion, cannot be too greatly blamed, let those take it to heart who have had so poor an opinion of Europeans as to think they could subject the public conscience here to a policy against which patriotism protests, and which the Gospel and humanity alike condemn.

"Be it so," some may exclaim. Admit that all the wrong is on the Southern side, but still the South desires to withdraw: she cannot live with the people of the North. The very war itself, no matter what its origin, is a new cause for disunion. By what right can 20,000,000 of men compel 10,000,000 of their fellow citizens to continue a detested alliance, to respect a contract that they desire to break, at any price? Is it possible to imagine that, after two or three years of fighting and of suffering, the conquerors and the conquered will live together? Can a country two or three times the size of France be subjugated? Will there not be blood between the parties? Separation may be a misfortune, but that misfortune is now irreparable. Admitting that the North has legality upon her side, as well as the letter and spirit of the Constitution, there still remains another indisputable point—the South desires to be free at home. You have not the right to crush a people that combats so valiantly. Therefore be resigned.

Were we less enervated by the amenities of modern life, and by the listlessness of a long peace; had we still in our hearts some remnants of that patriotism which in 1792 carried our fathers to the banks of the Rhine, the response would be easy, but today I fear it would not be understood. If tomorrow the south of France were to revolt and demand separation—if **Alsace and Lorraine** desired to isolate themselves, what would be not only our right but our duty? Would the votes be counted to ascertain whether a third or a half of the number of Frenchmen have the right to destroy the national unity, to make a nullity of France, to tear to pieces the glorious heritage which our fathers have acquired with their blood? No! we would grasp our muskets and march! Woe to him who does not feel that his country is holy! and that it is noble to defend it, even at the cost of every species of suffering and danger!

But America is not France; it is a confederation, not a nation. Who says this? The South, in order to justify her wrong. The North says contrary; and for two years past it is at the price of innumerable sacrifices that it affirms that the Americans are one and the same people, and that the country shall not be cut in two. This is fine—this is grand; and if anything astonishes me, it is that France remains insensible in the presence of such patriotism. Is not love of country the especial virtue of the French? What, then, is the South, and what is this right of separation so loudly vaunted? Is it a conquered people reclaiming its independence, as Lombardy has done? Is it a distinct race, refusing to continue in an oppressive alliance? No; they are colonists established on the territory of the Union by American hands, who revolt without any other reason than their own ambition. Take up a map of the United States. If we except Virginia, the two Carolinas, and Georgia, which are old English colonies, all the rest of the South is established upon territory purchased and paid for by the Union, which is equivalent to saying that the North supported the greater part of the expense. . . . In a few words, taking in all the rich regions that border the Mississippi and Missouri, from their sources to their mouths, there is not an inch of ground that has not been paid for by the Union, and does not belong to it. It was the Union that drove away or bought off the Indians; it was the Union that built forts, constructed navy-yards, light houses, and harbours; and it was the Union which gave value to these deserts, and rendered colonialization possible. The men of the North as well as the men of the South cleared and planted those regions, and made flourshing States of sterile solitudes. In old Europe, where, on all sides, unity has arisen from conquest, show us as sacred a title to property, or a country that is more the common work of a whole people. And now is a minority to be permitted to take possession of a territory belonging to all, and to select the very best part? Shall a minority be permitted to destroy the Union, and put in peril those who were its first benefactors, and without whom it would not exist? If this be not an impious revolt, then we must say that the whim of nations makes their right.

It is not merely a political reason that stands in the way of separation; the geography, the situation of the localities, oblige the United States to form but one nation. **Strabo,** contemplating that spacious country which is now called France, said, with certainty of genius, that considering the nature of the territory and the course of the streams, it was easy to see that the forests of **Gaul,** inhabited by a scattered population, were to become the residence of a great people. Nature had arranged our territory to be the theatre of a grand civilisation. This is not less true of America. It is, to speak correctly, but a double valley, with an insensible point of separation, and two great water-courses— the Mississippi and the St. Lawrence. There are no lofty mountains that separate and isolate the populations; no natural barriers, like the Alps and the Pyrenees. The West cannot live without the Mississippi; to possess the mouth of that river is for the farmers of the West a question of life and death. The United States have felt this from the very first. When the Ohio and the Mississippi were yet only rivers lost in the woods—when the first settlers were but a handful of men dispersed through the desert, the Americans already knew that New Orleans was the key of the front door. They were unwilling to leave it to either France or Spain. Napoleon understood this. He held in his hand the future greatness of the United States; and he was not averse to ceding to America all this vast territory, in order, as he said, to give England a maritime rival which, sooner or later, would humble the pride of our enemies. He could have dispossessed himself of the left bank merely, and have satisfied the United States, which, at that time, asked for nothing better; he did more (and here I think he made a great mistake); he gave up, with a stroke of the pen, regions as large as the half of Europe, and abandoned all our rights and claims to that fine river which we discovered.

Ere long sixty years will have passed since that cession. The States which are today called Louisiana, Arkansas, Missouri, Iowa, Minnesota, Kansas, and Oregon, the Territories of Nebraska, Dakota, Jefferson, and Washington, which will soon be States, have been founded upon the vast domain ceded by Napoleon. Without counting the slaveholding population that desires to break the Union, there are 10,000,000 citizens between Pittsburgh and Fort Union who claim the course and mouth of the Mississippi as having been ceded to them by France. It is from us that they hold their title and their right of possession. They have on their side the claims of sixty years, claims consecrated by labour and cultivation, claims which they have received as rights from a solemn contract, and, better still, from nature and from God. It is for defending this that they are reproached; they are usurpers and tyrants because they will not put themselves at the mercy of an ambitious minority. What should we say if, tomorrow, **Normandy,** in revolt, should pretend to hold for herself, exclusively, Rouen and **La Havre?** And yet, what is the course of the **Seine** compared to that of the Mississippi, which runs along 2,250 miles, and receives all the waters of the West? To possess New Orleans is to command a valley that includes two-thirds of the United States. "The river shall be made neutral," we are told. We know what such promises are worth. It has been seen how Russia managed the mouths of the **Danube;** why it cost the **Crimean war** to secure to Germany the free enjoyment of her great river. . . .

Now, suppose that the separation should be accomplished, and that the new Confederation should comprise all the Slave States, the North would lose, in one day, its power and its institutions. The Republic would be stabbed to the heart. There would be in America two nations face to face; two peoples, rivals and ever on the eve of quarrelling with each other. Peace, in fine, will not eradicate hatreds; you cannot efface the recollection of greatness passed away, of the Union destroyed; the South victorious would undoubtedly be none the less the friend of slavery, nor less in love of domination. The enemies of slavery, now undisputed masters of their policy, would not assuredly be softened by the separation. What will the Confederation of the South be to the North? A foreign power established in America, with a frontier of fifteen hundred miles, a frontier open on all sides, and consequently always menacing and menaced. This power, hostile owing to its very vicinity, and still more so through its institutions, will possess some of the most considerable portions of the New World; it will hold half the sea-coast of the Union; it will command the Gulf of Mexico, an interior sea one-third the size of the Mediterranean; it will be mistress of the mouths of the Mississippi, and may, at its pleasure, ruin the population of the West. Thus, the remnant of the Union would have to be ever in readiness to defend itself against its rivals. Questions of customs houses and frontiers, rivalries, jealousies—all the annoyances of Europe would overwhelm America together.

. . . Up to this point I have continued the hypothesis that the South remains an independent power. But unless the West join the Confederates, and the Union be reestablished without New England, this independence is a dream. It might last a few years, but in ten or twenty, when the West should have doubled or trebled its free population, what would the Confederation,

enfeebled perforce by its slave system, be, in the presence of a people number-
ing 30,000,000 and shutting it in on both sides? In order to resist the South
would have to lean on Europe; it cannot live unless protected by a maritime
power, and England alone is in a condition to guarantee its sovereignty. This
would be a fresh danger for free America and for Europe too. The South has
no navy, and with slavery, never will have. It is England that from the very
first day would grasp the monopoly of cotton, and furnish the South with capital and ships. In two words [sic], the triumph of the South would see England
reinstalled upon the continent from which the policy of **Louis XVI,** and of
Napoleon drove her, the neutral powers weakened, and France again involved
in all those questions of the freedom of the seas which cost two centuries of
struggle and of suffering. The American Union, in defending its rights, had
ensured the independence of the ocean; the Union once destroyed, the preponderance of England would spring up again. That would be peace banished
from the world; it would be the return of a policy which has served only our
rivals. This is what Napoleon felt, and what today is forgotten. It would seem
as though history were only a collection of narratives for the amusement of
children. No one is willing to heed the lessons of the past. If the experience of
our fathers were not thrown away upon our ignorance, we would perceive
that, in maintaining the national unity, in defending her independence, it is
our cause as well as her own that the North protects. All our wishes would be
for the success of our old and faithful friends. The enfeeblement of the United
States would be our own enfeeblement; and in the first quarrel with England
we would not regret, when too late, the abandonment of a policy that for forty
years past has been our security.

TERMS AND DEFINITIONS

Alsace and Lorraine: two provinces
in eastern France often occupied by
German rulers.

Mr. Cobden: Richard Cobden
(1804–1865), English statesman and
economist.

Crimean War: conflict in which
England, France, and their allies
defeated Russia (1854–1856).

Danube: main river of eastern Europe.

M. de Gasparin: Agenor Comte de
Gasparin (1810–1871), prominent
French legal scholar of the day who,
along with Laboulaye, authored the
widely-circulated *Reply To The
Loyal Legion Of New York.*

Gaul: former Roman province in
modern-day France.

La Havre: city in Normandy, France;
principal port for the importation of
cotton.

Lancashire: county on the northwest
coast of England.

Louis XVI: King of France (b. 1754)
who supported the United States
during the Revolutionary War and
was later executed during the French
Revolution (1789).

Mendicacy: begging.

Montesquieu: Charles-Louis de
Secondat, Baron de Montesquieu
(1689–1755), French Enlightenment

jurist and philosopher whose works influenced the American Constitution.
Normandy: province in northwestern France bordering the English channel.
Rouen and Mulhausen: French textile manufacturing cities.

Seine: river in northwest France connecting Paris to the English Channel.
Strabo: Greek father of geography (36 B.C.–A.D. 24).

KARL MARX

A CLASH BETWEEN TWO ANTAGONISTIC SOCIAL SYSTEMS

Most modern-day Americans would probably be perplexed to learn that one of the staunchest European proponents of the Union cause was none other than Karl Marx (1818–1883), founder of the Communist International and author of The Communist Manifesto *and* Das Kapital. *In Marx's view, a Union victory was both essential and inevitable because capitalism and wage labor had to supplant feudalism and slavery if the world was to continue its progress toward communism. Marx covered the Civil War as a correspondent for several newspapers, including the* New York Tribune, *and wrote the following article for the German newspaper* Die Presse *on November 17, 1861.*

In reality, if North and South formed two autonomous countries, like, perhaps, England and **Hanover,** their separation would then be no more difficult than was the separation of England and Hanover. "The South," however, is neither a territory strictly detached from the North geographically, nor a moral unity. It is not a country at all, but a battle slogan.

The counsel of an amicable separation presupposes that the Southern Confederacy, although it assumed the offensive in the Civil War, at least wages it for defensive purposes. It is believed that the issue for the slaveholders' party is merely one of uniting the Territories it has hitherto dominated into an autonomous group of states and withdrawing from the supreme authority of the Union. Nothing could be more false: "The South needs its entire territory. It will and must have it." With this battle-cry the secessionists fell upon Kentucky. By their "entire territory" they understand in the first place all the so-called *border states*—Delaware, Maryland, Virginia, North Carolina, Kentucky, Tennessee, Missouri, and Arkansas. Further, they lay claim to the entire territory south of the line that runs from the northwest corner of Missouri to the Pacific Ocean. What the slave holders, therefore, call the South, embraces more than three-quarters of the territory hitherto comprised by the Union. A large part of the territory thus claimed is still in the possession of the Union and would first have to be conquered from it. None of the so-called border states, however, not even those in the possession of the Confederacy, were ever *actual slave states*. Rather, they constitute that area of the United States in which the system of slavery and the system of free labor exist side by side and contend for mastery, the actual field of battle between South and

North, between slavery and freedom. The war of the Southern Confederacy is, therefore, not a war of defense, but a war of conquest, a war of conquest for the extension and perpetuation of slavery.

The chain of mountains that begins in Alabama and stretches northwards to the Hudson River—the spinal column, as it were, of the United States—cuts the so-called South into three parts. The mountainous country formed by the Allegheny Mountains with their two parallel ranges, the Cumberland Range to the west and the Blue [Ridge] Mountains to the east, divides wedge-like the lowlands along the western shores of the Atlantic Ocean from the lowlands in the southern valleys of the Mississippi. The two lowlands sundered by the mountainous country, with their vast rice swamps and far-flung cotton plantations, are the actual area of slavery. The long wedge of mountainous country driven into the heart of slavery, with its correspondingly clear atmosphere, an invigorating climate and a soil rich in coal, salt, limestone, iron ore, gold, in short, every raw material necessary for a many-sided industrial development, is already for the most part a free country. In accordance with its physical constitution, the soil here can only be cultivated with success by free small farmers. Here the slave system vegetates only sporadically and never struck roots. In the largest part of the so-called border states, the dwellers on these highlands comprise the core of the free population, which in the interests of self-preservation already sides with the Northern party. . . .

It will have been observed that we lay particular emphasis on the numerical proportion of slaves to free men in the individual border states. This proportion is in fact decisive. It is the thermometer with which the vital fire of the slave system must be measured. The soul of the whole secession movement is South Carolina. It has 402,541 slaves and 301,271 free men. Mississippi, which has given the Southern confederacy its dictator, Jefferson Davis, comes second. It has 436,696 slaves and 354,699 free men. Alabama comes third, with 435,132 slaves and 529,164 free men. . . .

For the oligarchy of three hundred thousand slaveholders utilized the **Congress of Montgomery** not only to proclaim the separation of the South from the North. It exploited it at the same time to revolutionize the internal constitutions of the slave states, to completely subjugate the section of the white population that had still maintained some independence under the protection and the democratic Constitution of the Union. Between 1856 and 1860 the political spokesmen, jurists, moralists and theologians of the slaveholders' party had already sought to prove, not so much that Negro slavery is justified, but rather that color is a matter of indifference and the working class is everywhere born to slavery.

One sees, therefore, that the war of the Southern Confederacy is in the true sense of the word a war of conquest for the extension and perpetuation of slavery. The greater part of the border states and Territories are still in the possession of the Union, whose side they have taken first through the ballot-box and then with arms. The Confederacy, however, counts them for the "South" and seeks to conquer them from the Union. In the border states which the Confederacy has occupied for the time being, it holds the relatively free highlands in check by martial law. Within the actual slave states themselves it supplants the hitherto existing democracy by the unrestricted oligarchy of three hundred thousand slaveholders.

With the relinquishment of its plans of conquest the Southern Confederacy would relinquish its capacity to live and the purpose of secession. Secession, indeed, only took place because within the Union the transformation of the border states and Territories into slave states seemed no longer attainable. On the other hand, with a peaceful cession of the contested territory to the Southern Confederacy the North would surrender to the slave republic more than three-quarters of the entire territory of the United States. The North would lose the Gulf of Mexico altogether, the Atlantic Ocean from Pensacola Bay to Delaware Bay and would even cut itself off from the Pacific Ocean. Missouri, Kansas, New Mexico, Arkansas and Texas would draw California after them. Incapable of wresting the mouth of the Mississippi from the hands of the strong, hostile slave republic in the South, the great agricultural states in the basin between the Rocky Mountains and the Alleghenies, in the valleys of the Mississippi, the Missouri and the Ohio, would be compelled by their economic interests to secede from the North and enter the Southern Confederacy. These northwestern states, in their turn, would draw after them all the Northern states lying further east, with perhaps the exception of the states of New England, into the same vortex of secession.

Thus there would in fact take place, not a dissolution of the Union, but a *reorganization* of it, a *reorganization on the basis of slavery,* under the recognized control of the slaveholding oligarchy. The plan of such a reorganization has been openly proclaimed by the principal speakers of the South at the Congress of Montgomery and explains the paragraph of the new Constitution which leaves it open to every state of the old Union to join the new Confederacy. The slave system would infect the whole Union. In the Northern states, where Negro slavery is in practice unworkable, the white working class would gradually be forced down to the level of **helotry.** This would accord with the loudly proclaimed principle that only certain races are capable of freedom, and as the actual labor is the lot of the Negro in the South, so in the North it is the lot of the German and the Irishman, or their direct descendants.

The present struggle between the South and North is, therefore, nothing but a struggle between two social systems, between the system of slavery and the system of free labor. The struggle has broken out because the two systems can no longer live peacefully side by side on the North American continent. It can only be ended by the victory of one system or the other.

If the border states, on the disputed areas of which the two systems have hitherto contended for mastery, are a thorn in the flesh of the South, there can, on the other hand, be no mistake that, in the course of the war up to now, they have constituted the chief weakness of the North. One section of the slaveholders in these districts simulated loyalty to the North at the bidding of the conspirators in the South; another section found that in fact it was in accordance with their real interests and traditional ideas to go with the Union.

Both sections have uniformly crippled the North. Anxiety to keep the loyal slaveholders of the border states in good humor; fear of throwing them into the arms of secession; in a word, tender regard for the interests, prejudices and sensibilities of these ambiguous allies, has smitten the Union government with incurable weakness since the beginning of the war, driven it to half measures, forced it to dissemble away the principle of the war and to spare the foe's most vulnerable spot, the root of the evil—slavery itself.

When, only recently, Lincoln pusillanimously revoked **Fremont's Missouri proclamation** on the emancipation of Negroes belonging to the rebels, this occurred merely out of regard for the loud protest of the "loyal" slaveholders of Kentucky. However, a turning point has already been reached. With Kentucky, the last border state has been pushed into the series of battlefields between South and North. With real war for the border states in the border states themselves, the question of winning or losing them is withdrawn from the sphere of diplomatic and parliamentary discussions. One section of slaveholders will throw away the mask of loyalty; the other will content itself with the prospect of compensation such as Great Britain gave the West Indian planters. Events themselves drive to the promulgation of the decisive slogan—*emancipation of the slaves.*

That even the most hardened Democrats and diplomats of the North feel themselves drawn to this point is shown by some publications of very recent date. In an open letter, **General Cass,** Secretary of State under Buchanan and hitherto one of the most ardent allies of the South, declares emancipation of the slaves the *conditio sine qua non* of the Union's salvation. In his last review for October, **Dr. Brownson,** the spokesman of the Catholic party of the North, on his own admission the most energetic adversary of the emancipation movement from 1836 to 1860, publishes an article for Abolition.

"If we have opposed Abolition heretofore," he says among other things, "because we would preserve the Union, we must *a fortiori* now oppose slavery whenever, in our judgment, its continuance becomes incompatible with the maintenance of the Union, or of the nation as a free republican state." Finally, the *World,* a New York organ of the diplomats of the Washington Cabinet, concludes one of its latest blustering articles against the Abolitionists with the words: "On the day when it shall be decided that either slavery or the Union must go down, on that day sentence of death is passed on slavery. If the North must triumph *without* emancipation, it will triumph with emancipation."

TERMS AND DEFINITIONS

A fortiori: by the same logic; an absolute necessity.

Dr. Brownson: Orestes Brownson (1803–1876), a leading American Catholic writer and editor.

General Cass: Lewis Cass (1782–1866), secretary of state in the Buchanan administration.

Conditio sine qua non: an absolutely necessary requirement.

Congress of Montgomery: constitutional convention that met in Montgomery, Alabama, which became the first capital of the Confederacy.
Fremont's Missouri proclamation: proclamation freeing all the slaves in Missouri issued by victorious Union General John Charles Frémont and revoked by President Lincoln.
Hanover: large state in northern Germany that produced Great Britain's ruling dynasty in the eighteenth century.
Helotry: system of servitude in ancient Greece equivalent to slavery.

HUO GUANGSHAN
AND GUO NINGADA

LINCOLN WAS A CAPITALIST REVOLUTIONARY

Writing nearly 120 years after the conclusion of the Civil War, two scholars from the People's Republic of China, Huo Guangshan and Guo Ningada, demonstrate both the continuity and change of Marxist thought over that time period. In "The Lincoln of the American Civil War," published in Chinese Studies in American History in 1983, they present a provocative interpretation of America's greatest president that places him squarely within the framework of modern Communist ideology. In the process, they betray a sense of admiration and respect for Lincoln's humanity that transcends ideological limitations.

In November 1860, Lincoln, the Republican, who represented the interests of the northern capitalists, was elected president, and within the country this evoked great repercussions. The southern slave owners declared that they would definitely not surrender in the face of the humiliating and shameless circumstance of Lincoln assuming office, stating that "to oppose Lincoln is to obey God." What the slave-owning class opposed was not Lincoln as a person, but the life-and-death class struggle. Marx profoundly pointed out that "The present struggle between the South and the North is therefore nothing but a conflict between two social systems, the system of slavery and the system of free labor. The struggle broke out because the two systems can no longer live peacefully side by side on the North American continent. It can end only with the victory of one system or the other."

Since there was no way to settle the contradictions and conflicts between the two social systems in the country, it was necessary to resort to force. The southern slave owners, relying on their advantage militarily and in the government, wildly schemed to subjugate the North by war, and thus to promote the slavery system throughout the entire country. Beginning in March 1861, the Confederate forces encircled Fort Sumter in the North [sic]. Lincoln immediately made his position known: "That to so abandon that position, under the circumstances, would be utterly ruinous. . . . This could not be allowed." In April the Civil War broke out in full force. During the early period of the

Civil War, if we compare the strength of the two parties, the North enjoyed relative superiority. In a comparison of manpower, the population of the North was over 23 million occupying 23 states, while that of the South was 9 million occupying 11 states. Of this 9 million, it was demanded that 4 million Negro slaves be emancipated. In an economic comparison, in the North was concentrated practically all the heavy industry, military industry, and light industry of the entire country; moreover, it had good transportation facilities and material abundance. In the South were mostly plantations and very few factories. Its economy was backward. The North held three-fourths of the gross national product. In a political comparison, the North was a capitalist system promoting the development of productive power. It opposed the old system; the war it was carrying out to establish a new system was a just one. The South was carrying out an unjust war to maintain the old system. In sum, the South proved definitely inferior in manpower, material and financial strength, and moral considerations. However, after the Civil War began, with the fall of Fort Sumter and the northern defeats at the Battle of Bull Run, even the capital, Washington, was frightened and ill at ease.

What created this passive position vulnerable to attack? Some people attributed the defeat to Lincoln's unwillingness to stir up the slavery system of the South. We feel that placing this responsibility on Lincoln's shoulders is not objective, is biased, and is not in accord with historical actuality. The military defeat of the North was brought about by concrete political, economic, and military causes. Politically, the contradictions between the capitalist class and the slave owners could not be reconciled, but the people did not hope to use revolutionary methods to seize political power. Rather, they sought to use peaceful means. Thus during the early period of the Civil War there was much hesitation, vacillation, and illusion; so everywhere in the war there was passive vulnerability. Economically, many slave owners of the South had debts with bankers and businessmen of the North, in an estimated amount of $212 million. If the South were subjugated, the debts would be called to question. At the same time, the cotton textile industry of the North needed the supply of cotton from the South. In the event the plantations were abolished, a shortage of raw materials might result. Thus the capitalist class did not make a complete and final decision to adopt military sanctions. Militarily, even before Lincoln assumed the presidency, President Buchanan used the final opportunity before turning over the reigns of power to dispatch troops, transport arms and ammunition, and appropriate military expenses to arm the South. When Lincoln assumed office, of the 1,108 officers and men in the service, 387 resigned to go over to the Confederacy to participate in the war against the Union. These were the reasons the North received temporary setbacks. These were circumstances created by objective history, and they could not be retracted by a single individual.

Lincoln had a deep understanding of the military reverses of the North. He once said: "As to the tide of the times, if we wish to ignore it, that cannot be done. I ask you [meaning the Abolitionists] to open wider your vision and coolly consider this kind of tide of the times; and if possible, place it above the political views of individuals and party factions." Marx also considered that if the question of the emancipation of slavery had been brought up too early, "it would bring utter defeat." We believe that Lincoln, on the one hand, understood that the conditions for emancipation of slaves were still premature and that it was not feasible to take action too early. On the other hand, strategically speaking, to avoid utter defeat there could only be temporary compromise. Thus we should be practical and realistic in evaluating Lincoln's goals and policies and his attitude in handling matters during the early period of the Civil War. We cannot use the temporary successes or defeats of the war as an argument to show that he did not want to abolish the slavery system. The harsh war tested the position and attitude of this statesman of the capitalist class. The fires of battle would again prove that he was an abolitionist and was an outstanding revolutionary of the capitalist class.

When the Civil War was in a tense phase, Britain, eyeing the situation **covetously,** sought to find an excuse to support the southern rebels. Marx said that this was possible to be brought about, "but not easily. . . . It does not seem to me that Lincoln will provide it such a pretext." But in November 1861, Lincoln's subordinates acted with undue haste and made it possible for Britain to find an excuse for intervening in the Civil War. This was the occurrence of the "Trent Incident." Northern troops seized two emissaries from a British liner who were sent by the South to Britain and France, namely **Mason and Slidell.** These two reactionaries had long been abhorred by many people. They were "the principal sponsors of the Fugitive Slave Act. . . . Both were the secret wirepullers of . . . measures . . . of Buchanan's administration." After the people received this news, they were filled with righteous indignation and resolutely demanded doubling the punishment. Secretary of State Seward made every effort to support this position, calling for the entire country to prepare for war against Britain, so that a war between Britain and the United States was about to break out at the slightest provocation. Lincoln, standing high and seeing far, carefully and earnestly analyzed the political tendencies of Britain and realized that it wanted to use this as an excuse to recognize the southern Confederacy as an independent state, conclude the U.S. sea blockade, make an armed invasion of the United States, and spread the slavery system to the entire country, making the United States become once again a colony. Under these conditions, Lincoln resolutely opposed an opportunistic diplomatic policy, saying, "During any one period, we can only fight one war at a time. The English didn't give us time to turn around. It was very humiliating, but we had one big war on hand and we didn't want two at the same time. England in the end will be the only one hurt." He resolutely and firmly made a tactical concession, avoiding war with Britain. This was the crystallization of success in his use of flexible tactics in the war.

In the tactical success this time, however, we cannot overlook the exceptionally important external condition—the support of international public opinion. At the time Marx and **Engels** published many newspaper articles explaining such questions as the origin and nature and war objectives of the American Civil War, they also published articles on the "Trent Incident" and the "British-American Conflict," exposing Britain's unjust and criminal aims in scheming to provoke a British–American war. In mobilizing the people of the world, especially the British, they aroused strong protest actions opposing the British government's aggression on the United States. All this had not a little effect. The British, suffering from the hardship of losing their source of cotton, which had caused their textile industry to verge on bankruptcy, firmly stated: "No matter what the suffering we may endure, no matter what the sacrifices we may have to undergo, we will not allow our Government to depart from the strict principle of neutrality on behalf of the slaveholding Confederacy." As for the British workers, because they maintained the struggle, "the unemployed population of many large cities constitutes 31.8 percent of the entire population, and many workers are on the verge of starvation." In this way, they were "carrying on a shameless crusade to make Western Europe avoid permanently maintaining and expanding a slavery system on the other side of the Atlantic Ocean."

After disposing of the "Trent Incident," Lincoln set about to solve the question of the North's defeat, adopting a series of measures to reverse the unfavorable war situation. First he dismissed and replaced Army Commander McClellan and other powerless generals. This "pulled out the pillars of support from the compromising faction in the Army." Next, from the experience of the war, he promoted a group of soldiers who had real knowledge and deep insight and were brave and skillful in battle, the lower-ranking officers becoming higher-ranking officers, in order to raise the command power and the fighting power of the troops. Third, during the first half of 1862 he put into effect a series of laws on such questions as resolving the land question of the farmers; proclaiming that the Negroes under certain conditions would receive the rights of freedom; and proclaiming that if the slave owners did not cease in their rebellion, they would be punished. These were effective revolutionary measures in regard to mobilizing the people to take an active part in the war, and especially in regard to developing the positive spirit of the Negroes in participating in the war. This shows that Lincoln clearly stood his ground in the capitalist class's democratic revolution. Fourth, he issued an order for conscription, carrying out the voluntary enlistment system, overcoming the negativistic emotion of abhorrence for the war that part of the people had, and guaranteeing the continued replacement of troops. Fifth, he issued the "Preliminary Emancipation Proclamation," arming the Negroes. In this way, he made the positive spirit of the participation of the people become fully mobilized. He also unified this positive spirit in the strategic objective of fighting to save the Union, and thus the Civil War experienced a basic turn in the course of events.

During the four years of war, Lincoln showed great concern in analyzing and studying the changes in the war situation, and in formulating the principles of strategy, maneuvers, and tactics. He always had as his war objective the saving of the Union, and later the abolition of the slavery system. Thus what he led was a just war—a war of progress, promoting the forward development of U.S. society. His unrelenting fighting stamina and the outstanding military exploits he accomplished should all be confirmed. Concerning the significance of the Civil War, Engels said, "A people's war of this sort, on both sides, is unprecedented ever since the establishment of powerful states; its outcome will doubtless determine the future of America for hundreds of years to come. As soon as slavery—that greatest of obstacles to the political and social development of the United States—has been smashed, the country will experience a boom that will very soon assure it an altogether different place in the history of the world."

Lincoln led the American people, through the means of war, to overturn the production methods of the slavery system. He overthrew the slave-owner class, which obstructed the power of production, and abolished the slavery system, which for such a long period had oppressed and exploited the Negro. Pushing U.S. society to become a capitalist society and at the same time making U.S. agricultural, industrial, and military enterprises develop at a flying pace, leaping rapidly forward to join the ranks of the world's most advanced capitalist countries—all these were great achievements accomplished by Lincoln in the very brief period of four years of the Civil War. This again proves the correctness of the conclusion of Marx and Engels regarding "the capitalist class in history having played an exceptional revolutionary role." Lincoln is an outstanding political representative of the capitalist class, which played an exceptional revolutionary role. Of course, with Lincoln serving as a representative of the capitalist class, ascending onto the platform of history, existing historical and class limitations could not be avoided. For example, he was satisfied with politically overturning the slavery system and did not have the power to continue to push the revolution forward. Economically, he considered that capitalists and laborers had a relationship of mutual benefit, which should not lead to a declaration of war against property, and even more, could not mean a declaration of war against proprietorship. Capitalism was the best system, and as for the racial question, although it was advocated that the various races were equal after the Civil War was concluded, this was no longer considered an important task of the revolution. The Negroes became free persons, but Lincoln had no power to eliminate their being confronted with racial discrimination. However, as compared to his achievements, these are of secondary importance. In any case, before he even had time to deal with these questions, he was tragically murdered. Some people overly emphasize Lincoln's class limitations, but we consider that this is not very appropriate.

Marx made an overall summary and completely fair evaluation of Lincoln. He pointed out: "Lincoln is not the offspring of a people's revolution. . . . he was an average man of good will." As to all that he did, "Never has the New World scored a greater victory. . . . Each step of his administrative career has been in the right direction, and has been stoutly maintained. He was resolved to exclude slavery from the territories. He was "one of the rare men who succeed in becoming great, without ceasing to be good. Such, indeed, was the modesty of this great and good man, that the world only discovered him a hero after he had fallen a martyr."

TERMS AND DEFINITIONS

Covetously: selfishly hoping to profit by a dissolution of the United States. **Engels:** Friedrich Engels (1820–1895), German collaborator and successor of Karl Marx.

Mason and Slidell: James Murray Mason (1798–1871) and John Slidell (1793–1871), Confederate envoys to Great Britain who were seized during the Trent Affair.

THINKING THINGS THROUGH

1. What assumptions differentiate Marx, Huo Guangshan, and Guo Ningada from the other three analysts?

2. Do you see any differences in perspective between Marx and the two modern-day Chinese scholars? What do you think accounts for the differences?

3. How does each writer regard the institution of slavery? the humanity of African-Americans?

4. How do you think that Dicey and Laboulaye would have responded to Lempriere's arguments?

5. How do you think that Lempriere, Dicey, and Laboulaye would have reacted to the reasoning of Marx and the two modern-day Chinese scholars?

CREDITS–VOLUME I

Chapter 1

Article 1: Reprinted with permission from Princeton University Press from Amerigo Vespucci, *Mundus Novus Letter to Lorenzo Pietro de' Medici.* Copyright (c) 1916, 1983.

Article 2: Reprinted with permission from Pierpont Morgan Library from Susan Tarrow's translation of Cèllere Codex, in Lawrence C. Roth, ed., *The Voyages of Giovanni de Verazanno.* Copyright (c) 1970.

Article 3: Reprinted from *A History of the New World in Reverse,* by Germán Arciniegas (Harcourt Brace, Fort Worth, TX, 1986).

Article 4: Reprinted by permission of the publisher from *The Old World and the New, 1492–1650,* by J. H. Elliott, Cambridge University Press. Copyright (c) 1992.

Chapter 2

Article 1: Reprinted from *Five Letters of Cortés to the Emperor,* by Hernando Cortés, with the permission of W. W. Norton and Cia. Copyright (c) 1969.

Article 2: Reprinted by permission of the publisher from *José de Acosta's Natural and Moral History of the Indies,* edited by Clements Markham. The Hackluyt Society. Copyright (c) 1949.

Chapter 3

Article 3: Reprinted with the permission of the University Press of New England from *Five Black Lives, the Autobiographies of Venture Smith, James Mars, William Grimes, the Reverend G. W. Offley, James L. Smith,* edited by Ana Bontemps. Copyright (c) 1971.

Article 4: Robert E. Conrad, *World of Sorrow, The African Slave Trade to Brazil,* (Baton Rouge, LA: Louisiana State University Press, 1986).

Article 5: Serge Daget, "Abolition of the Slave Trade," in *General History of Africa, VI, Africa in the Nineteenth Century until the 1800s,* edited by F. Ade Ajayi. Reprinted with the permission of UNESCO, 1989.

Chapter 4

Article 3: Reprinted by permission of Dover Publications, Inc. from Peter Kalm, *Peter Kalm's Travels in North America,* (New York: Wilson-Erickson, 1937), pp. 343–348.

Article 4: Reprinted by permission of the publisher from *Journey To Pennsylvania* by Gottlieb Mittleberger, pp. 42–48, edited by Oscar Handlin and John Clive, Cambridge MA: Harvard University Press, Copyright (c) 1960 by the President and Fellows of Harvard College.

Article 5: Reprinted with the permission of Yale University Press from *Journal of a Lady of Quality,* by Janet Schaw, pp. 151–157. Copyright (c) 1939.

Chapter 5

Article 4: Edward D. Seeber, ed., *On the Threshold of Liberty: Journal of a Frenchman's Tour of the American Colonies in 1777,* (Bloomington: Indiana University Press, 1959).

Chapter 6

Article 1: Reprinted with the permission of the University of Oklahoma Press from *The New Democracy in America,* by Francisco de Miranda, edited by Judson Wood and John Ezell, pp. 162–170. Copyright (c) 1963.

Article 3:   Reprinted by permission of the publisher from *Views of Society and Manners in America,* by Frances Wright, pp. 162–171, edited by Paul Baker, Cambridge, MA: Harvard University Press, Copyright (c) 1963 by the President and Fellows of Harvard College.

Article 4:   Lorenzo de Zavala, *Journey to the United States of America* (Austin, TX: Shoal Creek Publishers, 1980).

Chapter 7
Article 1:   Reprinted from *Michael Chevalier, Society, Manners, and Politics in the United States: Letters on North America,* (Peter Smith Publisher, Inc., Gloucester, MA., 1967), pp. 410–419, with the permission of the publisher.

Article 3:   Sarmiento, Domingo Faustino, *Sarmiento's Travels in the United States, 1847,* translated by Michael A. Rockland, pp. 184–185 and 188–195. Copyright (c) 1970 by Princeton University Press. Reprinted by permission of Princeton University Press.

Article 4:   Copyright (c) 1971 from *Travels Between the Hudson and the Mississippi, 1851–1852,* by Moritz Busch, pp. 273–281.

Reprinted with permission of The University Press of Kentucky.

Chapter 8
Article 5:   Francisco Barquín Bilbao, "The U. S. Threat to Latin America," in *Readings in Latin American Civilization,* edited by Benjamin Keen, copyright 1967. Permission granted by Benjamin Keen.

Chapter 9
Article 2:   Frances Ann Kemble, *Journal of a Residence on a Georgian Plantation in 1838–1839,* (New York: Random House, 1961).

Chapter 10
Article 4:   Reprinted from *The Civil War in the United States,* by Karl Marx and Frederick Engels, pp. 71–73 and 79–83, with the permission of the International Publishers Company, Inc. of New York, New York. Copyright (c) 1937.

Article 5:   Reprinted from "The Lincoln of the American Civil War," by Huo Guangshan and Guo Ningada, pp. 132–137 and 140–142, in *Chinese Studies in American History,* XVI (Fall–Winter, 1982–83).